IN PURSUIT OF C. S. LEWIS

Adventures in Collecting His Works

Edwin W. Brown, M.D.

...with an Introduction by Dan Hamilton

Proleptikos Press

Indianapolis, Indiana
proleptikos@aol.com

Dedications and Acknowledgements

To my patient and loving wife Pat, who has heard these and other stories repeated *ad infinitum*, somehow managing for more than fifty years to give silent assent to their retelling to others.

Ed Brown

To my wife Elizabeth, who has patiently shared me with books every day for twenty-five years – and frequently with Ed, for almost as long.

Dan Hamilton

And thanks to the following people at Taylor University, who helped make this project not only possible but delightful:

Dr. David Neuhouser, Director of the Center for the Study of C. S.
Lewis and Friends
Laura Constantine, The Edwin W. Brown Collection Assistant
Roger Phillips, Reference and Inter-Library Loan Librarian
Sharon Eib, Assistant Director of Technical Services

Cover design and artwork by Tim Sutherland, the winning artist in a Taylor graphics class under Shaun Casbarro, Spring 2006.

C. S. Lewis cover photograph used by permission of The Marion E. Wade Center, Wheaton College, Wheaton, IL.

Ed Brown photograph by Jim Garringer, Taylor University.

CONTENTS

4

Introduction

Every book tells at least one story. There is first the obvious tale of the print on its pages – but there is usually a story between the pages, and often an adventure behind the book itself. Book collecting is the process of discovering (and sometimes becoming!) the story behind the scene.

Ed Brown has been caught up in this delightful activity of book collecting for many years – and he has seemingly acquired as many stories as he has books. Whenever Ed tells these tales, a crowd gathers round. He was generally too busy to write down the anecdotes, and I eventually took it upon myself to film and tape Ed's storytelling – both formal and informal, at colloquiua and around restaurant tables – in order to preserve a more permanent record of the warm and human marvels behind the slow and painstaking assembly of his collection.

I've had the privilege of knowing Ed for more than two decades, and I've always been impressed – by his collection, by the strange and wonderful ways it came about, and by his attitude toward it. He has not been like the dragons of old, hoarding away his treasure against all comers; rather, he has freely welcomed the people (especially students, of all ages) who came to see the books and learn of them and from them.

In the 1980s, I often joined Taylor students touring his basement pub and took pleasure in watching the whole world behind the books unfold for the unsuspecting and dazzled audience. (I particularly enjoyed watching one young man's face when he realized that the old book he had casually leaned his elbow on was a first edition, second printing King James Bible, printed in 1611!)

Word of Ed's first-rate collection of pubbery, Lewis, MacDonald, and other writers spread quietly but steadily; people continued to call and visit, and eventually Ed realized that the whole collection deserved a more public setting.

His daughter Wende had attended Taylor, and he greatly appreciated the education she received there – as well as the intellectual climate which found Christian faith and humor and imagination to be wholly compatible qualities. So when the opportunity came along, he was glad to see his other "children" go to a new home where even more people could see and enjoy them.

His involvement has not ended there, for Ed remains an active participant in expanding, improving, and showcasing the Edwin W. Brown Collection at Taylor. Book collecting is not something one walks away from easily; Ed will readily admit that it's much more like a disease than a hobby.

Collecting of this sort values all manner of books, but two different kinds of books in particular:

First, there are pristine originals – as close as possible to the author's intent. This means an original handwritten (or typewritten) manuscript, where one exists; a publisher's proof copy, or a first edition, first printing, with no markings or wear (and, of course, the original dust jacket).

The thrill involves saying (or at least feeling): "*This* is what the author intended – and *this* is how it burst forth upon the world. The first copy placed in the author's hands looked like this. No-one had yet discovered how much a treasure this story was when this book was first placed on the shelf for sale."

Few writers are already famous when their first books appear. First books by unknown authors are usually small press runs – even private printings – which suffer from limited publicity and distribution, and are frequently subject to early liquidation when sales do not meet the publisher's expectations.

Early firsts, therefore, are generally more rare and valuable than first printings of long-awaited sequels and follow-ons from popular authors. Every book has a first edition, but some first editions may be the *only* edition!

For the Lewis collector, the hardest originals to find are *Spirits in Bondage* and *Dymer* – slim volumes of verse published long before Lewis became either a Christian or a public figure, although he was already struggling with the spiritual and intellectual issues that would lead him down the once-rejected path to God. *The Pilgrim's Regress* marks the beginning of the work of C. S. Lewis we are most familiar with. (Even then, the first three editions differ in presentation and content, so which of the three is most important? Collect them all and solve the dilemma!)

A second, and more fascinating, area involves association copies – books handled by someone of particular interest connected with the author – a friend, a family member, a colleague, a noted admirer. These tie the author to a particular person for a particular reason – and sometimes to a particular time and location. The most prized of all association copies is the presentation copy – a book given to someone by the author and inscribed by him. And rarest of all presentation copies is the book dedicated to a person, given and inscribed to him or her by the author.

The Holy Grail of this category for the Lewis collector could very well be a first edition of *The Screwtape Letters* (dedicated to his friend Tolkien), given to Tolkien, and personally inscribed and signed by Lewis. (Maybe even with Tolkien's scribbles in the margin!) Such a book may exist. If it does, Ed hasn't found it – yet.

Ed has, however, unearthed many worthy artifacts. These books have value and interest not so much by what they are but by where they have been, and because of the people who have held the books in their hands and often their hearts.

The realization dawns that *people hallow things.* We treasure the relics of the past because someone famous or beloved owned them or used them; their emotional or historic value far exceeds their intrinsic value. We keep our grandfather's chair or our mother's china not for the market value, but because we relish the connection we feel when we sit in that familiar, weathered chair or run our fingers across the kiln-fired surface. Something of the previous owner has passed into the object, and we honor the connection that is there. *Things do not hallow people, but people hallow things.*

There is an intangible pleasure – a thrill, in the old-fashioned sense of the word – that comes from handling a book that was owned and handled by Lewis, or received and read and enjoyed by someone connected with him. Though we are physically touching "only" a book, we are also touching the person standing behind it in the shadows of history – the author, an owner, a reader, a person who changed lives through the printed word or whose life was changed by the printed word.

The books and papers themselves are certainly valuable and often irreplaceable, yet these stories are human at their core. Book collecting is not an isolated pursuit; happily, the paper trail passes through many human hands, and is tangled up in all their lives.

I've greatly enjoyed playing Boswell to Ed's Johnson, and appreciated the many hours I've spent in the friendly confines of the Brown Collection – reading, learning, verifying facts, checking editions and dust jackets, and acting as occasional "bird dog" in spotting overlooked volumes and ephemera to be added to the shelves.

May you enjoy these stories, savor the books as you encounter them, and make good use of the bibliography – without losing sight of the One to whom Lewis so unfailingly pointed his readers.

> Dan Hamilton
> Indianapolis, Indiana
> April, 2006

Preface

The Edwin W. Brown Collection at Taylor University

What follows on these pages are some of what I hope are the more interesting stories behind the C. S. Lewis collection resulting from a hobby that began some thirty years ago – with no expectation that it would culminate in so gratifying an outcome in addition to the enormous pleasure afforded during its pursuit.

In December 2005 I was asked by the editor of a British magazine, *Rare Book Review,* if I would consider writing the feature article for their next issue, which was to give prominence to the works of C. S. Lewis following the December release of the long-awaited film, *The Lion, the Witch and the Wardrobe.* Somehow, word seemed to have reached that distinguished publication that there was an American over there somewhere in the cornfields of Indiana who had put together an impressive C. S. Lewis collection.

I was more than pleased to share with its readers some of my joy in having had the privilege of putting together a fine Lewis collection of all of his first editions, many letters, some manuscripts, and other items. When I received a copy of the February/March issue I was even more pleased to see how elegantly they had adorned the article with a beautiful scene from the movie and excellent pictures of some rare Lewis books and dust jackets (or dust wrappers, as they call them over there) which I provided them. I was not quite prepared for the accolades, beginning with *"Finding Narnia ... in the world's largest C. S. Lewis collection"* on the cover and *"the world's foremost C. S. Lewis collector Ed Brown guides Rare through his private collection of first editions"* in the introduction to the six-page article!

As most Lewis enthusiasts know, the "world's largest C. S. Lewis collection" – depending upon how one defines the term – is either at the Marion E. Wade Center at Wheaton College, Wheaton, Illinois, or the Bodleian Library of the University of Oxford. The Wade Center enjoys the advantage; its founder, the late Dr. Clyde Kilby, was a friend of the Lewis brothers, from whom he received priceless

11

unique materials. The Bodleian Library, as a copyright deposit library, not only receives the first edition of every book published in the United Kingdom, but houses an invaluable collection of Lewis manuscripts and other material deposited there by Walter Hooper, who served as Lewis's personal secretary in mid-1963 shortly before Lewis's death, and became the literary executor of the Lewis estate.

If anyone should be considered "the world's foremost C S Lewis collector," it is Walter, who for more than four decades has indefatigably devoted himself to preparing editions of Lewis's unpublished works and seeking to find the original appearance in print of every poem, essay, sermon, letter, or whatever else Lewis wrote – and I am humbled that he should defer to me in that respect as a private collector.

The Bodleian Library, however, does not retain the dust jackets of its books (which for the rarer and the more popular Lewis titles have become far more valuable than the books themselves) and many of those of the Lewis first editions at the Wade Center are not of the best quality. Thus, although the collection at Taylor University is only the third most extensive Lewis collection known, each of the first editions is of the finest quality I could find over the years – and I have found dust jackets for all but *Spirits in Bondage*, all likewise of the best available quality. I am still upgrading any books and jackets in need thereof when I can find them – and I am honored that the university has thus named the collection.

I had known Taylor University in Upland, Indiana (an hour's drive from our home in Indianapolis) as a respected nondenominational Christian institution of higher learning largely through friendship with Milo Rediger, its president at that time. Having encouraged our daughter Wende to attend there, my wife and I soon became keenly aware of its outstanding qualities as we followed her academic and spiritual growth through the next four years. However, I was not aware of any special interest on campus in the works of C. S. Lewis and his acknowledged mentor, George MacDonald, until I received a call one day from the professor of mathematics, Dr. David Neuhouser, quite some time after Wende's graduation.

It was thus I learned that David had for years been conducting classes on Lewis and MacDonald, and had written a book on the latter. One of his math students, Bruce Brown, son of my brother Paul, had told David of the uncle in Indianapolis who collected C. S. Lewis – and thus began a friendship of many years. David began bringing a group of students to my home each Fall, with whom I spent a delightful time showing them the collection; later he asked if I might consider donating the collection to Taylor at some future date.

Had I not just retired at that point, with a large investment in the collection on which I might have to draw to supplement our income, I would have been more than pleased to do so – but eventually a very generous and anonymous donor was willing to purchase the entire collection on behalf of Taylor, and the rest is history.

Finally, I would be remiss if I failed to give due credit to Dan Hamilton, friend and editorial assistant. Dan urged me for years to write this all down; used his extensive expertise as a published author to find us a publisher; and spent long hours as our deadline approached in arranging a competition for Taylor art students to design the covers, used his computer skills to format the text, and performed countless other tasks in preparation for the final submission of the manuscript. Without his tireless efforts and constant prodding, I would still be dreaming of getting this into print, so it is as much his book as mine.

But how did it all begin?

Blame the British

The British are entirely responsible for my having acquired that incurable disease, book collecting.

I visited England for the first time in 1963 while *en route* home from a two-year visiting professorship at Osmania Medical College in Hyderabad, India, and became enamored of the best of British pubs – those marvelous neighborhood social clubs and eating places, the heart of British society in a small community.

There is nothing quite like the British "public house", the traditional meeting place for people from the village or neighborhood to enjoy their friends over a glass of ale or other beverage and a snack – or a sumptuous meal in the finest of them. (While most pubs served only the traditional Scottish egg or Cornish pasty in the past, today this has given way to some of the better English fare to be had. With stricter laws for drinking drivers, pub owners found it necessary to offset their lower sales of alcoholic beverages by offering more and better food and at better prices than those offered by restaurants.)

A distinguishing feature of British pubs are the many unusual names and colorful signs adorning them – such as the Bear and Ragged Staff, the Slug and Lettuce, the Snooty Fox, *ad infinitum*. The early British tavern keepers began to adopt the use of such visual signs to advertise their ale and porter to the mainly illiterate populace, and inn signs began to appear by the roadside in towns and villages throughout the country.

When we moved to Indianapolis from Washington, D.C. in 1966, we bought an old brick-and-stone English tudor-style home on Meridian Street that simply cried out for a pub as the decor of the basement recreation room. But not a mere replica like Union Jack's or those other commercial establishments with their reproduction pub mirrors and signs. Only the real thing – or as near the real thing as one could get – would do.

My work as director of the Division of International Affairs at the Indiana University Medical Center took me frequently to such places as Iraq, Afghanistan, and India, always with a convenient stopover in England going or coming. In London's flea markets and "junque" shops were to be found a marvelous assortment of bits and pieces of old pub hardware, the result of the efforts of the breweries (who own most of the British pubs) to modernize their establishments. My luggage to be checked in at Heathrow soon began bulging with decorated beer pump handles of various design, beer mats, old pewter mugs, old bottles, menu boards, and the like.

These modernization efforts soon proved to be misguided, however, and much of such stuff began finding its way back into some of the pubs or into replicas of British pubs in other countries. No longer were these relics thus to be found cheaply – or indeed at all – in the dingy shops of Chelsea, but now only in a few upper-end antique shops. A knowledgeable cab driver eventually led me to Portobello Road's famous market place, where at erstwhile Trad's I was able to find such treasures as antique advertising mirrors, a stained glass window labeled "TAP ROOM," a brass dragon wine dispenser, and a beautiful brass "optics" stand – that unique, colorful device for dispensing the prescribed-by-law quantity of spirits.

Getting some of these larger pieces safely home proved to be a challenge, not only because of their fragile nature, but also their weight, when in those days one's total baggage allowance was a mere 44 pounds. Having on one trip carefully packaged a beautiful antique advertising mirror that took up two-thirds of my weight allowance, I was horrified to see it reduced to a carton full of broken glass by the time it was transferred to the flight to Indianapolis.

On my next trip I was determined not to let its replacement out of my grasp – not an easy task with a 25-pound, 2' x 3' framed piece of quarter-inch thick mirror glass. Prevailing upon the gate agent to let me board first, I quickly made my way to the rear of the aircraft, wrapped it in airline blankets, stowed it in the corner of a garment compartment, and then stood guard over it until everyone was seated – after pointing numerous passengers to other such compartments to hang their coats after telling them, "Sorry, this one's full."

My greatest achievement, however, was prevailing upon a friendly TWA agent in London to allow me to check in a huge carton full of brassware and pewter mugs, together with two pair of skis that my daughter and I had left behind in Switzerland two years earlier – a total weight of well over 150 pounds on a 44-pound allowance. (TWA is sadly missed.)

I was fortunate to find a fine mirrored back bar in Indianapolis that had just arrived from England in an antique wholesaler's container, but the 12-foot-long bar I required proved to be more elusive – and not something that even a friendly TWA agent would pass on. One eventually turned up in a barn down in New Harmony, Indiana, but considerable ingenuity was required to reduce it to two pieces without disfiguring it, in order to get it down the stairs into our basement.

The final touch was to be a large brass cash register recording sales in pounds, shillings and pence, of course. At 150 pounds weight-wise, this would definitely have to come by sea, but several trips to England failed to produce one. Fate smiled on me, however, when on one glorious day I found exactly what I had been looking for – a magnificent piece manufactured by National Cash Register in Dayton, Ohio, exported to England in 1901, and now being offered for sale at an antique show at the Indianapolis Fair Grounds!

My pub thus became a reality, with its walls covered in green felt, and its ancient brassware gleaming amidst the rich dark brown of the woodwork. But it lacked its most important feature – a pub sign. The trail that led not only to the choice of a sign but to the beginning of my book collection began not in jolly old England but in far-off Saudi Arabia.

So what has all this pub business to do with collecting books anyhow? Actually it has everything to do with my undertaking a hobby that has not only enriched my life and, I hope, that of others – not to mention one that came as a relief to my ever-indulgent spouse. Prior to collecting books, I had collected cars – not cute little toy cars but some of the most outlandishly oversized American behemoths, specifically Lincoln Continentals manufactured from

1961 to 1965. I shan't bore you with what drew me into this bizarre pursuit, but when reality at last dawned, and I realized it was time to give it up, I had some 13 of them – and only a two-car garage. The rest were parked in the driveway or stored in sundry barns around the county. Needless to say, replacing these with books immensely pleased the *memsahib*.

Introduction to Oxford

While on Indiana University business in Saudi Arabia in 1974 I had the pleasure of becoming acquainted with Miles Blackwell, co-managing director of Blackwell's, the great Oxford book-selling and publishing firm, whose bookshop has been at 50 Broad Street since 1879, when it opened its doors in a tiny room 12 feet square. Now Oxford's biggest bookshop, with more than 200,000 titles in stock covering every subject, discipline and interest, it includes the Norrington Room, a vast subterranean terraced chamber of over 10,000 square feet housing 160,000 volumes on over three miles of shelving. The room, opened in 1966 under Trinity College, gained a place in the Guinness Book of Records for having the largest display of books for sale in one room anywhere in the world.

Although it has drawn patrons from all over the world, few of them are aware that this is but the tip of the iceberg as far as Blackwell's worldwide book business is concerned. Brother Nigel, the other co-managing director of the firm, had his office at 50 Broad Street, where he looked after the shop as well as other aspects of the family business. Miles' office was in a large office building down near the train station, from where he roamed the world on company business. Saudi Arabia had recently established several new universities at that time, and Miles was essentially stocking their libraries.

My outbound flight from Riyadh to Athens had been delayed, and having already checked out of my room, I had no choice but to kill time in the hotel lounge, there being nothing outside to attract one's interest on a Friday, the Muslim day of worship. The only other person in the lounge that afternoon, suffering the same fate, was this pleasant young Englishman who invited me to a game of back-gammon.

I had the pleasure of meeting Miles on many occasions in subsequent years, particularly during a six-month leave spent in Oxford in 1985, and it was he who introduced me to another author – one who was alive and well and living in Oxford – Anthony Price. Anthony was editor of the *Oxford Mail*, a weekly paper, and each year for 19 years prior to his retirement he wrote a spy novel incorporating the main character, Dr. Audley, in each. Miles had introduced me to him at The Eight Bells (Miles' "local" near his home in Eaton, a few miles south of Oxford) where Anthony often came for lunch; when I next had lunch there and again saw him, I asked him to sign one of his first editions which I had fortuitously found at a second-hand bookstore the day before. Not only did he sign it, but he filled the entire blank space on the title page with a flowery inscription. Today I have a complete collection of his Audley spy thrillers in mint British and American first editions, together with proof copies of each, all duly inscribed. Would that I might have become a friend of C. S. Lewis in the same way!

I last saw Miles some years ago, and was saddened to learn recently that he had died not long after he and his brother were ousted from their posts by an uncle who somehow gained control of the business.

When I first visited Blackwell's antiquarian department, it was located in a loft near the city market, but soon thereafter moved to Fyfield Manor, a magnificent country manor house in the tiny village of Fyfield, 10 miles southwest of Oxford. Surely no rare book shop ever had a more glorious venue! Visiting its manager, Philip Brown, during those years and having lunch at the White Hart, Fyfield's ancient and superb pub was a great day's outing in itself. Today, my friend Philip holds forth in a tiny area at the back of the 3rd floor at 50 Broad Street – and Oxford has become a mishmash of one-way streets that will carry you out of town if you happen to make the wrong turning while heading for the center, with parking (when one can find a space) at exorbitant rates. If you're planning a visit to Oxford, go by train and buy a day pass for its excellent bus service.

A Pub and a Plaque

I made my first visit to Oxford at Miles' invitation some months after our meeting in Riyadh.

On the way to my hotel from the train station I passed a pub called The Eagle and Child, a name hitherto unfamiliar. The evening was warm and I was thirsty, so I popped in just as they were opening. (In those days, pubs were required by law to close in the afternoon, and at specified hours at night, whereas today they can largely set their own hours. "Time, gentlemen, please!" was the traditional cry of the publican (also called "landlord") – the licensee of the pub – just before closing.)

A small wooden plaque on one wall caught my eye – and I knew I had found the name for my pub:

C. S. Lewis, his brother, W. H. Lewis, Charles Williams and other friends met every Tuesday morning between the years 1939-1962 in this their favourite pub. These men, known popularly as the "Inklings," met here to drink Beer and to discuss, among other things, the books they were writing.

I had first become acquainted with the works of C. S. Lewis when a boyhood chum gave me a copy of *Perelandra* when I was in college, and while on my way to Switzerland in 1972 on sabbatical leave, I picked up half a dozen Lewis paperbacks in England for reading that winter – among them his marvelously lucid apologetic, *Mere Christianity*. I had known nothing of the role that "The Bird and the Baby" (as it's affectionately known in Oxford) played in the lives of these great Christian writers, but it was now clear that I could do no better than to adopt its name for my pub. When I told the landlord, Terry Reading, of my plan and that I would like to photograph the sign outside to have it reproduced, he suggested otherwise. Reaching behind the bar, he produced a picture of the sign that had hung there in Lewis's day, replaced some years earlier by the brewery. "I think you'll find this one much more interesting. It's now owned by Father Walter Hooper, who was Lewis's secretary."

I eventually tracked Walter Hooper down by mail in order to ask him if he could arrange to have a color photograph of the sign taken, so that I might have a reproduction made for my own Eagle and Child. On my next visit to Oxford my wife and I were invited to his flat on Beaumont Street, where he had the photo ready for me to take to London to have the sign made by a firm in London who reproduce old pub signs – and thus I became a friend of the man who has done more than anyone to introduce the general public to the writings of C. S. Lewis.

The sign depicts a soaring eagle with a chubby, curly-headed infant on its back. The child is Ganymede, who in Greek mythology was the most beautiful of all mortals. So beautiful was he that Zeus, the chief and head of all gods, sought him to live among the gods and fill Zeus's own cup. Taking the shape of a mighty eagle, he snatched the child and carried him from Mount Ida to Mount Olympus. It seems only fitting that a pub so named should become the place where mortals met and communed with the gods in their writings. (As for Ganymede, we're told that Zeus's wife Hera, "ever more jealous of lovely Ganymede, nagged her husband so much he grew fed up, and promised to send him away. Only later did she find out that he left Olympus to take his place among the stars, as the constellation Aquarius, where he can be seen to this day, still pouring nectar.")

Walter told me he had written the original text for the plaque commissioned by Terry and his wife Win. "It came about that so many people asked Terry and Win where the Inklings met that they asked me to write something they could hang on the wall. I wrote the bit you have seen on the plaque, typed it onto a piece of paper, and for some months that piece of paper was attached to the left-hand wall of the Rabbit Room. It soon became clear that this was to be permanent, and Terry and Win had the words painted onto that plaque which is in that room today. I was in the pub the day the plaque went up, and I was looking at what I had written when a student stopped, looked hard at it, and said, 'Why did he capitalize Beer?' I didn't answer him, but I capitalized Beer because I wanted to emphasize the *pub* atmosphere, as distinct from the atmosphere of a *bar*."

A warm and inviting place it is. This black-and-white picture is taken from a beautiful watercolor commissioned by Terry from a local artist. Sadly, Terry had died by the time I returned to Oxford in 1985; Win had just retired from running the pub on her own, and when I called upon her, she showed me this painting.

Then she generously gave it to me – to decorate my own Eagle and Child.

My pub was at last complete, but it then occurred to me that it might be useful to have some of Lewis's books on a small shelf on one wall, alongside the replica of Hooper's plaque. A dozen or so of the paperbacks readily available in any large bookstore should do nicely – but then that seemed a bit tacky for such a fine establishment. What about some hardbacks, in nice dust jackets? Fine – but there weren't many available in those days.

Well, what about the first editions of those paperbacks? Surely they must have first appeared in hardback. But where to find them?

A Bonanza in Belfast

Soon thereafter, Pat and I were scheduled to rendezvous in London with our friends, Hal and Betsy Guffey, for a trip through the Middle East. Hal was president of International Students, Inc., a Christian organization that carries on a friendship ministry to foreign students at American universities, and we were to visit their coworkers in Egypt, Saudi Arabia, and Afghanistan. Having never visited Ireland, Pat and I flew first to Dublin, where I made my first incursion into the world of book collecting – dubious, however, of finding anything of Lewis in a Catholic country. That misassumption was short-lived when I walked into the first second-hand bookshop on my list and inquired whether they might have any first editions of C. S. Lewis. "We may have one or two, but as a rule we sell them as soon as we get them." I did find one in Dublin, but when I went up to Belfast for a day, I struck gold – and like the '49ers of yore who acquired gold fever, I immediately became infected with that disease for which there is seemingly no cure – book collecting.

Downtown Belfast in 1975 was one British checkpoint after another, so instead of waiting in line for searches and questioning while wandering around looking for book stores, I decided to consult the yellow pages at the telephone office. Two antiquarian bookstores were listed for Belfast, but a policeman I queried about their location said that only one was reasonably nearby. His fellow officer, noting the address, said to his colleague, "Isn't that the store that was bombed a day or two ago? But you might as well phone them – perhaps it might not have been that bad." As it turned out, the number and address I had was for the home of Jack and Jean Gamble, who warmly invited me to stop by – and with whom I've enjoyed a warm friendship ever since.

Their store, Emerald Isle Books, had indeed been bombed by the IRA – and totally destroyed. Just three days earlier two men had visited the home to offer him an old book of Irish history, his specialty. Once inside the house they brandished revolvers, and asked where the children were. Jean had been about to leave to pick up their daughter at kindergarten, so they ordered her to go there directly, pick up the child, and come directly home. "If you're not

24

back in 20 minutes or attempt to contact the police," they warned, "we'll shoot your husband."

When she returned, one of the gunmen remained at the house while the other ordered Jack to phone the bookshop about a mile down the road and tell the manager he was bringing a customer. There he planted what the police later estimated to have been a 50-pound bomb, in a futile attempt to destroy a British police post next door. Detonated by a timer, the bomb destroyed the shop and 50,000 old books, but the police station was unscathed.

Despite this recent disaster, Jack welcomed me and showed me his stock of books on shelves in every room of the house, not yet consigned to the shop. Among them were a dozen or more Lewis first editions. Among them was *George Macdonald: An Anthology*, edited by Lewis. (MacDonald signed his name with an upper case "D", and it is usually seen thus in print today, although Lewis seemed to prefer the lower case "d".)

"If you collect Lewis, you'll surely be wanting to collect George MacDonald," he said, to which I weakly replied, "Of course!" – too embarrassed to confess that I had never heard of George MacDonald. He generously gave me the book as a gift to read on the train back to Dublin, saying he would wrap and post the others since I was only beginning my trip. I would learn much more about Lewis from Jack in subsequent visits to Belfast.

Born in Belfast in 1898, Lewis experienced the joy at age 7 of moving into a large house, "Little Lea," on the outskirts of Belfast, which his father Albert had specially built for the family. While working in Saudi Arabia in 1975, I received from Jack a newspaper clipping advertising the sale of Little Lea – at what would later prove to have been a tremendous bargain at £50,000 for any investor interested in Lewis. On our way home from Saudi Arabia at the end of my tour, we spent several days with the Gambles. The house had been sold, but the new owners had not yet moved in, so we had the rare opportunity to go through it while it was being renovated. What a marvelous place for the Lewis brothers to have lived during their later childhood!

Establishing a Fine Base in Oxford

Although becoming the owner of Little Lea was beyond my budget for extravagant purchases, a marvelous opportunity presented itself some years later for becoming part owner of another Lewis home – the house in Oxford where Lewis spent his life from 1930 until his death in 1963 – The Kilns.

The house had been purchased by the Thirsk family upon Warnie's death in 1973, ten years after his brother's death. In 1984, the Thirsks decided to sell the property, and when a Christian businessman in California heard that it was on the market, he went to Oxford to put an option on it. He then formed a limited partnership with himself as general partner in which he sold shares at $5000 each. Pat and I bought in, as did David and Ruth Neuhouser, Dan and Elizabeth Hamilton, and a dozen or so others.

By January 1985 when the sale was completed, the British pound was worth only $1.17 after having almost reached parity with the dollar shortly before – and enough shares had been sold that, with a bit more cash which could easily have been obtained from the existing investors, sufficient funds would have been available to pay cash for this highly desirable property. However, the general partner chose to use only half the proceeds received from the sale of shares, retaining the balance for ongoing expenses, and borrowed the equivalent of $50,000 from an Oxford bank to complete the purchase. This was a most unfortunate decision, for immediately thereafter the pound began to recover, with the result that the mortgage payment in dollars increased every month thereafter, leading to eventual dissolution of the partnership, with ownership finally being turned over to the C. S. Lewis Foundation of Redlands, California.

A privilege of ownership for the initial investors was that of being able to stay in The Kilns whenever they were in Oxford, when such was convenient for the resident managers, Michael and Judith Apichella, a young couple who had moved there from Illinois at the invitation of the general partner. I seized the opportunity to exercise that privilege for a week or so in July 1985 by scheduling a sabbatical leave from Indiana University, but when my wife joined me in mid-July we moved into a rental flat on Woodstock Road to give some breathing room to Michael and Judith. Judith was expecting their first child, and the tremendous influx of American tourists (as the result of the low pound) was bringing a flood of visitors to The Kilns – over 300 of them that summer, as the guest book later showed.

Our flat at 87 Woodstock Road was a perfect base from which to operate, being within a short walk in one direction to the center of Oxford and a short drive in the other direction to the ring road that quickly took us to the main highway to wherever we were headed.

Miles Blackwell had been immensely helpful in our acquiring a fine used car from his dealer – a recent model Saab – and in the next few months we covered enormous distances driving around England, Scotland and Wales as I sought out every second-hand bookstore within many miles of Oxford. (When I sold the car back to the dealer four months later, he was amazed to see that we had driven it more than 3000 miles without ever leaving Britain's shores – and thanks to the steady rise in the value of the pound, its value in dollars was the same as that which we had paid for it.)

Oxford is conveniently located next to one of England's most delightful areas, the Cotswolds, and as our much-marked-up map of the Cotswolds revealed upon our return home, we had driven on virtually every highway and byway therein (including those one-lane roads for which the area is famous – in which either you or an oncoming driver must pull into the nearest cut in the hedge rows on both sides in order for the other to go by.)

The interim history of The Kilns is not a pleasant story, but warrants being told. Michael Apichella's wife Judith is English, and when offered the opportunity to move to England and live at The Kilns, the young couple eagerly accepted the offer. Michael was a writer and both were Lewis enthusiasts, so this was a marvelous opportunity for them – and a delight to Judith's parents. The house needed much in the way of improvements, but they were determined to do their best to honor its heritage, which had essentially been lost during the previous ten years. Within their first four months they had made contact with the C. S. Lewis Society of Oxford and were scheduling Lewis-related meetings at the house. By the time I arrived in July, however, it was apparent that things were not going well.

Unfortunately, their "employer" had made no provision for their gainful employment, providing them only with a roof over their heads and barely enough to buy food and pay the utilities, having assumed that Michael would get a job to support the family – a naive assumption indeed, for he was an American for whom a work permit was essentially unobtainable at that stage. However, they were given permission to rent rooms to several students, which eased their financial situation somewhat. No provision had
been made for tools necessary to maintain the property, but when another of the partners arrived in Oxford for the summer, we bought a lawn mower, hedge clippers, and other tools and began to get the grounds in order, as well as making some major repairs indoors.

Within a year or two, however, the rising pound had put such a burden on the general partner in meeting the mortgage payments, paying for utilities, and making essential repairs that he asked the Apichellas to leave and turned the property over to a local rental agency to let it out to students in its entirety. Michael had by now obtained part-time employment as an instructor for the University of Maryland college extension program at nearby U. S. Air Force bases in England, and later became half-time director of religious programming for BBC-Oxford, enabling them to buy a little home south of Oxford for themselves and their two lovely girls.

But all's well that ends well. The C. S. Lewis Foundation eventually obtained ownership of the property and restored it to what it was in Lewis's day, and today it is used at various times as a Lewis study center. As for the Apichellas, I have had the pleasure of visiting them over the years, most recently in the lovely town of Bury St. Edmonds, north of Cambridge, where they now have a beautiful, large family and are doing very well. Michael had written a number of books and still teaches at the air bases, while Judith has also become a teacher.

My first week in Oxford in 1985 was memorable for another reason: the rarest of Lewis first editions became mine – Lewis's first book, *Spirits in Bondage*.

Serendipity, Thy Name is Golden

Serendipity: the faculty or phenomenon of finding valuable or agreeable things not sought for – as did the heroes of the Persian fairy tale, *The Three Princes of Serendip*

While the thrill of the chase is often enough to sustain the avid book collector, anticipation of something, like many things in life, often exceeds its realization. The newly acquired first edition, especially of a rare title, is fondly held, gently thumbed, and possibly even read, but then it becomes just another book on a shelf of marvelous books. Coming back to it from time to time renews much of the delight that accompanied its acquisition, but the original thrill isn't quite there still. Not so, however, when at a later date one finds some feature of a book that hitherto either escaped one's attention or was regarded as a flaw – only now revealed as an unrecognized blessing.

The serious collector seeks books in their original, pristine state, preferably seemingly untouched by human hands, and while one may tolerate a neat little owner's signature, something as gross as a complete address as well is anathema. They might as well have pasted therein a photo of themselves. Such was my reaction when I acquired a long-sought-after copy of Lewis's extremely rare first book, *Spirits in Bondage.*

At the age of seven, Lewis began writing about an imaginary "Animal Land" (published in 1985 as *BOXEN: The Imaginary World of the Young C. S. Lewis*). As a teenager, however, his first ambition was to be a poet. While under the tutelage of W. T. Kirkpatrick, to whom his father had sent him in 1914 when he was unable to tolerate the life at a private school, Lewis began voraciously studying the craft of poetry and writing verse himself during his holidays from school. At age seventeen he wrote two of the romantic lyrics which later appeared in *Spirits in Bondage.*

These and some 50 other poems written during the two-year period he was with Kirkpatrick were copied into a notebook which he titled The Metrical Meditations of a Cod ("cod" being a northern Irish term of humorous self-deprecation), fourteen of which are included in *Spirits of Bondage*. The other verses in his first published book were written while on army duty in France and during recovery from his wounds.

The theme of *Spirits in Bondage* – that nature is malevolent and that any God that exists is outside the cosmic system – reflects the influence of Kirkpatrick's atheism on the young scholar, but by the time he returned to Oxford after the war, Lewis began having doubts about the validity of his views of a remote and uninvolved God. For the next ten years he would continue to modify these views as he came closer and closer to a real understanding of God.

Published under the pseudonym, Clive Hamilton (using his mother's family name), and by an Oxford student, the book understandably was not a great success. The few reviews of the book appeared in such first-class papers as *The London Times* and *The Scotsman* and were quite favorable, but the book did not sell well, and after a few years the publisher destroyed most of the remaining copies. The book is extremely rare today – I am aware of only 5 or 6 copies having appeared on the market in the past 20 years. (A recent computer search of library holdings showed only 15 copies worldwide.)

My initial search for the book took me to the westernmost tip of the British Isles. Dr. Clyde Kilby, founder of the Wade Center at Wheaton College, had told me he had heard of a copy owned by someone in Penzance (whose name I've long since forgotten), but he had not had the opportunity to check it out. Pursuing that clue, I took a train from London, and upon arriving in Penzance inquired of the local postmaster, who informed me that the chap in question had died some years earlier. Further inquiry revealed nothing regarding the disposition of his library, and I returned to London empty-handed.

My first copy, obtained from a London bookseller in 1985, was initially a disappointment. The original owner had not only written both his name and address in indelible ink, but also hadn't the decency to do so on the blank endpaper where any reasonable person would have established ownership. Instead, he defaced the title page with his scrawl: *Richard Lewis, West dene, Helensburgh.* Lewis is such a common name, and Helensburgh is in Scotland, so I assumed no connection with the Lewises of Northern Ireland. I could only hope to find another copy while living in Oxford that summer.

Some weeks later, I acquired a copy of *They Stand Together: The Letters of C. S. Lewis to Arthur Greeves (1914-1963).* Lewis first met Arthur, with whom he was to become a friend for life, when both were in their teens. Although their parents were friends and neighbors, it was not until 1914 that Lewis first visited the family when he was told that Arthur was ill and would welcome a visit. Overcoming his natural shyness, Lewis hesitatingly made the journey across the street. "I found Arthur sitting up in bed. On the table beside him lay a copy of *Myths of the Norsemen.* 'Do *you* like that?' said I. 'Do *you* like that?', said he. Next moment the book was in our hands, our heads were bent close together, we were pointing, quoting, talking – soon almost shouting –– discovering in a torrent of questions that we liked not only the same thing, but the same parts of it and in the same way; that both knew the stab of Joy and that, for both, the arrow was shot from the North. Many thousands of people have had the experience of finding the first friend, and it is none the less a wonder; as great a wonder as first love, or even greater. I had been so far from thinking such a friend possible that I had never even longed for one; no more than I longed to be King of England."

Later that same year, when Lewis returned to school in England, they began a correspondence that lasted until only a few weeks before Lewis died, writing to each other weekly for many of those years. Much of this correspondence, together with many enormously helpful footnotes by the editor, Walter Hooper, fills the 566 pages of *They Stand Together.*

While reading through my copy later that summer I came across a footnote noting that Lewis's uncles, Richard and William Lewis, moved to Scotland in 1883 to go into business in Glasgow, but had their homes in Helensburgh, some fifteen miles from the city. Helensburgh! A light flickered in my brain, and with trembling hand I pulled my *Spirits in Bondage* off the shelf. There it was indeed, now clear as a bell: Richard Lewis, West dene, Helensburgh! It was his uncle Richard's copy, second only in significance to the copy given to his father, now lovingly housed in the vault of the Marion Wade Center at Wheaton College. Bless you, Richard, for including your address!

(In 1995, when ordering a book from dealer Brian Annesley in Helensburgh, I mentioned this entry. He confirmed that the local telephone directory of 1933, of which he had a copy, still listed "Richard Lewis, West dene, 1 Sutherland Crescent lower T588". "West dene is the name of the house," he noted. "There is also a Sutherland Crescent upper – i.e., there are two concentric crescents, one behind the other. Lewis lived in the lower one, nearer the Clyde. The house is reasonably spacious, but not grand by the standards of the day, and is semi-detached – i.e., shares a wall with another house. It is Victorian, built sometime before 1877, according to my earliest record. The T stands for telephone, and 588 is the number.")

Other than this and the Wade Center's copy of the book, I have not seen any of Lewis's books given by him to members of his family. Some years ago, however, a gentleman in England, Mr. Lewis Dodd, offered me a book he had been given by an old friend of his, George Sayer – a copy of *Surprised by Joy*, which had belonged to Joy Davidman. George and his wife Moira were close friends of Lewis, and as he describes in his Lewis biography, *Jack: A Life of C. S. Lewis*, he was invited to the luncheon at which Jack first met the woman who was eventually to become Jack's wife, Joy Davidman Gresham.

"Joy desperately wanted advice from Jack about her marriage (*to William Gresham*). She also wanted to discuss with him the book she was writing on the Ten Commandments. She wrote to him from London and invited him to have lunch with her and Phyllis Williams (*her friend in London*) early in September. He returned the invitation by inviting her and Phyllis Williams to lunch in his Madgalen College rooms. The fourth member of the party should have been Warren, but he withdrew, and I was asked to take his place."

At their lunch, Jack gave Joy a copy of his latest book, *Mere Christianity*, which had been published a few weeks earlier. After their marriage, when Jack gave Joy another copy of the book lovingly inscribed by him, Joy gave the first copy to George as a memento of their first meeting. Some time later she wrote on the flyleaf, "*Given me by C. S. Lewis September 17, 1952. Joy Davidman,*" and on two pages are intriguing notes written long before their subsequent friendship blossomed and grew into marriage:

Page 78: *What are all these kissings worth if thou kiss not me?*
Page 86: *What if the quieter love does not come? It cannot be achieved alone.*

Standing Together

Another unusual acquisition was a first edition of a 3-volume set of a George MacDonald novel, *Alec Forbes of Howglen* which had come from the personal library of C. S. Lewis purchased by Wroxton College near Banbury. The college is the British branch of Fairleigh Dickinson University of New Jersey, housed in Wroxton Abbey, the magnificent 17th century estate of Sir William Pope. The abbey underwent considerable restoration in preparation for its becoming a study center, upon completion of which the university planned a magnificent "housewarming" – only to realize that the library was devoid of books. An agent was hastily commissioned to scour the countryside for books – any books. Luck was with him, for just at that time Lewis's personal library of some 2500 volumes was being auctioned in Oxford.

In 1985, when the college needed the shelf space taken up by the Lewis collection (which was not pertinent to the academic needs of the college), the principal, Nick Baldwin, decided to sell it on condition it would remain in England where any Wroxton student interested in it might still have access to it. When our general partner learned of the Lewis collection at the college, he offered to buy it when a price had been established. Nick gave him an option to do so, provided it would be housed at The Kilns, where their students would still have ready access to it.

Nick had asked my opinion of its value, but I wasn't much help to him. My own knowledge of book values was limited to those I had been collecting, and Lewis's friends had been invited by him to help themselves to copies of their own books in his personal library after his death. There were, however, four books of George MacDonald in the Wroxton College collection – the only ones, as I told Nick, that were of any interest to me.

Upon returning to Indianapolis later that year, I learned that Nick had obtained an appraisal, and our general partner had asked the director of the Wade Center at Wheaton College to evaluate the collection and to exercise his option to purchase it. One of the other limited partners had offered to fund the purchase, and together they went to England to complete the transaction. Pending the anticipated restoration of The Kilns, however, it would be necessary to store the books at the Wade Center until such time as they could be securely housed at The Kilns.

Much to my amazement I later received a parcel from England containing these four books. There was no accompanying letter, and the return address of the sender on the Customs label was written simply as "Anonymous." Before turning the collection over to the buyers, Nick had generously set these aside for me. I was thrilled to obtain the books, one of which had been given Lewis by Arthur Greeves.

Some years later, again while reading *They Stand Together*, I came across a letter to Arthur dated December 24, 1930, in which Lewis thanks Arthur for notes, "*Yesterday I picked up for 4/6 Alec Forbes in three half leather volumes. Do you know it?*" The "4/6" rang a bell. I eagerly removed Volume I from the shelf – and there on the flyleaf was the penciled price "*4/6*" (4 shillings, 6 pence), just as it had been written there by the dealer from whom Lewis purchased the book some 65 years earlier. Not only did I now have absolute proof of its having belonged to Lewis, but knew the precise date on which he bought it as well. Fellow collectors, never remove those penciled notations that used-book dealers are prone to enter in their stock. You never know what value may come of them.

Worth Repeating

But there was more to come ...

In 1999, while examining the same Alec Forbes triple-decker, David Neuhouser began to wonder about some strange inscriptions in the back of each volume.

("Triple-decker" or "three-decker" is the term given to the peculiar practice in 19th century Britain of publishing novels in three volumes. Between 1842 and 1894, Charles Edward Mudie's lending library influenced Victorian literature, particularly fiction, by demanding that publishers print all novels in three volumes, and offering only fiction suited to the middle-class family. An astute businessman, Mudie ordered books in large quantities, often taking thousands of volumes and occasionally buying up entire printings, thus insuring his power with both publishers and public, since his large stock meant that readers did not have to wait long for popular works. By offering a novel in three volumes, he could obtain three rental fees for a single novel. With the growth of public libraries, however, he eventually lost this control, and the three-decker went the way of the dodo.)

David, now retired, but still at Taylor as director of the C. S. Lewis Study Center which houses the Edwin W. Brown Collection, found similar notations in the back of Lewis's copy of *Annals of a Quiet Neighbourhood*. He eventually realized that the scribbled numbers, each with an alpha or beta marking, were Lewis's "quality" rankings of chapters from which Lewis had extracted a total of exactly 365 selections in his George MacDonald anthology. All of the alpha passages made it into the book; none of the beta passages were used. Thus a book that afforded me a pleasant surprise some years after it came into my possession brought yet another surprise to David after being in his possession for several years.

Friends and Family Trees

In his preface to the MacDonald anthology, Lewis wrote: "I have never concealed the fact that I regarded him as my master; indeed I fancy I have never written a book in which I did not quote from him."

Lewis shared this interest in MacDonald with Arthur Greeves, and Arthur often sent his own copies of MacDonald to Jack. On August 31, 1930, he wrote to Arthur, "I have had two delightful moments since I last wrote to you. The first was the arrival of the Macdonalds. Thank you over and over again!"

In the copy of *Annals of a Quiet Neighbourhood* received as a gift from Nick Baldwin, Lewis had diagrammed on the flyleaf the family tree of the characters in the story. (I had previously seen a photograph of this page, taken years before at Wroxton College by Douglas Gilbert, in *C. S. Lewis: Images of His World*, by Kilby and Gilbert.) I was so intrigued at studying this Lewis entry that it was not until months later that I saw what I had long overlooked – the ownership signature of Arthur Greeves on the other side of that page.

After reading MacDonald books received from Arthur, Lewis normally returned them, but apparently neglected to return this one. Many years later, my friend Jack Gamble of Emerald Isle Books in Belfast was pleasantly surprised to find the rest of Arthur's MacDonald books among 25,000 books of the Linenhall Library in Belfast which he had purchased, to which Arthur's nephew had donated them. He kindly sold them to me, and all of the MacDonald books loaned to Lewis are once again together in the collection at Taylor University.

The family tree turned out to be another common thread that eventually brought Dan Hamilton into the same orbit with Dave Neuhouser and me. When Dan was preparing his modern edition of *A Quiet Neighborhood* in 1982, he had been forced "in self-defense" (as he claims) to sketch out the tangled Oldcastle, Weir, and Walton family relationships in order to unravel the plot. This edition, with the tree printed in the back, came to Dave's attention and then to mine.

To anyone who has not read any of those paperback editions of MacDonald novels edited by Dan, I highly recommend doing so. Although I had bought every one of the very rare MacDonald "triple-deckers" I came across in my early years of collecting those authors other than Lewis, I had never done more than thumb through one of them. Dan's condensed version was the first I had read all the way through, giving me an appreciation for all of MacDonald's exciting novels – and his "EDITOR'S AFTERWORD" at the end of *The Seaboard Parish* spurred me to visit the west coast of England on my next trip there, primarily to see what he describes:

Kilkaven and Tintagel and St. Nectan's Glen are all real places as well, and may be seen today. Kilkhaven was MacDonald's name for Bude, a town on the northern Cornish coast where MacDonald and his family spent the summer of 1867.

My wife and I visited Bude in the summer of 1984, and found much of it exactly as described – the marvelous cobbled breakwater protecting the harbor from the daily ravages of the sea; the curious cottages at the end of the quay near the canal; and even the ornate boathouse – not the one used now (at the head of the canal) but the one which still stands a few hundred yards away from the sea.

Tintagel is exactly as MacDonald saw it, except that wide stone steps with sturdy handrails ease the climb to the top, making an otherwise perilous ascent possible even for the visitors (such as myself) who have no head for heights. The stone arch through which Connie saw the sea still stands, affording an unparalleled view of the waves crashing between the cliffs hundreds of feet below.

Merlin's Cave burrows under the peninsula where the castle stands, and the old church and graveyard still huddle atop the land's edge overlooking the castle ruins. St. Nectan's Glen, a few miles away, is also preserved as a tourist stop and tea garden.

(MacDonald's son Greville recollected the family's time in the area of Bude as among the happiest of his childhood – and largely because his father was more involved in the lives and play of his children then than at any other time within his memory.)

I took the paperback with me, using those paragraphs as a guide to be sure I missed nothing. With book in hand, Pat and I surveyed the area as we approached the castle's ruins in Bude and ascended "the wide stone steps with sturdy handrails." It was truly exciting to keep that paragraph before us as we looked through the stone arch and saw what Dan describes. Without Dan's help I might have had to carry the heavy triple-decker in a backpack and thumbed laboriously through it to fully enjoy the view!

A Tale of Two Geoffreys

The popularity of C. S. Lewis has grown steadily over the years, but the release of the film *Shadowlands* resulted in an abrupt surge of interest in his writings. Among both old and new collectors of his books there has been an ever-increasing demand for a book signed by him, but such books have always been in short supply, with no more than a few turning up in any given year.

Some time ago my good friend Laura McMullan in Alabama asked if I could find for her a set of British first editions of the Chronicles of Narnia that she might leave to her grandchildren. Although such sets appear on the market from time to time, they are invariably ones put together by dealers who may obtain each of the seven volumes from as many as seven different sources. I was aware of such a set being offered by a prominent London dealer, two volumes of which had been inscribed by Lewis for the original owners – both, strangely enough, with the same first name. In *Prince Caspian* he had written: *Geoffrey Barfield, with love from Jack Lewis.* The other, *The Silver Chair*, was inscribed: *Geoffrey Corbett, with love from C. S. Lewis.*

Both names were very familiar. Geoffrey Barfield was the son of Lewis's best friend, Owen Barfield. Lewis had dedicated *The Lion, the Witch and the Wardrobe* to Geoffrey's sister, Lucy, to whom Lewis was godfather, and Geoffrey Corbett was the dedicatee for *The Voyage of the 'Dawn Treader.'* In all my years of collecting, however, I had never taken the time to find out who Geoffrey Corbett was and why he was so honored. Although five of the first six Narnia books were dedicated to children of Lewis's friends (*The Last Battle* had no dedicatee), to my knowledge Lewis never had a friend named Corbett.

When hard-pressed for any information about C. S. Lewis, I invariably turn to the Oracle of Delphi – Walter Hooper, the man who knows more about Lewis and his works than any living person, and who has edited the vast majority of the many posthumous editions of Lewis's writings. A phone call to Oxford quickly solved the mystery, confirming what I had by now begun to suspect: the two Geoffreys were one and the same person.

Jeffrey Barfield (as he now spells his name) came into the Barfield household as Geoffrey Corbett, born on June 6, 1940 to a London mother who was unable to take care of him. Maud and Owen Barfield learned of her plight and offered to take care of him for a time. When Jeffrey became of school age and was to have been returned to his mother, she had no money for his school fees and was willing to give him up for adoption. The Barfields, on the other hand, were very willing to adopt him, but neither could they afford the school fees. Like the Barfields, Lewis had come to adore this child, so he offered to pay the fees, and Jeffrey thus became a permanent member of the family – and today is the only survivor.

Although baptized in the Church of England, Jeffrey at the age of 20 or so became very much involved with a local Pentecostal congregation and began preaching in a number of evangelical churches. When he began receiving letters addressed to "Pastor Barfield," Owen suggested that he change his name, and this he did when he reached 21, the legal age of majority.

Laura was thrilled to have a first edition set of the Chronicles of Narnia with two such inscriptions and was most grateful for my "research," having been unaware that *The Voyage of the "Dawn Treader"* had originally been dedicated to Geoffrey Corbett. It seems that, unbeknownst to me, the Lewis "expert" who collected only first editions, that later editions of the Narnia books show Geoffrey Barfield as the dedicatee.

Readers of *The Lion, the Witch and the Wardrobe* may recall that Lewis dedicated it to Lucy Barfield, the only daughter of Owen Barfield and for whom Lucy Pevensie in the book was named. She was 15 years old at the time, and some time after the book appeared, she was stricken with multiple sclerosis. She received many letters from readers wishing her well and asking about Narnia, which some believed she had actually visited. Despite struggling with the disease her entire adult life, she devoted her life to working with children, even when severely disabled. She died in 2003.

The Lewis Legacy in the Market Place

The past decade has seen a bull market developing for first editions and early reprints of Lewis books, and with the release of Disney's hugely successful *The Lion, the Witch and the Wardrobe* in December 2005, a further surge in the market was anticipated as the result of many becoming interested in an author of whom they may have been only vaguely aware. Book collectors are a strange breed, and when they see something new that had not previously attracted their attention, their antennae begin to vibrate.

Book collectors fall into many different categories, of course, with some specializing in juvenile fiction, others in fantasy and science fiction, and so on. The truly serious collector may limit himself to first editions, whereas less discriminating (or less well-heeled) collectors may be satisfied with early reprints, or "reading copies" of first editions – copies in such poor condition that they sell for very little, but which give pleasure to the reader who revels in reading a book just as it first appeared in print.

For any given first edition, condition is all-important. As I've indicated earlier, discriminating collectors want a book in as nearly the same condition as when it left the printer – and in a dust jacket (or dust wrapper as it's known in Britain) in like pristine state if it originally had one. Since dust jackets are often discarded or lost, and much more fragile than the book, there are far fewer first edition dust jackets in existence than the books themselves.

Later printing dust jackets may thus be found on books offered by booksellers, either because some previous owner wanted to improve the appearance of the book in his library, or because the bookseller can more readily sell it. The seller will usually inform a prospective buyer that the jacket as being from a later printing, but in some instances he may be unaware that it is – as I have seen from time to time. As I've pointed out in the bibliography herein, if the publisher has not indicated on the front flap of the jacket that it's a later printing, one needs to look at any advertising of other books (usually on the back of the jacket) that may list a book that was published later than the book on which the jacket appears.

In one instance, as the result of having acquired multiple copies of the same title, I became aware of two significant differences between two jackets on copies of the same first edition. One was a slight difference in the wording of the brief publisher's blurb on the front flap; the other was the listing of one title on the back, not identified by date of issue but by the number of the printing – 14th *large impression* on the one; 13th *large impression* on the other. Clearly the latter was the true first edition dust jacket – not put on that book by the seller but by the publisher himself, who decided to change the wording on the front flap and put the new jacket on remaining copies of the first printing of the first edition.

With the publication of *Out of the Silent Planet* Lewis found that he could incorporate Christian theology in fiction in a way that might almost be described as subliminal. His biographer, George Sayer, wrote: *"Out of the Silent Planet* initially received about sixty reviews, quite a large number for a book by a little-known writer. Only two reviewers showed any awareness of the book's Christian theology. It was typically regarded as just science fiction. ... The reviewers' failure to see the point of the book gave Jack the idea that would be basic to all his children's stories. If there was only someone with a richer talent and more leisure I think that this great ignorance might be a help to the evangelisation of England; any amount of theology can now be smuggled into people's minds under cover of romance without their knowing it."

The book did not sell well, but was re-issued in 1940 as "The First Cheap Edition" in a different binding with a price of 3s 6d. The binding was rose-red cloth instead of mauve, with the same style lettering on the spine as the first edition, but in black instead of gold. I recently learned from an old Blackwell employee that the cheaper edition was printed in 1940 by Basil Blackwell from Lane plates, something done commonly by Blackwell during the war, but with the top-edge not dyed. Because the reprinted text is precisely the same as that of the first printing, and on the same kind of paper, only the different binding distinguishes it from the first edition, resulting in unjacketed copies being sold as first editions – at first edition price – by dealers who are not familiar with the First Cheap Edition.

The original Harold Jones jacket was used with the original price of 7s. 6d. clipped by the publisher, removing a large triangular piece from the lower right corner. Overprinted in red, immediately below the publisher's blurb on the front flap, is: RECOMMENDED BY THE BOOK SOCIETY. Also overprinted in red, below the original last line on the flap, Jacket by Harold Jones, is: FIRST CHEAP EDITION 3s 6d net.

In 1943, the book was again reissued, in light blue cloth and black lettering on the spine, with *Reprinted 1943* added beneath *First published in 1938* on the back of the title page.

The original jacket by Harold Jones is so rare that few dealers have ever seen one. This is one of only three copies I have been able to find in over thirty years:

Books printed during World War II in Britain often went through many printings because paper supplies were rationed to publishers, who had to decide how to allocate their monthly quota among books being published. A striking example of this – and an illustration of how collectors value a first printing of a book versus later printings – is the publication record of *The Screwtape Letters*.

The book was first issued on February 9, 1942 in an unknown quantity. Whether the publisher did not anticipate the success of the book or was simply limited to that number of copies is also unknown. In any case, the supply of first printings disappeared so quickly that it was reissued *twice* in March 1942 and six more times by the end of the year – and many times thereafter. Fortunately, each subsequent printing was duly noted on the front flap of the jacket in red – for example the printing of December 1942 is noted as *Fourth edition*. (For a brief discourse on the use of "edition," "impression," etc., see the second paragraph of the introduction to the bibliography.)

The difference in price between the first printing of the first edition is dramatically shown by that for *The Screwtape Letters*. As this is being written, there are two copies of the first printing, in dust jackets, being offered on the Internet for $5000 and $6000 respectively. In that same listing a copy of the March 1942 second printing, in fine condition in the dust jacket, is being offered for $350! Except for the words, *FIRST PUBLISHED FEBRUARY 1942, REPRINTED MARCH 1942*, on the back of the title page, there is no difference whatsoever between the two books – same cloth binding, same printed pages throughout – and except for <u>*Second Edition*</u> at the top of the front flap of the dust jacket and some reviews, the jackets are identical.

Without the dust jacket, those $5000 and $6000 copies would be worth no more than $1500 each – and in the case of a first British edition of *The Lion, the Witch and the Wardrobe* the spread is even greater. A fine first edition of the book in a fine dust jacket is currently being offered for $15,000, whereas the book alone should be priced at no more than $2000. Such is the crazy world of book collecting.

The Chronicles of Narnia are by far the most widely collected Lewis first editions, with *The Screwtape Letters* the second most popular. Among collectors of science fiction, Lewis's space trilogy is in high regard, yet while a British first edition of *Out of the Silent Planet* is so rare in the dust jacket that the few that have appeared in recent years have sold for $8000 or more, one can find copies of *Perelandra* and *That Hideous Strength* for as little as a few hundred dollars. The first American edition of any Lewis book, including the Chronicles of Narnia, are considerably less valuable than the first British edition.

The prices of British first editions of the Chronicles of Narnia have soared so out of reach of most collectors that some are satisfying their desire to have a set by opting for first editions that have been rebound in leather. Used for such sets are genuine first editions whose bindings are in such poor condition that no serious collector would buy them, yet the pages within may be in fine condition. Bound in the British tradition by some of England's finest binders, with raised bands, handsome gold tooling of the leather, and gilt edges, such a set can be had for about $8,000 these days, compared to $30,000 for a set in the original bindings and dust jackets. Still not able to afford such a luxury, other collectors are turning to sets of early reprints of the Narnia books in dust jackets essentially unchanged from the original ones, at a fraction of the cost of a set of first printings.

Actual manuscripts, of course, are the rarest of all. Lewis entrusted a duplicate manuscript of *The Screwtape Letters* to Sister Penelope at the Anglican convent in Wantage, in case the other copy that had been sent to the publisher in London in 1942 should be bombed. After the war she wrote to him to ask him if he wanted it back. He told her: *If you can persuade any "sucker" (as the Americans say) to buy the MS of Screwtape, pray do, and use the money for any pious or charitable object you like ... I understand some people are paying good money for my things.*

She did sell it, using the money to refurbish their chapel, and it is now in the Berg Collection in the New York Public Library. If he thought people were crazy to buy such of his things in those days, he must be shaking his head in utter astonishment today.

Dressing Up Tired First Editions

As I've noted elsewhere, there has been an increasing interest in recent years in having first editions of Lewis's more popular books rebound in leather, using copies with worn or damaged exteriors which can then be sold at a fraction of the cost of a fine copy in the dust jacket. My first venture into this area began some fifteen years ago when I first began visiting Eastern Europe just after the collapse of Communism to see the changes taking place since my many earlier visits to the region.

In Romania, where I had known nary a soul nor had a single contact when I first went there in March 1990, just six weeks after their revolution, I had the good fortune through some incredible circumstances to meet the new Minister of Health in his office just six hours after my arrival in Bucharest. At ten o'clock that evening he generously offered me the services of an English-speaking guide to conduct me around some health facilities the following day – a feat he was able to accomplish at that hour by phoning his sister and asking her to tell her son, a student in the university, to take the day off and host this American visitor. It was thus that I met an amazing young man, Bogdan, who was to serve me in that role for two more visits that year and in the immediate years to come – whom my wife and I now view almost like a youngest son and whose family in Bucharest are now part of our extended family. But that's another story ...

Learning how impoverished the citizens of Romania had become under the tyrannical dictatorship of Nicolae Ceausescu, I asked him before my second visit what he might like me to bring him. "Books – any kind of books!" Sensing that his religious upbringing in the Orthodox church may not have exposed him to good modern Christian literature, I brought him two copies of *Mere Christianity,* one in English and one in Romanian – a gift I had received from Romania's foremost Christian exile in America, Josif Ton, its translator and founder of the Romanian Missionary Society in Wheaton, Illinois, before returning to Romania immediately after the revolution. For lighter reading I brought him a set of the *Chronicles of Narnia.*

Learning of my interest in book collecting, in my next visit he led me to a government-operated bindery he had discovered, where I could have some of my old books rebound in leather, thanks to his having made special arrangements with the manager of the facility. (Bogdan had a knack for making special arrangements in many areas, I was to discover, affording me privileges of many kinds during my many visits to that country in the past 15 years – not through bribery of any kind but just through convincing people that I was a distinguished American visitor!) On my following visit, I brought a number of old books to be rebound, including several Lewis first editions that had seen better days. The results were highly rewarding, and the price could not be beaten – less than ten dollars per volume.

My most notable undertaking was having a set of deluxe paperbacks of the Narnia books specially bound for each of our six grandchildren. Encased in beautiful red leather, each volume in each set had an introductory page bound in, as though it were part of the original publication. Prepared on my word processor on exactly the same kind of paper, it read for example: "This edition of C. S. Lewis's ever popular classic, the Chronicles of Narnia was specially prepared and bound for Kiersten Camp, daughter of Jeffry and Wende Camp as a gift from her grandparents, Dr. Edwin Brown and Patricia Brown. The books were printed in the United States and taken to Romania where they were bound by hand in leather by craftsmen in Bucharest." If Lewis is as popular fifty years from now, they should be able to supplement their retirement by passing them off as unique Limited Editions!

The Romanian binders were hampered, however, by ancient equipment that sometimes produced undesirable results – such as a line of gold type along the spine that veered southward as it progressed. Moreover, their attempts to mimic the raised bands and other niceties of the best of British binding didn't pass muster, so I eventually turned to England for this kind of work. Needless to say, my British binders have not been able to meet the Romanian pricing, but since collectors seem willing to pay as much as $2000 for a finely bound first edition of *The Lion, the Witch and the Wardrobe*, the binding cost of about $500 per volume is cost effective.

Nonetheless, even these ancient and honorable establishments are not exempt from the occasional blooper – such as one of my binders whose workman must have been half asleep when he confused the title of the third volume of the Space Trilogy, *That Hideous Strength*, with that of the first volume, *Out of the Silent Planet*, resulting in a beautifully bound copy, embossed in the finest of gold, *That Hideous Planet*. I now use another binder, in Oxford, who ranks among the finest in Britain.

Occasionally, he will replace a damaged page or two with a good one taken from another first edition of the book which has too many marred pages to be itself rebound. In one instance, I received from him a superbly bound *The Lion, the Witch and the Wardrobe* in which two pages from such a copy had been skillfully inserted for two pages covered with scrawled crayon marks by the former owner. Unfortunately, the workman had neglected to remove the damaged pages in so doing. (I would hope he is no longer employed there. Fortunately, with some skillful surgery with a razor blade I was able to excise the cancer without evidence of its having been there.)

The Prodigal Stepson Who Never Returned Home

One of the most intriguing Lewis letters acquired in recent years was this one of March 20, 1962:

Dear Roth,

Thank you very much for your kind and most cheering letter. I cannot tell you how much I appreciate your kind interest in the whole matter. If David opens out and gives me the least encouragement I'll try to say something much as you suggest. Otherwise it wd. be like trying to open an oyster with a paper knife!

Yours
C. S. Lewis

"David" was most likely the older stepson, David Gresham – but who was Roth and what could he have suggested that would have been so encouraging to the ailing Lewis?

A search of the reference sources usually consulted turned up no one by that name, so I emailed younger brother Doug in Ireland to see if he might be able to give me a clue. Unfortunately, the name meant nothing to him either nor was he aware of what might have been suggested. He only remembered that David was accustomed to leaving for school early in the morning, coming home just in time for dinner, and then secluding himself for the rest of the evening. On weekends he was at home only for meals.

So much for that mystery! Months later, however, when someone raised a question about David Gresham on "MereLewis," an Internet discussion group, I made reference to this letter and Doug's response to my query. One of the other participants at that moment recalled having seen something about Roth in one of the Lewis biographies, *Clive Staples Lewis: A Dramatic Life*, by William Griffin.

Although I bought a copy of this book when it was published in 1986, I had somehow misplaced it before reading it. A frantic search of my less-than-well-organized library soon turned it up, however, and on page 428 there it was: " '*Thank you very much for your kind and most cheering letter ...*' Lewis had written to Cecil Roth, reader in post-biblical Jewish studies at Oxford." But Griffin did not give the source of his knowledge of this letter, and the letter itself had not been published in Warren Lewis's book, *Letters of C. S. Lewis*, so now having a first name for Roth I turned to the source of all knowledge, Google.

In precisely 0.05 seconds (by its self-acclaim) Google came up with a list of some 18,200 websites in which the name Cecil Roth appears, the 61st of which led to my learning more than I could possibly have hoped for about this letter. Entry number 61 was an advertisement for a book, *Cecil Roth, Historian Without Tears*, by his wife Irene. I immediately ordered it, and on pages 152-153 I discovered the whole, fascinating story:

Soon after our arrival in Oxford, we inaugurated a tradition of weekly Saturday afternoon "At Homes" at which undergraduates and other Jewish visitors were welcome. .... One never knew who might turn up at our Sabbath "At Homes" .... I remember how one Saturday afternoon during the early 1960's I saw a young boy, accompanied by two undergraduates, walking toward the house. He appeared to be about sixteen years old, still a schoolboy rather than a university student.

Cecil never found it easy to start a conversation with strangers and since only a few visitors were present at the time, the silence became strained. Finally I broke the ice and asked the young man what college he was attending. Perhaps, I thought, our new guest was older than he looked.

"I am at Magdalen College School," he said. "My friends from the synagogue brought me here today because they thought you would not mind my joining them." Then he turned to Cecil and, in a very superior voice, said, "My name is David Gresham. I believe you know my stepfather, sir. He lives at Headington. He's C. S. Lewis."

Cecil could hardly believe his ears. Was it possible that Lewis, the famous author and Anglican theologian, could have a stepson sufficiently interested in Judaism to attend the synagogue and to invite himself to our Sabbath afternoon reception?

It was, and he had. Joy Davidman Lewis was of Jewish descent, though her parents had long since abandoned any substantial faith for atheism. She herself had married William Gresham, a Gentile; together they wandered through the morasses of atheism and Communism and eventually came to Christianity. (Their pilgrimage is one of those related in the book, *These Found The Way*; in which their mutual friend with Lewis, Chad Walsh, is also featured.)

Their troubled marriage ended when Bill divorced Joy in favor of another woman; she came to England with her two sons, where her friendship with C. S. Lewis blossomed into love and marriage. She died just a few years later at age forty-five. (Her full story is unfolded in Lyle Dorsett's book, *And God Came In*.)

Her two sons were left in the charge of Jack and Warnie Lewis. The younger, Douglas, sporadically attended the Church of England, finding it then mostly as boring as he now believes hell to be. He has ably told the story of his years with Jack and his own spiritual pilgrimage in *Lenten Lands* and *Jack's Life*.

But David, the elder, turned back to the faith of his mother's bloodline, embracing ultra-Orthodox Jewish beliefs.

As Irene Roth relates, *His mother's writings had featured the Jews, particularly one shohet (ritual slaughterer), in an unsympathetic manner. David informed his stepfather, and later also Cecil, that he was going to become a ritual slaughterer in order to present this type of Jewish religious functionary to the world in a more favorable light. Lewis had no idea what all this meant, but he showed great patience and tolerance for the boy's demands, far more than did the Jewish undergraduates with whom David had begun to associate.*

Eventually David taught himself Yiddish, purchased traditional Hassidic garb, fur hat and long caftan (which, however, he was restrained from wearing) and frequently refused to speak to women, including myself.

Eventually Cecil advised C. S. Lewis to remove David from Magdalen College School, where the headmaster was even more unhappy with his pupil than the boy was about being there. Cecil suggested that the boy be sent to an Orthodox Talmudic academy.

C. S. Lewis's reply to Cecil's letter reflects the dilemma which the Hassidic boy presented to his Christian stepfather. "Dear Roth," he wrote. "Thank you very much for your kind and most cheering letter ..."

And thus was the mystery solved through the keen memory of a stranger chatting on the Internet and the incredible power of Google. When spending a weekend with the Greshams at Rathvinden, their country estate in Ireland, I asked Doug about his brother. Apparently they have rarely seen each other in recent years, although they occasionally keep in touch by email. David is married, has two children, and is probably living in India.

The Closest Thing to Meeting Lewis Himself

Sadly, my interest in C. S. Lewis came fairly late in life. Prior to 1963 I had read only *Perelandra* and knew almost nothing about their author. I vividly recall, however, opening the November 1963 issue of *Time* which featured the assassination of President Kennedy, and noting on the obituary page a name that caught my eye – *Clive Staples Lewis*. I couldn't understand why it somehow seemed familiar, but as I continued to stare at it, suddenly the light broke through: Clive Staples Lewis – good grief, that's C. S. Lewis! And at that moment I felt a tinge of remorse that I'd never had the privilege of meeting him.

Years later, as I became more familiar with his work, I had a longing to meet those who knew the man behind the words – and as fate would have it, I could not have done better than to have Walter Hooper become the first of these. As noted earlier, this good fortune was the result of learning from Mr. Reading, landlord of The Eagle and Child, that the original pub sign had been given to Walter Hooper when the Ind Coope brewery refurbished the Bird and Baby some years earlier.

Walter Hooper first became aware of C. S. Lewis when he read Lewis's preface to J. B. Phillips's *Letters to Young Churches* in 1953 as an undergraduate at the University of North Carolina in Chapel Hill. Drafted into the Army soon thereafter, he came across a copy of *Miracles*, which he kept beneath his shirt during the whole of his basic training, for reading during short breaks from "firing the bazooka, crawling under barbed wire, and peeling potatoes while on K.P. I went to that book as a man in the desert might go to a well." In 1954, as a chaplain's assistant at Fort Bragg and after reading whatever of Lewis he could get his hands on, he wrote to him to thank him for what he had received from Lewis's writings – never imagining that he would receive a reply. But Lewis did, and Walter became known among the chaplains as "The Soldier Who Had Heard From C. S. Lewis." Less than ten years later he had the opportunity to meet Lewis in Oxford, and as described elsewhere herein, his life changed forever.

Two years later, again in Oxford, I phoned Walter to see if he might have time for us to get together. He graciously invited me to meet him at the Randolph Hotel that afternoon for their regular high tea, apologizing, however, that he had to keep an engagement soon thereafter, so he would be able to spare only 20 minutes or so. Early in the conversation he noted that he had recently been in America for a tour with the Lewis film, *Through Joy and Beyond*. He then told of a particularly unpleasant experience in Los Angeles when the religion editor of the *Los Angeles Times* questioned him at length about allegations that certain Lewis documents had possibly been forged by someone.

When the interviewer became particularly obnoxious, Walter rose and politely told him that the interview was over because he had other commitments to keep. Although the interviewer rose as if to leave, he continued his questioning. Also present was a young man who had been giving his time to Walter, driving him wherever he needed to go in Los Angeles. This friend, a former college football player, eased up to the visitor, and chest to chest nudged him toward the door with the parting woods, "Father Hooper says the interview is over!"

When I asked Walter who the young man was, I was pleased to learn that it was my own new friend, Jerry Root, then a youth pastor at a church in the Los Angeles area. I had become acquainted with Jerry through an advertisement of a Los Angeles bookseller in a magazine for book collectors and booksellers, the erstwhile *AB Weekly*, now defunct with the advent of the Internet-based book exchange, abebooks.com. *WANTED: First editions of C. S. Lewis*, the ad read – and caught my eye because I had been contemplating submitting the same ad and was disturbed that someone had beat me to it.

Phoning the bookseller, I learned that he had submitted it on behalf of a customer who wanted to amass "the best C. S. Lewis collection on the West Coast." He kindly offered to pass my name and phone number to the customer, and thus began a long friendship with one of the great C. S. Lewis scholars, now on the faculty of Wheaton College, and much in demand as a writer and speaker on Lewis.

Jerry had indeed been a football player, and while on leave in Oxford in 1985 I learned that he, too, was in Oxford for a time, where in his spare time he was coaching a semi-professional Oxford football team – not European football (soccer) but American football, which had begun to take hold in England. (I've not heard anything about it in recent years.)

But back to my afternoon tea with Walter –

The minutes passed rapidly as he expanded on the story of that American tour and four hours later glanced at his watch in alarm, remembering that he had not only missed his late afternoon appointment but was to have joined a friend for dinner an hour earlier. Thus I learned how deeply offended he was by allegations of impropriety in the handling of the Lewis literary estate. He has consistently refused over the years to dignify these allegations with a formal response – and those of us who know him have been disturbed by these allegations as well.

Walter and I still have a chat whenever I visit Oxford, and whenever I have a question about some aspect of Lewisiana I ring him up or email him. Of the many posthumous collections of Lewis's work edited by Walter, none has been more demanding than the three-volume series of Lewis letters on which he worked non-stop for the past eight years! In undertaking this monumental work he has attempted to locate the original or a copy of every letter ever written by Lewis – a prodigious task, considering that Lewis never failed to answer any of the many thousands of letters he received. Copies of most are in the Bodleian Library in Oxford and the Marian Wade Center in Wheaton, Illinois, but many are still in the hands of the recipients, their heirs, or collectors. Thanks to my purchases of Lewis letters, I've had the privilege of supplying many of the letters in this new series.

Prior to undertaking this great work, he devoted many years to the most exhaustive and interesting reference work on Lewis ever published: *C. S. LEWIS: A COMPANION AND GUIDE.* First published in 1996, this 940-page gem should be in the library of everyone with any interest whatsoever in C. S. Lewis.

Friends and Family

The next Lewis associate I met, whose friendship I have been privileged to enjoy, was Dr. James Houston. We were introduced by a mutual friend, Jim Hiskey – a professional golfer who works with the national Prayer Breakfast movement, at one of whose annual gatherings in Washington, D. C. we met. As a young lecturer at Hertford College on Oxford, Jim enjoyed the acquaintance of Lewis through the room Jim shared with Nicholas Zernov, lecturer on Eastern Orthodox Culture at Oxford. For seven years Lewis regularly visited their residence for Saturday evening discussion parties.

Jim told me of his friendship with Jean "Davy" Van Auken, wife of Sheldon Van Auken, whose story of the Van Aukens' friendship with Lewis is beautifully told in Sheldon's book *A Severe Mercy*. Davy, who had become a Christian after coming to Oxford, attended the daily prayer meeting of the Oxford Intercollegiate Christian Union, of which Jim was the faculty representative. Much daily prayer was made for Sheldon's conversion, and one day Davy announced that Sheldon had also become a Christian. That evening, Jim was with Lewis and reported to him the good news about Sheldon. "Lewis was not one to show much personal emotion, so he responded, 'I'm so glad,' then abruptly changed the conversation." Jim had reminded him of the faithful correspondence Lewis had maintained with Sheldon, but "Lewis was never one to take credit for what was truly God's Spirit."

Jim is now the emeritus Professor of Spiritual Theology of Regent College, which he founded in 1970 – an outstanding evangelical seminary on the campus of the University of British Columbia in Vancouver. "I was inspired by the effective integration that Lewis made between his professional skills and the intelligence of his faith, whereas so many gifted Christians in professional life play 'Mickey Mouse' with their faith." It was this same vision that led him to establish New College on the Berkeley campus of the University of California, and in 1976 he and Jim Hiskey created the C. S. Lewis Institute on the nation's capital. Their goal was to have people who would follow the example of Lewis in taking their faith as seriously as their profession, with equal intelligence and competence. Similarly, the eminent British theologian, scholar, and preacher, Dr. John Stott, was encouraged to found the London Institute for Contemporary Christianity – all part of the same movement as originally inspired by the example of Lewis.

All too many years ago I spent part of two summers as a student at Regent College, taking a few courses from their distinguished summer school faculty. One of these was the late Dr. John White, Christian author of some 25 books and professor of psychiatry at the University of Manitoba. The other was Rev. Michael Green, also an author and then rector of St. Aldate's Church in Oxford – the finest lecturer I have every had in any subject in any school I've ever attended. I will always remember his comment on C. S. Lewis: *God took that mighty intellect and turned it to His own purposes.*

Another close friend of Lewis whom I was privileged to know was George Sayer, author of *Jack* – by far the best of the several Lewis biographies – and a pupil of Jack at Oxford from 1933 to 1936. He and his first wife Moira became lifelong friends of Jack, and later, Joy. Jack often visited the Sayers in Malvern, where he became Senior English Master at Lewis's old school, Malvern College, and the Sayers were frequent guests at The Kilns. Whenever he was in Oxford on a Tuesday, he was asked to join the Inklings at the Bird and Baby.

A letter I recently acquired when his present wife, Margaret, put some of his books and letters at auction illustrates the closeness of their relationship. Lewis replies to an invitation from the Sayers to come and visit soon:

The Kilns, Headington Quarry, Oxford 18 Dec. 1960

My dear George, It would be the very thing I pine for and you have both (bless'd pair of Sirens) been much in mind. But I already have to be away from home for some days after Christmas – on that evaluating commission on the Psalter – and I don't feel I ought to hew another cantle out of so short a vacation.

Perhaps you'll ask me in the Easter one! Who is Gnonwy (Sorowy? Inowy?) Sir Henry's successor I take it. Blessings on you, and a thorough thanks.

Yours, Jack

Any chance of your spending a night at Magdalene next term. You'd be very welcome.

I've also had the good fortune to obtain ownership of George's copy of *Spirits in Bondage*, bearing his inscription, *George Sayer 1936* – the year he graduated from Oxford.

Several years have passed since I last visited the Sayers, and while I have spoken with Margaret from time to time by phone, there will be no more lively conversations with the two of them. George was confined to a nursing home more than two years ago, suffering from severe dementia, and died in October 2005 – a sad end for one of the last of the Inklings.

A late footnote to this story: George successfully conveyed his enthusiasm for Lewis to his pupils at Malvern. One of them, Mike Tiley, decided in 2004 to have his family heirloom 1938 radio restored and presented to the Kilns for display and use there. The gift is appropriate; during the long dark days of World War II, Lewis gave "broadcast talks" to the embattled English, reminding them of the eternal values that alone made anything worth fighting for. The only voice on the BBC more familiar than Jack's was Winston Churchill's; Lewis would later use these radio messages as the foundations for three books which would eventually be combined into his durable classic of Christian apologetics, *Mere Christianity*.

A Very Special Lewis Friendship

In 1931, Lewis's friend Hugo Dyson, then teaching at Reading University, recommended a Reading student to him as a pupil. Her name was Mary Shelley, but when the secretary at Reading, Miss Seaton, sent Lewis a request to take her as his pupil, he wrote back that he had no more room for another pupil. Sadly disappointed, Mary wrote to Lewis herself, apologizing for her importunity and begging him to accept her because Dyson had recommended her. To her joy, he responded thus on June 18, 1931:

Dear Miss Shelley, Yes, rather. When I got the letter from Miss Seaton I did not know that the pupil mentioned was the Dysonian one – nor, I think, did Mr. Dyson mention your name when he spoke about you to me. ... It is I who shd. apologise for my muddle rather than you for your "importunity" – the latter, being in any case, the more flattering offense. I shd. be obliged if you would explain all to Miss Seaton. The (unnamed) "Dysonian" pupil was one of the people I was leaving room for by my refusal to take "a pupil" from her. In fact you were being crowded out by yourself among other people.

He invited her to meet with him at her earliest convenience, and in the meantime recommended a number of books to read in preparation for their first meeting. Mary did not do as well as she expected in her university examinations at Oxford, receiving only a Fourth Class degree, and was very discouraged with the results. Lewis, however, tried to encourage her with the following letter:

Dear Miss Shelley, If you are not, at the moment, too sick of me and all my kind to read further, it may be worth saying that you must not run away with the idea that you are a Fourth Class mind. What really ruined you was an NS and a S on language, which would of course have spoiled even very good work elsewhere. In the Lit. your highest mark was B?+(XIXth century). Why your literature papers were not better I do not understand. I blame myself for not having extorted more essays from you – but I doubt if that was the whole cause. You were very short and general. But I am quite clear in my own mind that you have not done yourself justice and that your real quality is far beyond the work you did in Schools. This is cold comfort to you with the world to face! – but at least it is said quite sincerely and not merely for the sake of consoling you. Try to forgive me both as an examiner and as a tutor. If there should at any time be any way in which I can be of use to you, let me know at once. Till then, good-bye and good luck.

Mary had been brought up in the Anglican church, but in her early teens lost whatever faith she may have had as the result of the influence of a family friend. Just before graduation, however, she bought a copy of Lewis's just published *The Pilgrim's Regress*, which reminded her of much of her own spiritual journey thus far and which, with Lewis's previous discussions with her, led her to become a believer.

She became a teacher at the Dartington Hall School in Surrey after graduation, married a young man named Neylan, and began what was to become an extensive correspondence with Lewis. Because of her interest in the writings of George Macdonald, he dedicated *George Macdonald: An Anthology* to her, and at her request became godfather to her first child, Sarah.

About two years ago I received a call from my friend Jack Gamble of Emerald Isle Books in Belfast, informing me of an upcoming auction in London of two collections of Lewis letters. I immediately phoned the auction house and asked them to fax me the catalogue pages describing these letters, so that I might bid on them. Included were a collection of 27 letters to Mary Neylan and another of 10 letters to a clergyman friend of Lewis, H. A. Blair.

No significant collections of Lewis letters had appeared on the market in many years, so after seeing the descriptions of the letters, I immediately booked a flight to London – only to develop a kidney stone that laid me low only a few days before the auction. A dealer friend in England came to my rescue, however, and attended the auction for me.

Upon arriving at the auction, however, she learned that the Neylan letters had suddenly been withdrawn from the sale – a great disappointment. She did, however, acquire the Blair letters for me, and then a few days later called to say that the auction house could arrange a private purchase with the seller, which they did.

The Neylan collection, now at Taylor University, shows the development of an increasingly warm relationship between Mary and Jack, particularly after the premature death of Mary's husband (whom Lewis always referred to as "the gudeman"). After his death, the salutations changed from "Dear Mrs. Neylan" to "Dear Mary," and the signature from "C. S. Lewis" to "Jack." Mary Neylan died in 1994 at the age of 86.

Included with the letters was a special "bonus" – a pencil portrait of Lewis done by Mary only a few months before Jack's death. It had never been published, intended only for Mary's pleasure – and when I made reference to it in a Lewis "chat channel" on the Internet several years ago, the late Kathryn Lindskoog, author and Lewis scholar, asked if she might have a copy of it, fondly remembering having seen it hanging in Mary's house when Kathryn visited her many years ago. I also sent a copy to Doug Gresham in Ireland, who commented that it was a very good likeness of the then very ill Jack.

Many of the letters in the collection were published anonymously, in whole or in part, in Warnie Lewis's 1977 *Letters of C. S. Lewis*, in which she is identified (in accordance with her own request to Warnie) as "To a former pupil." Of the published letters, however, one was missing in the collection obtained at auction – an important letter, dated 4 January 1941, in response to Mary's decision to deal at last with a serious spiritual problem she had been facing. (The nature of the problem is not indicated in Lewis's letter, but it was obviously a serious one, for which he offers advice as to how she should now proceed, after self-examination, repentance, and restitution.) I contacted the auction house to see if by some chance the letter had been misplaced, but they did not have it. The next step was to try to contact the person who sold the letters in the hope he or she could explain its absence.

Since the auction house keeps information about its sellers and buyers in the strictest confidence, I asked them if they would forward a letter from me, which they did. No reply was forthcoming, however, and on the assumption that the seller may have been Mary's oldest daughter, Sarah, I began trying to track her down.

A Google search of the Internet provided the first help, from an obscure genealogy website that gave her married name as Tisdall and the names of her two sons and a daughter. Another Internet search of British telephone directories turned up phone numbers for the two sons, but when I phoned those two numbers I was told in each case that someone of that name had previously lived at that address five years ago but their whereabouts was unknown.

I phoned Walter Hooper, of course, but he too had been unable to locate Sarah. However, when I visited him some months later, he remembered that Mary had told him back in 1988, when he was working on a revised edition of *Letters of C. S. Lewis*, that Sarah was "either working at the Radcliffe Infirmary" or "was doing a work at the Radcliffe Infirmary." We knew from an article Mary had written in 1991 for *The Chesterton Review* that Sarah was an artist, so having just an hour to spare before another friend was to drive me back to London, I went over to the hospital, only a few blocks from Walter's house. The receptionist was not familiar with the name Sarah Tisdall nor of any artistic work done by her, but she took me to the person who headed the art committee – and indeed Sarah had done a work there in 1988. The entire four walls of the huge vaulted ceiling waiting room in the Radiology department were covered with a magnificent mural – and in the files of the art committee was Sarah's current address and telephone number!

I had no time to contact her before leaving England – nor in any case would I have known how to go about it, lest she be offended after already refusing to answer my letter. After returning home, I mulled over the problem for several months, only to be abruptly relieved by the arrival of a warm e-mail from Sarah, apologizing for the lengthy delay, occasioned by her having been in the throes of moving to a new home when my letter arrived.

We have since become good friends, first by e-mail and later through my visits to London and through her participation in a Lewis colloquium at Taylor University in 2004. In January 2005 she moved to Mexico City, where she continues her art career.

Only recently did I learn why she had abruptly withdrawn the letters from the auction, only to turn around a few days later and offer to sell them. The night before the auction the auction house informed her that they had received a call from an American institution claiming that the letters belonged to them! The auction house therefore recommended that she withdraw them from public sale, and having no idea of the basis on which such a claim was made, she felt that she had no choice but to follow their advice. Fortunately for me and for Taylor University, she decided to go ahead with a private sale. As far as the missing letter was concerned, she had no knowledge of what happened to it; she had sent to the auction house all the letters left by her mother.

In December 2004 Brazos Press published *Seeking the Secret Place: The Spiritual Formation of C. S. Lewis* by Lyle Dorsett, former director of the Wade Center. In the draft sent me earlier by the publisher for my review, the author devotes some nine pages to an interview he had with "a widow who resided in a small village in southern England," whom for sake of anonymity, he calls "Grace Jones." From Prof. Dorsett's more detailed descriptions of some of the letters, and her account of her spiritual journey, it is obvious that "Grace Jones" was Mary Neylan.

But what about that very important missing letter which was published in 1977 but was not among the collection obtained from Sarah?

I mentioned earlier a letter among George's books and letters put up for auction at Sotheby's by his wife Margaret. George's illness had put him in a nursing home, and she had been forced to sell their large house and move into a much smaller accommodation. As the result of George's close friendship with both Lewis and Tolkien, there was a large amount of correspondence from both in George's files, much of which Margaret had to sell in order to meet the expense of the nursing home. I was fortunate in having bid successfully by phone at the auction for a group of five letters, described by Sotheby's as from C. S. Lewis to George Sayer.

Surprisingly, only three of the five letters were from Jack to George; the other two were from Jack to Mary Neylan! I phoned Margaret to ask what she might know of this, but she had no knowledge of how they had come into George's possession. Nor would George be able to cast any light on the mystery in his state of dementia.

When I told Sarah of this strange matter, she remembered that her mother had once sent her Lewis letters to her friend George Sayer, asking if he could sell them to Wheaton College. George must have written to the Wade Center at the time, but before anything could be concluded, Mary had changed her mind about selling them and asked George to return them. Presumably these two had somehow gotten mixed up with his own letters from Lewis, and were long since forgotten.

The strangest aspect of this, however, was that one of the letters was the published one missing from the collection! Almost two years after Sarah Neylan had put her mother's letters up for auction at Phillips, the missing letter turned up among the George Sayer letters purchased at a Sotheby's auction. Coincidence? I think not! Given the many instances in which important Lewis pieces came into my possession through very unusual contributing events and the importance of the collection to Taylor University, I have no question that divine guidance has been a major factor in all of it.

A Very Special Gift

Sarah also blessed the collection at Taylor University with one of its most prized acquisitions – her mother's copy of the George MacDonald anthology, given to her by Lewis, with this inscription:

with affectionate compliments and congratulations from
C. S. Lewis 1946

The dedicatory copy of any first edition – i.e., the copy given by the author to the person to whom he has dedicated the book – is in itself a rarity of rarities, being unique among all the first editions of that book that may still be in existence. Among Lewis first editions, this copy may be the only one of its kind as far as we know. Only 26 of Lewis's books had a dedicatee, and some were dedicated to groups of indefinite number. *The Problem of Pain*, for example, was dedicated *"To the Inklings"* – those friends of Lewis who first met in Lewis's rooms at Magdalen College and later at The Eagle and Child to read and discuss the works they were writing – while *Perelandra* was dedicated *"To Some Ladies at Wantage"* – the nuns at The Community of St. Mary the Virgin, an Anglican convent in Wantage, Berkshire, not far from Oxford. (The dedication of the Portuguese translation of *Perelandra* translates back into English as "Some wanton ladies"!)

Some of the dedicatees were persons not very well known except to Lewis and his closest friends. One, for example, was Marjorie Milne. Although the 1926 first edition of *Dymer* has no dedicatee, Lewis dedicated the 1950 second edition to Marjorie, to whom he was introduced in the 1940s by Owen Barfield. A devout Roman Catholic, Miss Milne became such an admirer of Lewis that she thought he should head a new religious movement.

By 1947, she had become so overbearing in her admiration of Lewis that he wrote to Owen Barfield, *Never communicate any troubles of mine again to M. Milne. Through no will of my own I occupy already a larger place in her thoughts than I could wish, and the degree of her sympathy is such as to make her miserable and to embarrass me.*

In his diary of 19 September 1950, Warnie wrote, *J. had by appointment that indefatigable talker Marjorie M, at 5 p.m. She had come to 'consult' him, but supplied at least 90 percent of the conversation. This is the woman of whom Owen Barfield remarked in his dry way, 'She's a good creature when all's said and done: especially when all's said and done!'*

The Pilgrim's Regress is dedicated to Arthur Greeves, Lewis's lifelong friend in Belfast.

The Allegory of Love is dedicated to Owen Barfield, another lifelong friend.

Out of the Silent Planet is dedicated to his brother, Warren Hamilton Lewis ("Warnie"). The story of the intimate, lifelong relationship of the two brothers is beautifully told in *Brothers and Friends*, edited by Clyde Kilby and Marjorie Mead, and in several of the letters to Lady Jill Freud, now at Taylor University, he indicates his devastation over the loss of his beloved brother – from which he never recovered in the ten years thereafter until his death in 1973.

He served in France, as did Jack, during the First World War, and remained in the Royal Army Service Corps, serving in Sierra Leone, West Africa, and in China. In 1930, when standing before the Great Buddha of Kamakura, he became convinced of the truth of Christianity. In his diary on May 13, 1931 he wrote: "I started to say my prayers again after having discontinued doing so for more years than I care to remember ... The wheel has now made the full revolution – indifference, scepticism, atheism, agnosticism, and back again to Christianity." (*Brothers and Friends: The Diaries of Major Warren Hamilton Lewis*, 1982)

Recalled to active duty during World War II, he was sent to France again in 1939 but was evacuated at Dunkirk the following year and transferred to the Reserves. The brothers lived together at The Kilns in Headington Quarry, Oxford, where in 1943 Warnie became Jack's secretary. Jack was by then receiving large quantities of mail from his admirers as the result of the success of *The Screwtape Letters*, but he never learned to use the typewriter, so Warnie typed most of his letters.

Warnie had a problem with alcohol that became serious in the 1940s. During a holiday in Ireland in 1947 he collapsed and was rushed to a hospital run by the Medical Missionaries of Mary – who frequently cared for him throughout the years thereafter whenever he went on an alcoholic binge in Ireland. A major contributing factor to his illness was a change in personality that gradually occurred as his brother became more and more famous and mingled with a large variety of people. Whereas Jack had been something of a recluse in his early years, Warnie was the opposite, getting along with many different people. In time these positions seemed to reverse, and Warnie withdrew more and more into his books. He was nonetheless a regular contributor to the discussions of the Inklings and was well-liked by all.

Warnie was a successful writer in his own right, with seven excellent books resulting from his hobby of studying seventeenth and eighteenth century France, on which he became an expert. Many of the letters I acquired from Lady Jill Freud are his own, in which he shows a keen wit and a charming way of expressing himself.

Rehabilitations and Other Essays is dedicated to Hugo Dyson. Dyson was Lecturer and Tutor at Reading University in 1931 when he referred Mary Shelley (Neylan) to Lewis as a pupil, and later became a Fellow of Merton College, Oxford. Dyson had become a very close friend of Lewis by 1931, when he and Tolkien were instrumental in bringing Lewis to believing in Jesus Christ in an after-dinner conversation with Lewis at Magdalen College which lasted until 4 in the morning – as he wrote to Arthur Greeves shortly thereafter: *I have just passed on from believing in God to definitely believing in Christ – in Christianity.*

The Screwtape Letters is dedicated to J. R. R. Tolkien, another of his closest friends.

A Preface to Paradise Lost, Lewis's review of the work of Milton, which he greatly admired, is dedicated to Charles Williams, another close friend and fellow Inkling. Williams and Lewis "discovered" each other's writings simultaneously in 1936, when Williams wrote to Lewis to praise the manuscript of *The Allegory of Love* he had reviewed as an editor at Oxford University Press, and Lewis at the same time wrote to Williams to praise his book, *The Place of the Lion*. The two quickly became friends, and when Oxford University Press moved its office from London to Oxford at the beginning of World War II, Lewis was elated. With the end of the war, Williams was preparing to move back to London when he suddenly became ill and died.

Five days later, in a letter to Mary Neylan, Lewis wrote: "I also have become acquainted with grief now through the death of my great friend, Charles Williams, my friend of friends, the comforter of all our little set, the most angelic man. The odd thing is that his death has made my faith stronger than it was a week ago. And I find that all that talk about 'feeling that he is closer to us than before' isn't just talk. It's just what it feels like – I can't put it into words. One seems at moments to be living in a new world. Lots, lots of pain, but not a particle of depression or resentment."

That Hideous Strength, the final book of the Space Trilogy, is dedicated to J. McNeill – Jane Agnes "Janie" McNeill, Lewis's life-long friend in Belfast. Janie hated the book, however, and expressed the wish that he had dedicated any other book to her.

The Great Divorce is dedicated "To Barbara Wall, Best and most suffering of all scribes." In Warnie's absence during World War II, Lewis was looking for someone to type his books. His friend, Colin Hardie, fellow Inkling and Oxford colleague, recommended his sister-in-law, Barbara Wall, herself a published author, who was living in Oxford at the time. She typed this, his previous book, *That Hideous Strength*, and his next book, *Miracles*.

Miracles is dedicated to Cecil and Daphne Harwood. Lewis says of Cecil Harwood in *Surprised By Joy*:

"He was ... a wholly imperturbable man. Though poor (like most of us) and wholly without 'prospects', he wore the expression of a nineteenth century gentleman with something in the Funds. On a walking tour when the last light of a wet evening had just revealed some ghastly error in map-reading (probably his own) and the best hope was 'Five miles to Mudham (if we could find it) and we might get beds there,' he still wore that expression. In the heat of argument he wore it still. You would think that he, if anyone, would have been told to 'take that look off his face.' But I don't believe he ever was. It was no mask and came from no stupidity. He has been tried since by all the usual trials and anxieties. He is the sole Horatio known to me in this age of Hamlets; no 'stop for Fortune's finger.' "

Arthurian Torso: Containing the Posthumous Fragment of 'The Figure of Arthur,' by Charles Williams and A Commentary on the Arthurian Poems of Charles Williams by C. S. Lewis (usually referred to as *Arthurian Torso*!) is dedicated "To Michal Williams, without whose permission this book could not have been made." Michal was William's widow, and although the book was partly hers in any case, Lewis generously arranged for all the royalties to be paid to her.

The Lion, the Witch and the Wardrobe has the best-known of all Lewis dedications – to his goddaughter Lucy Barfield, Owen Barfield's adopted daughter:

TO LUCY BARFIELD

MY DEAR LUCY,

I wrote this story for you, but when I began it I had not realised that girls grow quicker than books. As a result you are already too old for fairy tales, and by the time it is printed and bound you will be older still. But someday you will be old enough to start reading fairy tales again. You can then take it down from some upper shelf, dust it, and tell me what you think of it. I shall probably be too deaf to hear, and too old to understand, a word you say, but I shall still be your affectionate Godfather,

C. S. LEWIS

It had always been assumed, and correctly so, judging from Lewis's opening words, that Lucy Pevensie was "named after" Lucy Barfield. Like the lovely (and perfectly cast!) little English girl who portrayed her in the 2005 film, Lucy Barfield was a very lively and happy child – apt, for instance, as her father described her, "to be seen turning somersault-wheels in the garden immediately after a meal." Aspiring unsuccessfully to become a ballet dancer, she became a teacher of music at a well-known girls' school in Kent, but, stricken with multiple sclerosis soon thereafter, she was forced to abandon all hope of a normal life. Confined to a wheelchair for decades that followed, she devoted her life to working with children, even when almost totally disabled. She received many letters from readers wishing her well and asking about Narnia, which some believed she had actually visited. She died on May 3, 2003.

Elsewhere in this book, I make mention of my friend Kathryn Lindskoog, who also suffered from multiple sclerosis. When she alleged that some of Lewis's work published by Walter Hooper after Lewis's death may have been forged, Owen Barfield wrote a strong letter to her in defense of Walter Hooper, to no avail. I later wrote to Owen and to Walter, offering to bring Kathryn to England if she were willing and could travel, hoping this might thus enable them to convince her that there was no substance to the allegations. Owen replied on their behalf:

"Thank you for your thoughtful letter to Walter and myself. There is not much fear of my lacking sympathy with anyone afflicted with multiple sclerosis, since my own daughter has been suffering it for the last 25 years. Nevertheless, we feel that we should not enter into any further discussion of Mrs. Lindskoog's reckless allegations. It is not uncommon for MS to affect the mind as well as the body."

Prince Caspian is dedicated to Mary Clare Havard, daughter of Lewis's personal physician, friend, and fellow Inkling, R. E. Havard. A regular at the meetings of the Inklings, he acquired various nicknames from them. The one given him by Hugo Dyson, "Humphrey," was that by which he became generally known in Oxford, where he conducted his medical practice, and in *Perelandra* Lewis named the doctor "Humphrey" in his honor. Because of the bright red beard he grew while serving in the Navy, Lewis dubbed him "The Red Admiral." When Warnie became annoyed on one occasion because Havard did not show up with his car when expected, he called him "The Useless Quack," and many of the Inklings enjoyed referring to him as "U.Q."

The Voyage of the Dawn Treader, as noted elsewhere, is dedicated to Barfield's foster son, Geoffrey Corbett, who later officially changed his name to Jeffrey Barfield. Later editions of the book give his name as Geoffrey Barfield.

The Silver Chair is dedicated to Nicholas Hardie, son of Colin Hardie, another of the Inklings and colleague of Lewis at Magdalen College. The two shared a particular interest in Dante, and both were members of the Oxford Dante Society, an exclusive society founded in 1876 and limited to twelve members – who met but once each university term.

The Horse and His Boy, as also noted elsewhere, is dedicated to David and Douglas Gresham.

The Magician's Nephew is dedicated to an American family, the Kilmers – a Washington, D.C. family whose eight children corresponded with Lewis in 1954, shortly before publication of the book. Many of the letters from Lewis to the children may be found in *Letters to Children*, by Dorsett and Mead, Macmillan, 1985. Writing to them early in 1954, Lewis said:

"Dear Hugh, Anne, Noelie (There is a name I never heard before; what language is it, and does it rhyme with oily or mealy or Kelly or early or truly?), Nicholas, Martin, Rosamund, Matthew, and Miriam ... You are a fine big family! I should think your mother sometimes feels like the Old-Woman-who-lived-in-a-Shoe (you know that rhyme?). I'm so glad you like the books. The next one, The Horse and His Boy, will be out quite soon. There are to be seven altogether."

Thus were six of the seven Chronicles of Narnia dedicated to children of Lewis's friends. *The Last Battle* has no dedicatee.

Surprised by Joy is dedicated to a former pupil of Lewis's at Magdalen College, Dom Bede Griffith, OSB (Order of St. Benedict). Born Alan Richard Griffiths, he became a Christian the same year as Lewis but elected to join the Roman Catholic Church, later becoming a Benedictine monk and changing his name to Bede after St. Bede "The Venerable." He outlived Lewis by thirty years, but for the previous thirty years the two had carried on an extensive discourse on the merits of their respective positions, but in which Lewis insisted on speaking only of those things which unified Christians.

Till We Have Faces: A Myth Retold, which Lewis regarded as his finest work, is dedicated to Joy Davidman, whom he had married in a civil ceremony earlier in 1956 in order for her to be allowed to remain in England. They did not live in the same house, however, until he married her in a Christian ceremony the following year when she was dying of cancer.

Reflections on the Psalms is dedicated to Austin and Katherine Farrer. Austin was a distinguished philosopher, theologian, and biblical scholar, whose wife Katherine became a close friend of Joy soon after Joy and Jack met for the first time. Joy was still living in her own home when, on the evening of October 18, 1956, Katherine had had a premonition that something dreadful had happened to Joy and immediately phoned her. When she went to answer the phone, Joy tripped over the phone cord and the bone in her leg snapped when she fell to the floor. She could hear Katherine's voice, shouted for help, and the Farrers were able to get her to the hospital, where she was found to have far advanced cancer that had eaten through her thigh bone.

The Four Loves is dedicated to Chad Walsh, a distinguished American scholar whose first book about Lewis, *C. S. Lewis: Apostle to the Skeptics*, had attracted the attention of Joy Davidman Gresham in 1949. Joy and her husband, William Lindsay Gresham, became friends of the Walshes, and in 1955 Chad, his wife, and two of their daughters visited Jack and Joy in Oxford. Chad's book had not only done much to make Lewis known in America but had been partly responsible for Joy eventually becoming Lewis's wife, hence the dedication to this particular friend.

Studies in Words is dedicated to Stanley and Joan Bennett, whom Lewis had known since the 1930s, and during his time at Cambridge he was a frequent visitor in their home. Stanley was a distinguished scholar at Cambridge, where for 25 years he served as librarian to Emmanual College. Joan was a Fellow of Girton College and Lecturer in English at the university for 28 years.

The Discarded Image: An Introduction to Medieval and Renaissance Literature, Lewis's last book, published the year after his death, is dedicated to Roger Lancelyn Green. As a student at Oxford, he had attended Lewis's lectures on medieval and renaissance literature, and soon thereafter became a life-long friend of Jack, and later Joy. He and his wife accompanied Jack and Joy on their memorable trip to Greece only three months before Joy's death. He was the author of many successful books, including many biographies, one of them with Walter Hooper on Lewis. He also wrote a monograph entitled *C. S. Lewis*, which he dedicated:

"TO
 JACK and JOY
 in memory of
 'A pub-crawl through the golden isles of Greece.' "

How many of the dedicatory copies were inscribed by Lewis is not known – but I do know that *The Allegory of Love* dedicated to Owen Barfield was not inscribed. It is very likely, therefore, that fewer than a handful of inscribed dedicatory copies of Lewis first editions exist today.

Kids at The Kilns

One of the persistent legends about Lewis was that he was a confirmed bachelor who was bothered by women and children. It simply isn't so, but it's a side of him that has been known to but a few and has only recently come to light in my experience.

Some years ago, while in Oxford on holiday, my wife and I touched base with an American tour group after learning they were to have meetings with three of my longtime friends: George Sayer, Walter Hooper, and Doug Gresham.

We first joined them in Malvern, a lovely Worcestershire town in the West Midlands region some 65 miles northwest of Oxford, on the slopes of the beautiful Malvern Hills, and the home of George and Margaret Sayer. It is also the home of Malvern College, to which Albert Lewis had sent Warnie in 1909 and Jack in 1913. Although Warnie was delighted with Malvern and wore a Malvern tie most of his life, Jack was not very happy there; with Warnie's departure upon graduating, Jack begged his father to send him elsewhere.

Some years after studying English under Lewis at Oxford, George Sayer became Senior English Master at Malvern College, where he remained until his retirement in 1974. He became a close friend of both Jack and Warnie, who were often visitors to the Sayers' home. "The most unselfish man I have ever gone about with," Lewis once wrote about him to a friend.

Following a breakfast talk and question-and-answer period, George took the group on a tour of the college. Pat and I had previously been invited by his wife Margaret to have lunch with her and George, where we enjoyed some marvelous conversation relating to visits to The Kilns by George and his first wife Moira, who died in 1977 after a long illness. Although I had previously been an overnight guest of the Sayers, I had not had the opportunity to see his extensive library, with its many Lewis first editions – and for which he asked my advice on how best to protect the dust jackets of his Narnia books after I told him how valuable these had become in recent years.

We drove to Oxford that evening, and rejoined the group the next day for lunch with Doug Gresham at The Eagle and Child. The next morning we again joined them as they were just finishing breakfast with both Doug and Walter Hooper at their hotel. (Hotel prices in Oxford, as well as in much of England, are exorbitant, so we had lodged the night before in a much less expensive B&B. In our many visits to England over the years we have rarely stayed in a hotel, much preferring the more intimate atmosphere of a B&B, where one not only becomes acquainted with the owners but often meets interesting guests. Once, at a small B&B in Pitlochry, Scotland, we were joined at breakfast by another American couple. Learning that their name was Kliewer, I mentioned that I had a close friend in medical school whose name was David Kliewer, with whom I had lost touch over the years. "Why, he's my uncle – and here's his address and phone number in Portland, Oregon, so you can renew the friendship.")

It was great to see these friends again, but an even greater and unanticipated pleasure was the discovery of the identity of their tour guide in Oxford. We had learned from some new friends whom we had met the previous evening that she was none other than C. S. Lewis's cousin, Joan Lewis Murphy, daughter of their uncle, Dr. Joseph Lewis. Joan told us she had moved to Oxford from Belfast many years ago, and when her marriage broke up there, she was left to care for her 10-year-old son.

Jack had encouraged her to go to graduate school at Oxford, and when she told him this was impossible because of the need to look after her son when he wasn't in school, he and Warnie said they would personally assume that responsibility. One or the other of the brothers then looked after the boy in Jack's rooms at Magdalen College while Joan spent the necessary hours in the Bodleian library. The lad clearly had the finest babysitters ever available to a 10-year-old!

I had known that some children had spent short lengths of time at The Kilns when evacuated from London during the war, but only later did I learn about a teenage girl who had spent almost two years working at The Kilns during the war.

Several years ago I was offered the possibility of purchasing a collection of nearly 100 letters from the Lewis brothers to a distinguished British actress, Lady Jill Freud, wife of Sir Clement Freud, M.P., grandson of Sigmund Freud, the father of modern psychoanalysis. The offer came from Sophie Dupré, a prominent British autograph dealer and friend, whose mother is a cousin of Lady Freud, and the letters had never been made public. Taylor University was interested, of course, and asked me to negotiate the sale when an anonymous benefactor offered the funds for the collection.

Lady Jill Freud, as teenage June Flewett, had lived with the Lewis brothers for almost two years during the war, where she helped Mrs. Moore with the household chores. In the summer of 1943 Mrs. Moore, who was a friend of her mother, had invited June to spend two weeks at The Kilns before entering the Royal Academy of Dramatic Arts that fall. When June saw how hard-pressed Mrs. Moore was as the result of the shortage of hired help during the war, she volunteered to delay her studies and stay on.

This bright 16-year-old totally captivated the affections of both brothers. In his diary, Warnie wrote:

I have met no one of any age further advanced in the Christian way of life. From seven in the morning till nine a night, shut off from people of her own age, almost grudged the time for her religious duties, she has slaved at The Kilns, for a fractional one pence an hour. I have never seen her other than gay, eager to anticipate exigent demands, never complaining, always self-accusing, in the frequent crises of that dreary house.

Jack likewise adored her. When she returned home shortly before the end of the war to take up her delayed studies at the Royal Academy of Dramatic Arts, he wrote to her mother,

Oh, what a sad waking up this morning when we realized June was gone! – But I try to comfort myself by realizing that there was a correspondingly happy waking in your house and thinking how long you and she have waited for it and how you deserve it. This is really

just a covering letter (as one might say, 'Daughter enclosed') and to try, once again, to express some part of our great gratitude. I have never really met anything like her unselfishness and patience and kindness and shall feel deeply in her debt as long as I live.

Although June adopted the stage name Jill Raymond upon entering the theater, the brothers always called her June, which Warnie always spelled "Juin" in his many letters to her. To her, C. S. was always "Jack," and it was only after some time at The Kilns that she learned to her astonishment that this new friend was in fact *the* C. S. Lewis.

(Jill Freud writes of her experiences at The Kilns in a fascinating book by my friend, the late Stephen Schofield, *In Search of C. S. Lewis*, copies of which are available via www.abebooks.com, the most comprehensive Internet source for used and rare books.)

Among their letters to June is a delightful one from Warnie describing the impending visit of Joy Davidman Gresham and her two boys, David and Douglas, to The Kilns:

We are looking forward with a certain gloom to Thursday, when an American woman, a "fan" of Jack's, comes down for the week end with her two boys; she has been before but not the boys, and is easy, though expensive, to entertain – having a pretty taste in cocktails. But the boys? How the dickens are two elderly bachelors to entertain two boys aged eight and six respectively? (Hideous thought, perhaps they will demand cocktails too?)"

Two weeks later he writes:

The American visit went off very well, and the boys turned out to be delightful, but very, very exhausting; e.g., when they had reached the ground after climbing Magdalen tower, their first remark was 'Now let's do it again.' It was impossible to remember that they were aged nine and seven and a half respectively, for they were amazingly adult and could take their part in any conversation, and were not as you might think, little prigs."

Four years later, after Jack married Joy, and she and the boys came to live at The Kilns, Warnie was not quite so enamored of David, the older boy:

Though life is now very different to what you will remember it, and there are times when I get tired of the role of 'family man'; not that I don't get on well with my sister-in-law; it is her detestable spoilt brat of an elder boy who is the fly in the ointment. But the other one is a decent little kid, so I suppose I shouldn't grumble.

Warnie, himself a confirmed bachelor, was 62 years old at the time.

Another Lewis Friend and a Strange Tale

Several years ago Pat and I had the privilege of meeting Val and Mary Rogers, and elderly couple, both of whom had been students of Lewis and later close friends. We spent a delightful evening with them, learning much new information about life at The Kilns during the '40s and '50s. It was also from them that we learned that Joan Murphy, about whom I spoke earlier, was Lewis's cousin.

The Kilns was still undergoing restoration at that time, and Mary asked how it was coming along, having not seen the house for many years. In particular, she asked if there was still an iron ladder – a series of iron "staples" – attached to the side of the house below Lewis's bedroom on the second floor – or if not, were they planning to restore that. Having lived at The Kilns in the summer of 1985, after a group of us had bought the house in order to preserve it, I told her there was no such ladder even back then, and I had no knowledge of there ever having been one. She then explained its origin.

Jack, Warnie, and Mrs. Moore bought The Kilns in 1930 in order to provide a permanent home for Mrs. Moore and her daughter Maureen. Although there has been much conjecture over the years about the exact nature of Jack's relationship with Janie Moore, the Rogers confirmed that they were aware (as were the Sayers) that there had been a sexual relationship prior to Jack's conversion in 1931. Following his conversion, he abruptly ceased that aspect of their relationship, and thereafter slept in an adjoining bedroom – which, however, had access to the rest of the house only through Mrs. Moore's bedroom. Because he was an early riser and did not wish to disturb her, he had the iron ladder installed outside his bedroom window as his means of exiting at an early hour!

By the time we acquired The Kilns in 1985, there was no evidence of the ladder having been there. However, Doug Gresham remembers an iron stairway fire escape at that site, so we can assume that fire regulations required replacement of the ladder long ago.

Autograph Hunting

Finding first or even later editions of Lewis books signed by him is one of the joys of collecting – but there's also much pleasure in personally obtaining the signatures of those who knew him on books by Lewis or about him. Walter Hooper was my first target in that respect. Many years ago, when he was the main speaker at a weekend conference sponsored by the C. S. Lewis Society of New York, I took with me several books for him to sign. Since that time I had not taken books to England for him to sign, but when he was a guest in my home two years ago following a C. S. Lewis Colloquium at Taylor University at which he was the main speaker, I couldn't resist: I had him sign every unsigned book on my shelf that he had edited.

One of the books taken to New York was *Light on C. S. Lewis*, a 1965 compilation of essays about Lewis by nine people who knew him – Owen Barfield, Austin Farrer, J. A. W. Bennett, Nevill Coghill, John Lawlor, Stella Gibbons, Kathleen Raine, Chad Walsh, and Walter Hooper. I was a novice in learning about Lewis when I first found a copy of the book in the early 1980s, and thinking it would be a grand thing to get all nine of those signatures, I began with Walter, whom I had recently met. His name is at the bottom of the list of contributors printed on the front of the dust jacket, so I then began at the top with Owen Barfield, whom I met soon thereafter. Continuing down the list to determine who might still be around, however, I was dismayed to find that all but Walter had already left this earth for heavenly realms. But two out of nine isn't all that bad – and the next time I visited Owen Barfield, I had in hand a lovely copy of *The Allegory of Love*, of which he is the dedicatee, to sign.

My major effort in this kind of venture, however, resulted from a momentous acquisition in 1985. Early that year I received a letter from England addressed in a hand I didn't recognize, nor was I familiar with the imprinted name at the top of the notehead – Mr. and Mrs. F. O. Gasch – at an address in Surrey. Turning to the signature, I was astonished to see that it was from Pauline Baynes:

Dear Dr. Brown,

Dr. Clyde Kilby suggested I should write to you. He thought you might be interested in acquiring the complete set of drawings, including the endpaper map, of "Prince Caspian", by C. S. Lewis. These drawings, which are of the same size as in the book, came to light last month after being lost for around 30 years, and were returned to me by Collins, who had them for the Penguin Books, where they had been hidden away since the paperbacks were first published! I long ago disposed of all the other Lewis originals, either privately or in exhibitions – so these are all that remain from the Narnia books, or, at least, have a scarcity value. I'm not sure of how much else: – but I intend, should I not sell them privately, to hand them over to Sothebys to auction later this year.
Forgive me writing if you are not interested, but Dr. Kilby thought you might be.

Yours sincerely,
Pauline Baynes

"... if you are not interested" ! What an incredible offer! There was a phone number at the top of the notehead, which I immediately called, to confirm that indeed I was. She apologized for not being able to give me a price, but said she would have them appraised at Sothebys and immediately let me know. I assured her that I would buy them, whatever the price, and when she wrote soon thereafter to give me the price, I sent her a check and told her I would pick them up personally within a few weeks as soon as I arrived in England for a six-month sabbatical.

What amazed me was that Dr. Kilby would have referred her to me rather than acquiring them for the Wade Center – until I remembered that he had retired as its founder and director some years earlier, shortly before I first met him. But why would he not have urged the Wade Center to buy them when she obviously wrote to him earlier to tell him of their return? As strange as that may seem, I think it entirely possible that he didn't want them to go to the Wade Center.

I first called upon him at his home in Wheaton shortly after he had retired as director of the Wade Center. He received me most graciously, and offered to take me through the Wade Center, but expressed regret about having been forced into retirement. It was after hours, and as he took me downstairs to the stacks in the basement to show me his most-prized Lewis acquisition – the inscribed copy of *Spirits in Bondage* inscribed by Lewis to his (Lewis's) father – he commented, "We have to go in the vault, if they haven't changed the lock on me!"

I learned later that the reason for the college having urged him to retire was that his short-term memory had become so compromised that when he traveled on Wade Center business, he would have to call his office in Wheaton to find out the reason for his being wherever he was, whether in the United States or abroad. While he probably accepted this change when proposed, it's likely that it weighed upon him as time passed – as so often happens with men who have poured themselves into their work for decades, and suddenly find themselves unprepared for breaking away from the demands, contacts, and other perquisites of their former position. I passed my concerns for him to a close friend on the board of trustees of the college, hoping that something might be done to ameliorate the situation, but I was not aware of the outcome, and he moved to a southern city some time thereafter, where he died in 1986. As a professor of English who introduced countless Wheaton students to C. S. Lewis, as a friend of the Lewis brothers and others of their contemporaries, and founder of the Wade Center, which he developed into the world's finest archive of Lewisiana and six other great Christian writers, Dr. Clyde Kilby left us a monumental legacy.

Not only did I acquire those precious drawings but the ongoing friendship of that talented lady as well, whose illustrations for the Chronicles of Narnia were a major factor in the success of the books, as Lewis himself acknowledged. When she congratulated him on the awarding of the Carnegie Medal for *The Last Battle* as the best children's book of 1956, he replied, "Is it not rather 'our' medal?"

The following year, while in London, I took advantage of that friendship when I bought a pristine set of Narnia first editions, which I had her sign, and she has since obliged me by signing books of friends whom I referred to her.

It was also a great pleasure to become acquainted with her late husband Fritz. He was a charming German, who was very fond of America as the result of having been kept there as a prisoner of war for much of the time of our involvement in World War II. He had been captured in North Africa, and spent his time as a POW in America.

Lewis employed Pauline to illustrate *The Lion, the Witch and the Wardrobe* after being impressed by illustrations she had done for Tolkien's children's books – and was so impressed with her work that she illustrated the entire series. She has an enormous list of credits for her art, both for books and magazine articles of others, and for books she published on her own. At 84, she is now essentially retired, still living in the same cottage in Surrey which she has occupied for many decades – and always a joy to visit.

Snatched from the Fire

The collection at Taylor is blessed with two Lewis manuscripts. One is a well-known exchange between Lewis and his closest friend, Owen Barfield, *Clivi Hamiltonis Summae Metaphysices Contra Anthroposophos, Libri II* – known simply as *The Summa* to Lewis scholars. The other is a five page "fair copy" (the final draft of a work, as submitted to the publisher) of a short story entitled *Light*, written about 1929.

During the war, when Warnie was in the Army, Lewis was looking for someone who would type his books, and Colin Hardie introduced him to his sister-in-law, Barbara Wall, who was living in Oxford. Barbara was the sister of Christian Hardie, wife of Colin Hardie, Inkling and colleague of Lewis at Magdalen College. She typed *That Hideous Strength, The Great Divorce,* and *Miracles.*

Lewis manuscripts are extremely rare, most of them having ended up in the "w.p.b." (waste paper basket) as he called it, the result of his frugality. Fair copies are only written or typed on one side of the sheet, so when he received a manuscript back from the publisher, he routinely tore the sheets in half, turned them over, and thus acquired a double-size stack of scratch paper.

Even when consigned to the w.p.b., the manuscript scraps were often further utilized by Jack, who would retrieve one, fold it into a spill, and use it to light the gas grate, the burner of which was too deep to reach with an ordinary match. One such twice-utilized half of a manuscript page was retrieved by Jill Flewett as a souvenir while emptying a waste basket one day at "The Kilns" – and which I purchased from Sophie Dupré several years before acquiring Lady Freud's collection of Lewis letters. It is now one of my most prized possessions.

This many-folded fragment, containing the verbatim text found in the first British edition of *Christian Behaviour*, Chapter 5, line 5 of page 38 to line 6 if page 39, is charred only along the left edge.

exactly. As a matter of fact, the only man I know to whom I do love as I love myself is myself. So apparently "Love your neighbour" does not mean "feel fond of him" or "find him attractive." I ought to have seen that before, because, of course, you cannot feel fond of a person by trying. Do I think well of myself, think myself a nice chap? Well, I'm afraid I sometimes do (and those are, no doubt, my worst moments) but that is not why I love myself. In fact it's the other way round: my self-love makes me think myself nice, but thinking myself nice is not why I love myself. So loving my enemies does not apparently mean thinking them nice either. That is an enormous relief. For a good many people imagine that forgiving your enemies means making out that they are really not such bad fellows after all, when it's quite plain that they are. Go a step further. In my most clear-sighted moments not only do I not think myself a nice man, but I know that I'm a very nasty one. I can look at some of the things I have done with horror and loathing. So apparently I am allowed to loathe and hate some of the things my enemies do. Now that I come to think of it, I remember Christian teachers telling me long ago that I must hate a bad man's actions but not hate the bad man: or, as they would say, hate the sin but not the sinner. For a long time I used to think this a silly, straw-splitting distinction: how could you hate what a man did and not hate the man? But years later it occurred to me that this was the very thing I had been doing all my life — namely myself. However much I might dislike my own cowardice or conceit or greed, I went on loving myself. There had never been the slightest difficulty about it. In fact the very reason why I hated these things was that I loved the man. Just because I loved

While it's most certainly the only surviving fragment of the fair copy of his second book of BBC talks, *Christian Behaviour*, it has even greater significance because of the penciled notes on the back – another serendipitous discovery made after I brought it home from London:

With the fragment in the vertical position, the notes begin at the unburned edge and are partially burned away at the bottom. Even electronically enhanced and enlarged, the legibility is poor:

My best deciphering efforts over the years have resulted in the following transcription of this fragment:

Have passed from Atheism to Xnity – and more & more <u>definite</u>.
Doctrinal.
Wing Commander Snooks.
Quite right in thinking experience more "real."
But a map (a) Based on innumerable real experiences
         (b) Necessary for sailing.
(a) Knowledge = experience + logic.
In religion the instrument is the whole man
(Keep in good order).
Behind Xty   (1) The continuous systematic Jewish experience.
            i.e. the unity of God & it <u>does</u> matter
            (2) Experience of Xt.
            What that experience really means.
            Either a lunatic or _____
            (3) The corporate experience of a Society He founded.
When you work all that out you get the Creeds.
Anyone vaguely thinking about "religion" & ignoring all this, like
a man starting Physics "on his own."
(b) "Does it matter what men worship provided it's good?"!
   Yes! matters whether it's <u>there</u>
<u>1.</u> Right & wrong conceptions of God's Love
   Master – dog: father – son: man – woman
<u>2.</u> Conception of Man.
   Not an imperfect creature who needs development but
   a rebel who must remember.
<u>3.</u> Wrong conception of Matter.
   "Our bodies drag us down" "the animal vices are the worst"
   God created matter. Our words get us into more trouble than
   our bodies. All the <u>worst</u> pleasures are spiritual.
<u>4.</u> Wrong conception of what <u>to do</u>.
   -----t our own efforts. Prayer [&] sacraments ----- is -----

But who was the mysterious Wing Commander Snooks in line three? Again, as I read the name and the notes immediately following, a light began to flicker in my brain. (My brain had by now become rather adept at producing flickering lights.) Where had I seen some of those words?

Christian Behaviour, published in 1943, was soon followed in 1944 by *Beyond Personality* – and it was there that the mystery was solved. On the opening page Lewis wrote:

In a way I quite understand why some people are put off by Theology. I remember once when I'd been giving a talk to the R.A.F. an old, hard-bitten officer got up and said, 'I've no use for all that stuff. But, mind you, I'm a religious man, too. I know there's a God. I've felt Him: out there alone in the desert at night: the tremendous mystery. And that's just why I don't believe all your neat little dogmas and formulas about Him. To anyone who's met the real thing they all seem so petty and pedantic and unreal!'

Now in a sense I quite agreed with that man. I think he'd probably had a real experience with God in the desert. And when he turned from that experience to the Christian creeds, I think he was really turning from something quite real to something less real. In the same way, if a man has once looked at the Atlantic from the beach, and then goes and looks at a map of the Atlantic, he also will be turning from something real to something less real. ... The map is only coloured paper, but ... it is based on what hundreds and thousands of people have found out by sailing the real Atlantic ... and if you want to go anywhere, the map is absolutely necessary.

And there, on that single scrap of paper, I not only learned the name of that old, hard-bitten R.A.F. officer (and at the time was the only person in the world who knew it!), but had in my hand the first notes of his third book of BBC talks! Lady Freud, of course, had no idea of what she had, nor did I until I was able to study it at home. Consider the sequence of events that resulted in the survival of what is undoubtedly the most significant and only fragment of that manuscript because of the penciled notes on the back: a page ripped in two, used, discarded, used again for a very different purpose, again discarded, consigned to the trash fire in the garden, but retrieved as a souvenir by a teenage girl who kept it for 50 years – and now a trophy displayed in the Taylor University library, to be shared with all. The odds of this incredible sequence defy calculation.

The Last of the Inklings

Owen Barfield was born in 1898, the same year as Lewis, but outlived him by 36 years. They first met as students at Oxford University, becoming the closest of friends for the remainder of Lewis's life. In his biography, *Surprised by Joy*, Lewis writes of him:

"There is a sense in which Arthur and Barfield are the types of every man's First Friend and Second Friend. The first is the *alter ego*, the man who first reveals to you that you are not alone in the world by turning out (beyond hope) to share all your most secret delights. There is nothing to be overcome in making him your friend; he and you join like raindrops on a window. But the Second Friend is the man who disagrees with you about everything. He is not so much the *alter ego* as the anti-self. Of course he shares your interests; otherwise he would not become your friend at all. But he has approached them all at a different angle. He has read all the right books but has got the wrong thing out of every one. It is as if he spoke your language but mispronounced it.

How can he be so nearly right and yet, invariably, just not right? He is as fascinating (and infuriating) as a woman. When you set out to correct his heresies, you find he forsooth has decided to correct yours! And then you go at it, hammer and tongs, far into the night, night after night, or walking through fine country that neither gives a glance to, each learning the weight of the other's punches, and often more like mutually respectful enemies than friends. Actually (though it never seems so at the moment) you modify one another's thought; out of this perpetual dogfight a community of mind and a deep affection emerge. But I think he changed me a good deal more than I him. Much of the thought which he afterward put into *Poetic Diction* had already become mine before that important little book appeared. It would be strange if it had not. He was of course not so learned then as he has since become; but the genius was already there."

(For a fascinating read, see *Owen Barfield on C. S. Lewis*, edited by G. B. Tennyson.)

I first met Owen Barfield in 1988, with a mystery in hand – the *Light* manuscript.

The *Light* manuscript was never published, but had apparently been sent to an unknown magazine for publication, as suggested by the entry in the upper right-hand corner of the first page: *From C. S. Lewis, Magdalen College, Oxford.* Entirely handwritten on five pages of "foolscap" (a lined sheet of paper, 8"x13", in standard use in Britain in those days), the story was neither published nor returned, turning up some 50 years later among some books and papers acquired from an unknown source by an obscure London book dealer. Seeing Lewis's name on it, he sold it for £100 (a very small sum for a Lewis manuscript) to a more knowledgeable dealer, who immediately sold it for £500 to Peter Jolliffe, a dealer who specialized in Lewis and from whom I had bought many first editions. Needless to say, the price increased considerably when he offered to me.

The first draft of the story, however, was published in 1977 in *The Dark Tower and Other Stories*, edited by Walter Hooper, who had found it in a composition book among Lewis's papers after his death. Jack had not given the story a title, so Walter entitled it *The Man Born Blind*. (The title *Light* is written in the same color of ink as the entry in the upper right-hand corner of the first page, which is different from that used for the story, so it appears that Jack didn't decide on a title until just before he sent it off.)

I had long wanted to meet Owen Barfield, this great friend of Lewis and the last living member (at 90) of the Inklings, but modesty had forbade my simply calling on him and announcing myself as a Lewis "fan" (as Warnie had referred to Joy). On that memorable trip in 1988 I had taken with me a photocopy of the manuscript to show to Walter Hooper, assuming from his having entitled the earlier version of the story *The Man Born Blind* that he had never heard of this final version. He had not.

Returning to London from Oxford, I began making my usual visits to the major antiquarian bookshops in central London. Among the first was the venerable Charing Cross Road Bookshop. I inquired of the assistant whether he knew if they had any first editions of C. S. Lewis – and was shocked by his reply, "Well, we did have Owen Barfield's copy of *Spirits in Bondage* last week, but it's been sold." (I learned only a short time ago from the buyer, a fellow collector in Tennessee, that he just happened to wander into the shop as the book was being placed on the shelf!)

"Do you know where it came from?" I asked. "Yes, my boss bought it directly from Owen Barfield when he heard that Barfield was selling some of his library." I thanked him and raced out of the shop to the nearest telephone, to call Walter and ask for Owen's address – ostensibly to be able to show him the copy of the *Light* manuscript but more importantly to see if any of his Lewis first editions were still available.

He was just leaving the house when I drove up. I introduced myself as a friend of Walter, apologized for just dropping in, and told him I just wanted to leave with him a copy of a Lewis manuscript, hoping he might know something about it. I also mentioned that I understand he had been selling some of his Lewis first editions, to which he replied that Blackwell's had bought most of them, and the rest had been picked up by some other dealers. The only thing left was *The Summa*, which was to be auctioned at Sotheby's the following week.

He apologized for having to be on his way to check out a retirement home he was considering and said he would drop me a line after he had read the *Light* manuscript. I thanked him and headed back to Oxford to have a look at the books bought by Blackwell's.

On the desk of Philip Brown, manager of Blackwell's antiquarian department and a longtime friend, was a pile of a dozen or so Lewis first editions. He hadn't yet priced them, so while I sat there, he took them one by one, noted what he had paid for them, penciled a price on each one, and handed it to me. Most were inscribed by Jack, some in very warm terms, so I chose a few representative samples thereof, thanked him, and left with my treasures, wondering how I was going to explain the next American Express bill to Pat.

The most interesting of these is a first edition of *The Problem of Pain,* given to Barfield with the following letter on Magdalen College stationery, and sent to him two days before its release on October 18, 1940:

Oct 16th 1940 My dear Barfield, A book on this subject from me at Oxford (wh. continues to be Gideon's fleece) to you in the front line seems rather impertinent. When wd. you like a few quiet nights here? Do come and spend one or two. You are daily in my thoughts. Yours, C. S. Lewis (This was during the Battle of Britain, when London was being bombed regularly by the German Luftwaffe.)

Barfield had pasted the letter to the front pasted-down endpaper, but only at the bottom of the letter, rather than the top, so that the following notes written by him on the back of the letter could be read:

Either redemption is better than innocence or the Parable of the Prodigal Son is sentimental bilge. Obedience, as an element in response, varies directly with the extent to which the response is either (a) mechanical or (b) contrary to inclination and first judgment. Therefore, (i) never an end in itself (ii) an unsatisfactory trope for the unique response of created to creator.

Barfield's penciled notes appear throughout the book.

It was too late in the day to phone Sotheby's about the upcoming auction of *The Summa,* and I was scheduled to fly home early the following morning. I reached them by phone from Indianapolis, only to learn that the auction was only two days hence. Fortunately, I was able to reach David Mayou, a dealer friend in London, who agreed to represent me at the auction – and for an amount that would have bought us a late model second-hand car, I became the proud and impecunious owner of a fascinating piece of Lewisiana. (Anyhow, the old car was running just fine.) I phoned Owen to tell him the good news. Sotheby's hadn't yet told him the result of the auction, and he was amazed at the price – which made me wonder how much Blackwell's and the other dealers had paid him for all those Lewis first editions, many of which were presentation copies with inscriptions by Lewis.

He later wrote to tell me that he had never seen the final version of the story. Although Jack had shown him the first draft in the composition book sometime around 1929, he was not aware that he had rewritten it for publication – and added that he preferred some of the revised portions of the earlier version. Most significant, however, was his noting that Jack had written the story for Owen's benefit, as a further argument against anthroposophy, the subject of their "Great War" debate in *The Summa*. How providential that the only two Lewis manuscripts to have become available for sale in the past several decades, from vastly different sources, were so clearly connected!

Over the next decade I was able to visit Owen at The Wallhatch, his retirement home in Forest Row, a small community about 30 miles southeast of London. On the first visit I phoned him from London to tell him what train I was taking, and that I would get a taxi from the station in East Grindsted to Forest Row. He would have none of that, saying that he would meet me at the station. Not only did he drive his own car, but his driving skill at age 88 was such that I would have had difficulty keeping up with him if I had been following him.

I was curious to know more about *The Summa*. When in 1923 Barfield became an adherent of Rudolph Steiner's Anthroposophy, Lewis later wrote in *Surprised by Joy*, "Barfield's conversion to Anthroposophy marked the beginning of what I can only describe as the Great War between him and me. It was never, thank God, a quarrel, though it could have become one in a moment if he had used to me anything like the violence I allowed myself to him. But it was an almost incessant disputation, sometimes by letter and sometimes face to face, which lasted for years. And this Great War was one of the turning points of my life."

Although the manuscript itself was never published as such, it was discussed at length in *C. S. Lewis's 'Great War' with Owen Barfield,* by Lionel Adey (1978). It fills 123 pages in the same sort of composition book in which Lewis wrote the first draft of *Light,* beginning with a title page, *Clivi Hamiltonis Summae Metaphysices Contra Anthroposophos, Libri II.* The next three pages, also in Lewis's handwriting, is an index: *Part I – Being,* with 21 subheadings, and *Part II – Value,* with 25 subheadings. Lewis then proceeded to fill 68 handwritten pages covering the 46 points in these subheadings, ending with *November 1928, Headington.* The next page (71) has only a tiny drawing of a hand pointing to the following page. He then mailed the book to Barfield in London.

Page 72, in Barfield's handwriting, is simply the title of his reply, *Replicit Anthroposophus Barfieldus.* He then takes 37 pages to respond to those points with which he disagrees, having written in red pencil *concedo* or *nego* on Lewis's pages after each subheading or portion thereof with which he agrees or disagrees. He concludes with a 14-page *AUTEM* (summary), and mailed the book back to Lewis.

Lewis responds with 10 pages of commentary – with no further response by Barfield! Tired of waiting for a response (and the book), Lewis wrote an additional 14 pages of comments on 8"x10" foolscap, which Barfield read, underlined in places, and neatly folded into the back of the book, where they remained in his possession for the next 60 years. My question to Barfield was simply, "Why didn't you reply and send the book back to him?" His response: "Why, I think I just tired of the whole thing!"

My last visit to The Wallhatch was in 1987. Driving to Gatwick airport for the flight home after two weeks in and around Oxford, I realized I would be checking in rather early and wondered how far it might be to Forest Row. Although I had spoken with him by phone from time to time, I hadn't seen Owen for about two years, and the last time I spoke with him, he had just returned from the hospital. Parking my car in the rental car lot without turning it in, I checked in for the flight, then retrieved the car and drove the 20 miles or so to the retirement home to check on his state of health.

He was in his room when I arrived, and it was apparent that he had gone downhill considerably since my previous visit. I apologized for just dropping in (reminiscent of our first meeting!) and explained that I had to leave for the airport in about 20 minutes. I don't remember what we chatted about, but I was grateful for having been able to see him again – and especially grateful for having made that last-minute decision to visit him, for he died less than two months later.

He was born in 1898, just two weeks before Lewis's birth, and it was clear that it had been difficult for him to have outlived his best friend by more than 25 years. Although survived by his adopted son Jeffrey, he outlived both his other son and his daughter Lucy.

Again, I marveled at the sequence of events – an inquiry of a knowledgeable clerk in just the right London bookshop that led to the acquisition of a major Lewis manuscript and the development of a warm friendship with Owen Barfield for the last decade of his life.

Shedding Light on *Light*

In his introduction to *The Dark Tower and Other Stories,* Hooper notes: "The next piece in this book, 'The Man Born Blind,' was found in one of the notebooks given me by Lewis's brother. It has never been published before and, as far as I know, was not seen by anyone during the author's lifetime with the exception of Owen Barfield and possibly J.R.R. Tolkien. Though I regret never having asked Tolkien about the story, I was interested to learn that he mentioned it to Professor Clyde S. Kilby who says in *Tolkien and the Silmarillion* (1976):

'Tolkien told me of C. S. Lewis's story about the man born with a cataract on each eye. He kept hearing people talk of light but could not understand what they meant. After an operation he had some sight but had not yet come to understand *light*. Then one day he saw a haze rising from a pond (actually, said Tolkien, the pond at the front of Lewis's home) and thought that at last he was seeing light. In his eagerness to experience real light, he rushed joyfully into it and was drowned. ... Owen Barfield tells me that The Man Born Blind was written during the late 1920s when he and Lewis were deep in the 'Great War' debate over Appearance and Reality which Lewis refers to in his autobiography, *Surprised by Joy.*'"

Hooper then goes on to say, "The story was written on the right-hand pages of one of his notebooks. On the left-hand pages, in a script penned some years later, are revisions ... (which) cannot be linked together with the rest of the original version and I have had to content myself with publishing the original, and only complete version of the story there is."

In 1985 I had the opportunity to examine this notebook at the Bodleian Library in Oxford, and obtained photocopies of the seven right-hand pages on which the original story appears, as well as the revisions on the left-hand pages.

(Getting into the Bodleian takes some doing, I discovered. I assumed that my Indiana University faculty ID card would admit me without difficulty, only to be told by a rather haughty library official that I would need to make application and that this would have to be signed by a referee known to the library. The Bodleian office is just across the street from Blackwell's, so I casually asked if Miles Blackwell's brother Nigel would be suitable as referee. Somewhat taken aback, the keeper of the keys replied that this would be satisfactory. I completed the application form, took it to Nigel's secretary, and asked if Nigel could sign it when he returned from lunch. I soon had a five-year pass to the Bodleian.)

The first of these revisions, opposite page four, is a six-line effort to revise the paragraph immediately opposite. On the next left-hand page, opposite page five, is a much more extensive revision of that same paragraph on page four. The left-hand page opposite page six is blank, but that opposite page seven is a still further revision of the same paragraph. When I came into possession of the *Light* manuscript the following year, my first step was to compare it with the original version published under the title given it by Hooper, *The Man Born Blind*. Lewis had extensively revised the story, including one little touch, that of changing the wife's name from Mary to Anne. One can only wonder if there were other drafts between my manuscript and that in Hooper's notebook, but I found a very interesting connection between these two.

Both the second and third revisions on the left-hand pages of the notebook were extensive, and each very different from the other, but only one sentence and the first part of the following sentence appear in the final version of the story. These word for word from that third revision – appear in the *Light* manuscript: "*About 6 weeks passed before he did so. During that time he had passed through every fluctuation of hope and despair ...*"

At this time I was also able to examine the manuscript of *The Dark Tower* – the name given by Walter Hooper to an unfinished story on 62 large sheets of ruled paper in Lewis's handwriting, found among a large quantity of notebooks and papers about to be burned by

Warnie a few weeks after his brother's death. On the back of the first page was what appeared to be the beginning of another story:

This book is about four children whose names were Ann, Martin, Rose and Peter. But it is mostly about Peter who was the youngest. They all had to go away from London suddenly because of the Air Raids, and because father, who was in the army, had gone off to the war and Mother was doing some kind of war work. They were sent to stay with a relation of Mother's who was a very old Professor who lived by himself in the country.

Thought to have been written about 1939, when children were being evacuated from London – and some of whom had come to live at The Kilns – this brief introduction to what was to become the beginning of the Narnia series some ten years later had been for the time being set aside by Lewis in favor of another story of space travel begun just after *Out of the Silent Planet.*

Eager to have a photocopy of the pages from the notebook with what was clearly the first draft of my *Light* manuscript, as well as this interesting first note on what was to become the Chronicles of Narnia, I asked the curator if it would be possible to have such copies. "I'm sorry, but you would have to have permission of the Lewis estate," was the disappointing reply – until a sudden thought crossed my mind.

"Would that by any chance be something Walter Hooper could arrange? He's a good friend of mine." Indeed it was, and a quick phone call to Walter was all that was needed. "Come back in an hour or so, and you can pick them up."

I later found these copies invaluable in comparing them with the *Light* manuscript. Making further copies of both, cutting identical lines from each, and putting one from the notebook above the same one from the manuscript produced uncanny results. The handwriting was so identical in every detail that there could be no doubt that it was that of Lewis.

In 1988, author Kathryn Lindskoog claimed in *The C. S. Lewis Hoax* that the manuscripts of both *The Dark Tower* and *The Man Born Blind*, said by Hooper to have been found among Lewis's papers, were forgeries. Although she had never seen either manuscript, she said of *The Man Born Blind*, "The writing is so flat, talkish, and amateurish that is seems impossible that Lewis could have written it." This was, of course, a startling claim, for the handwriting is certainly that of Lewis, and while the story may have left something to be desired (perhaps even in its final form, and thus the reason for not been accepted for publication), it was, after all, the first short story he had ever written.

Except for Walter Hooper, Owen Barfield, and the three dealers who had handled the *Light* manuscript, no one other than myself had ever read it. I thought it only fair, therefore, to let Mrs. Lindskoog, with whom I had never had any contact, know of its existence. Obtaining her number from directory assistance, I phoned her at her home in Orange, California, to tell her about it – and was a bit taken aback when she assumed that it, too, was a forgery! "I hope you can get your money back from the dealer!"

No one at the Bodleian Library, nor anyone else who has seen both *The Dark Tower* manuscript and the two versions of the short story has, to my knowledge, doubted that the handwriting is that of Lewis – and needless to say, Peter Jolliffe, the dealer from whom I bought *Light*, would today be more than delighted to take it back.

Mrs. Lindskoog acknowledged that the handwriting may very well look like that of Lewis. "After all, that's what forgers are usually able to do." The obvious question, then, is why would someone have forged the *Light* manuscript? Most forgeries are done for monetary gain, but as I noted earlier the dealer who first sold it did so for only £100 – and had probably paid far less for it. There thus could have been no significant monetary gain to the forger.

Some months after informing Kathryn Lindskoog of the existence of the manuscript, while visiting family in California I was able to visit her and her husband John in their home in Orange. For four delightful hours we talked about many things relating to Lewis and

The Kilns – without once touching upon the forgery issue. She was a truly remarkable person. Afflicted with multiple sclerosis for many years, she eventually become so incapacitated as to be bedridden, with only the use of her right hand. Yet despite her infirmity, she continued to do an enormous amount of reading and writing, and published several books in the years just before her death in October 2003. Despite our disagreement, she was a warm friend, and I am sure she is having a marvelous time discussing this and many other matters with her friend Jack.

In *The C. S. Lewis Hoax* Kathryn also disputes the bonfire from which Walter said he retrieved all those notebooks and papers. Not many years ago I had an interesting conversation with a retired Blackwell's employee, who told me how he first met Walter Hooper back in 1964. He had not heard of *The C. S. Lewis Hoax* until I happened to tell him about it and the bonfire episode, to which he responded with a very interesting tale.

He had become friendly with the young American the previous summer when Walter was helping Lewis with his correspondence in the absence of Warnie, who was in Ireland on one of the extended drinking bouts to which had become victim in his later years. Walter had returned to Oxford soon after Lewis's death, and had been helping Warnie sort through Jack's many papers and other effects, much of which Walter and Doug Gresham had brought back from Magdalene College in Cambridge the summer before, after Jack's resignation due to his deteriorating health.

One day early in 1964 Walter came into Blackwell's in a mild state of panic to ask his friend if he might use their copier, one of the first xerographic copiers in Oxford. He explained that he had just retrieved a large quantity of Lewis papers that were about to be burned by Lewis's brother, Warnie, and he needed to make copies of those that had not yet been destroyed. "We told him we would help him during our lunch hour, and day after day Walter showed up with stacks of paper." Seems a pity that the Blackwell brass in those days didn't know what a contribution the company had made to the Lewis legacy!

Lewis Sightings

C. S. Lewis is generally acknowledged in Christian circles as the greatest Christian writer of the 20th century. He is undoubtedly the most quoted writer outside St. Paul and other writers of the New Testament, and I have heard him quoted in countless sermons in many different churches.

Sometimes, however, he appears in unlikely places, such as in one brief episode in the novel *Swan Song*, by Oxford writer Edmund Crispin. One of Crispin's characters, sitting in the lounge of the venerable Randolph Hotel, just down the street in Oxford from The Eagle and Child, looks out the window and remarks, "It must be Tuesday. There goes Lewis on his way to the Bird and Baby."

More recently, Lewis fans who were also followers of the Inspector Morse series on television had a special treat. In one episode, Morse and Sergeant Lewis were having a pint in a pub (as was often their habit), when Lewis noticed a plaque on the wall opposite. The scene is best described in Oxford writer Colin Dexter's *The Secret of Annexe 3*, on which the TV episode was based:

"In the back bar of the Eagle and Child in St. Giles', the two men [Inspector Morse and Sergeant Lewis] sat and drank their beer, and Lewis found himself reading and reading again the writing on the wooden plaque fixed to the wall behind Morse's head:

C. S. LEWIS, his brother, W. H. Lewis, J. R. R. Tolkien, Charles Williams, and other friends met every Tuesday morning, between the years 1939-1962 in the back room of this their favourite pub. These men, popularly known as the "Inklings," met here to drink Beer and to discuss, among other things, the books they were writing.

Sergeant Lewis's mind ... was waxing the more imaginative as he pictured a series of fundamental emendations to this received text, "CHIEF INSPECTOR MORSE, with his friend and colleague Sergeant Lewis, sat in this back room one Thursday, in order to solve ..."

(As noted earlier, the plaque was placed in the pub in the early '70s. When I first saw it in 1974, it was the only reference to be found in the pub to Lewis and the Inklings. Today, it is surrounded by photographs and other memorabilia of the Inklings, the Eagle and Child having become in recent years a major feature of the "Lewis Trail" followed by individuals and tour groups.)

My own special Lewis sighting wasn't really a Lewis sighting at all – and I wonder if any others of the countless thousands who've seen it have known of the Lewis connection. It happened one day when I was traveling home from Skopje, Macedonia, via Zurich, Switzerland, where my connecting flight was delayed by several hours. I left the airport to visit the town and its beautiful lake, the Zurichsee. At the head of the lake is a park, graced by a statue of a naked young man standing beside an eagle. The only inscription thereon is *GANYMED*! Why the city of Zurich became so enamored of the beautiful young man Ganymede as to erect a statue in his honor I have yet to learn.

The original large rectangular sign on The Eagle and Child, replaced by the present small oval sign, has two different versions of the picture of Ganymede. On the one side, the infant Ganymede is reclined on the back of the flying eagle; on the other side he is being carried in a cloth sling clutched in the eagle's beak. It's certainly a more interesting rendition of Ganymede than the Zurich statue – and who would want a pub to be known as the Bird and Big Boy?

A Christian Forum at a Secular University

Oxford is an historic and unique institution. As the oldest English-speaking university in the world, it can lay claim to nine centuries of continuous existence. There is no clear date of foundation, but teaching existed at Oxford in some form in 1096 and developed rapidly from 1167, when Henry II banned English students from attending the University of Paris. Unlike American universities whose individual colleges, institutes, or whatever they may be called on a single campus – or even multiple campuses – Oxford comprises a host of colleges (39 at last count) which are essentially independent in their administration from the parent university, although the degrees are awarded by and in the name of the university.

Like so many of our great universities in America, however, those colleges of Oxford which were established as religious institutions of higher learning – with names such as Trinity, Jesus, St. Edmunds (and seven others with saintly names), Christ Church, etc. – have long since relinquished their Christian heritage. Established in 1941 by Stella Aldwinckle, with C. S. Lewis as its first president, the Socratic Club became the best-known and best-attended of all the Oxford student societies.

Stella, a graduate of St. Anne's College, taught divinity at two other British universities after leaving Oxford, but returned to Oxford in 1941 in a pastoral ministry to students as a member of the Oxford Pastorate, a team of workers associated with St. Aldate's Church who gave spiritual counseling primarily to undergraduates. (St. Aldates church remains to this day a great evangelical church, which my wife and I were privileged to attend during a sabbatical in Oxford in 1985, when Michael Green was its senior minister.) Soon after her arrival, she posted a notice inviting "all atheists, agnostics, and those who are disillusioned about religion or think they are" to meet together – a meeting from which emerged the Oxford University Socratic Club.

Thereafter green posters were to be seen all over Oxford at the beginning of each term, stating that "in view of the present struggle between a Christian and a 'Nazi' Order of Society, this club has been formed for those who do not necessarily wish to commit themselves to Christian views but are interested in a philosophical approach to religion in general and to Christianity in particular, in a spirit of free enquiry and in the light of modern thought and knowledge". Printed on the cheapest of paper, there are almost none in existence today, but in 1985 I was fortunate to have obtained one for each of two different terms, together with an admission card for another term's meetings, issued free upon application to Stella Aldwinckle.

Oxford University

SOCRATIC CLUB

President: C. S. LEWIS, M.A.

In view of the present struggle between a Christian and a ' Nazi ' Order of Society, this Club has been formed for those who do not necessarily wish to commit themselves to Christian views but are interested in a philosophical approach to religion in general and to Christianity in particular, in a spirit of free enquiry and in the light of modern thought and knowledge.

OPEN DISCUSSION will follow the introduction of the subjects by speakers who will include both Christians and non-Christians.

MEETINGS

Trinity Term, 1945

| May 7th. | Justification by Faith. | Rev. J. HICKENBOTHAM |
| | | Fr. T. M. PARKER |

(By Request : Joint Meeting with the S.C.M.)

May 14th.	Resurrection.	Mr. C. S. LEWIS
May 21st.	Reason and Faith.	Pastor KRAMM
May 28th.	Can Myth be Fact ?	Rev. A. M. FARRER
		Mr. C. S. LEWIS
June 4th.	Christian and Non-Christian Mysticism.	
		Rev. GERVASE MATHEW, O.P.

Meetings at 8.15 p.m. on MONDAYS, the first three in St. Hilda's J.C.R., the last two in Oriel J.C.R.

The Papers will be followed by Questions and Open Discussion.

Oxonian Press, Queen Street.

One of the speakers would present his paper on the subject, the other would reply, and there would then be general discussion. The Socratic Club was enormously popular among Oxford students, but when Lewis left to Cambridge in 1955 interest began to decline and by 1972 it had come to an end. Between 1943 and 1952,the club published five issues of the occasional *Socratic Digest*, each containing some of the papers presented during some terms. These are extremely rare today, although I have been able to assemble two complete sets and am looking for nos. 4 and 5 to complete a third set.

Lewis wrote a Preface for the first issue, in which he said:

"In any fairly large and talkative community such as a university, there is always the danger that those who think alike should gravitate together into *coteries* where they will henceforth encounter opposition only in the emasculated form of rumour that the outsiders say thus and thus. The absent are thus easily refuted, complacent dogmatism thrives, and differences of opinion are embittered by group hostility. Each group hears not the best, but the worst, that the other group can say. In the Socratic all this was changed. Here a man could get the case for Christianity without all the paraphernalia of pietism and the case against it without the irrelevant *sansculottisme* of our common anti-God weeklies. At the very least we helped to civilize one another ..."

More Than a Signature

With the enormous increase in interest in C. S. Lewis in recent years – particularly after the release of the films *Shadowlands* and *The Lion, the Witch, and the Wardrobe* – his signature, or even his initials, adds considerably to the value of any of his books. If the book is a first edition, so much the better, but his signature in any of his books increases its value many-fold.

Far more desirable than a signature alone is an added inscription, whether a simple "To George with best wishes" or something more personal, especially if the book is a presentation copy – one Lewis gave to a friend. Rarely, one finds a book signed "Jack". At about four years of age Lewis announced that his name was Jacksie (later shortened to Jack) and refused thereafter to answer to Clive.

Although he thus became Jack to everyone who knew him, only infrequently did he sign his name as such. I have, for example, a presentation copy of *The Problem of Pain* sent a few days before its release to his best friend Owen Barfield – and even for Owen he signed it simply *Yours, C. S. Lewis*. On the other hand, the copy of the 1950 revised edition of *Dymer* he gave Barfield is inscribed, *Owen Barfield from Jack Lewis, October 1950.*

Of all the signed books I've owned, none is so extensively inscribed as a first edition of *The Screwtape Letters* belonging to John Arlott, whom he met at the BBC. Arlott, a former police detective, joined the staff of the BBC, where, as a cricket commentator on radio and television, he became one of the country's most recognizable voices. But he was also a major collector of fine literature, a writer, and an accomplished poet – all of which must have appealed to Lewis. This is possibly the most unusual inscribed copy of any Lewis book, given the amount of his handwriting on both the front and back blank endpapers.

Filling the entire front pasted-down endpaper is the complete handwritten text of a Lewis poem, *Experiment,* published earlier in the *Spectator* of December 9, 1938, but titled therein, *Metrical Experiment*, signed *C.S.L.* at the end:

Metrical Experiment

(Copyright belongs to The Spectator)

Some believe the slumber
Of trees is in December
When timber's naked under sky
And squirrel keeps his chamber

But I believe their fibres
Awake to life and labour
When turbulence comes roaring up
The land in loud October;

And plunders woods and sunders
And sends their leaves to wander,
And undisguises prickly shapes
Beneath the golden splendour.

Form returns. In warmer
Seductive days, disarming
Its firmer will, the wood grows soft
And spreads its dreams to murmur.

Into conceit winter
With soul worked it enter.
The hunter Frost and the keen wind
Have quelled the green enchanter.

C.S.L

Opposite, on the flyleaf, is Lewis' signature, followed by an asterisk, with the footnote, *I never could develop a nice grown-up "signature" so I just have to write my name like any other word*:

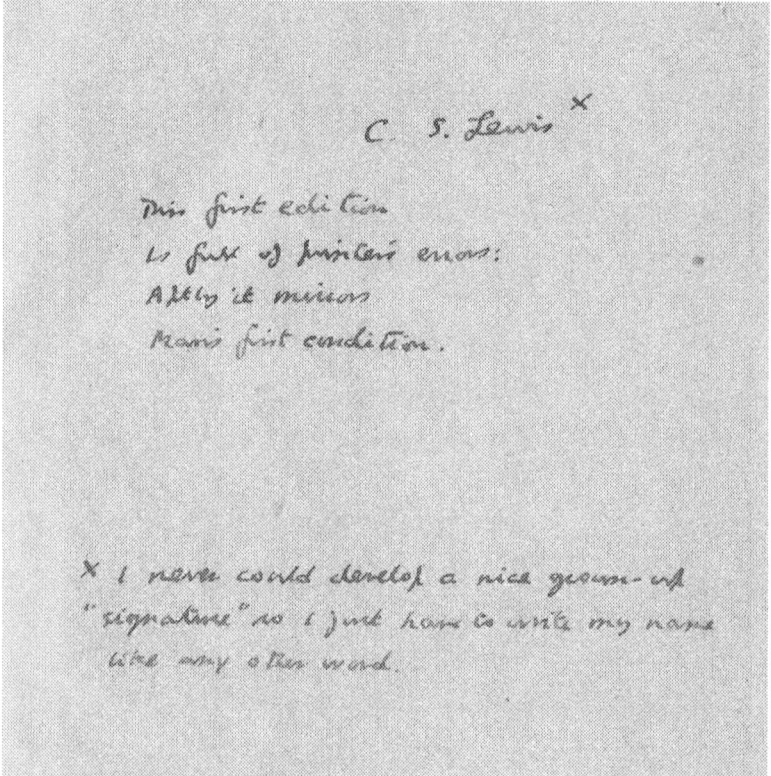

His footnote about a "grown-up 'signature' " is interesting. Years ago my friend Jack Gamble in Belfast gave me a copy of a book Lewis had owned as a teenager, *Here Are Ladies*, by James Stephens, his favorite author at the time. On the flyleaf is his teenage signature:

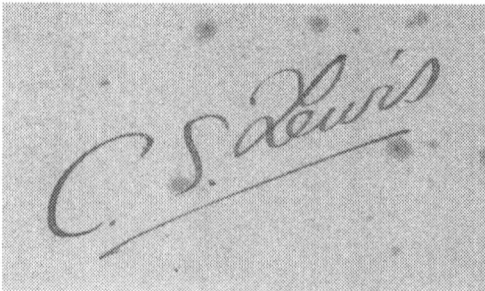

Between the signature and footnote is a brief four-line poem:

This first edition
Is full of printer's errors:
Aptly it mirrors
Man's first condition.

At the end of the book, on the blank page opposite page 160, is this cryptic note:

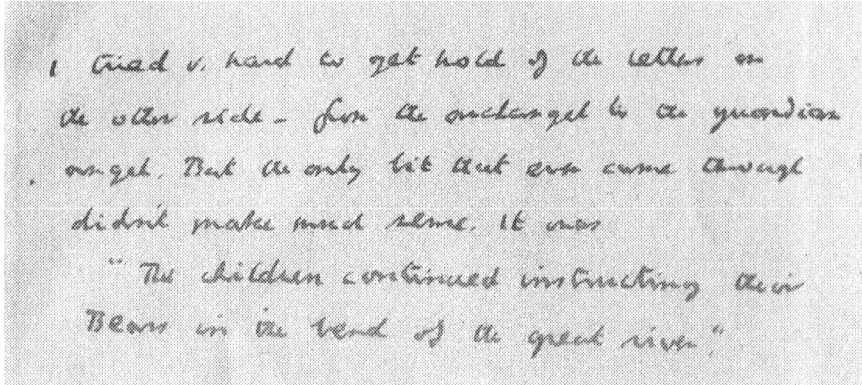

I tried v. hard to get hold of the letters on the other side – from the archangel to the guardian angel. But the only bit that ever came through didn't make much sense. It was "The children continued instructing their Bears in the bend of the great river."

I have yet to find a Lewis scholar who can interpret that mysterious response from the heavenly realm!

The book was acquired at a Christies auction in London in 1992 by Peter Jolliffe, the British dealer from whom many of my Lewis first editions and the *Light* manuscript were purchased – and to whom I owe a debt of gratitude for having been responsible for many fine acquisitions. Ten years later I found a copy of that auction catalog on eBay: *The Library of the Late John Arlott, O.B.E.*, with his full-page photograph on the cover and lot number 106: LEWIS, C. S., *The Screwtape Letters*, London, Geoffrey Bles, 1942. Such provenance of any rare book is invaluable, leaving no doubt whatever of its origin in the mind of a prospective purchaser of such a book.

Serendipitous Wonderment Yet Again

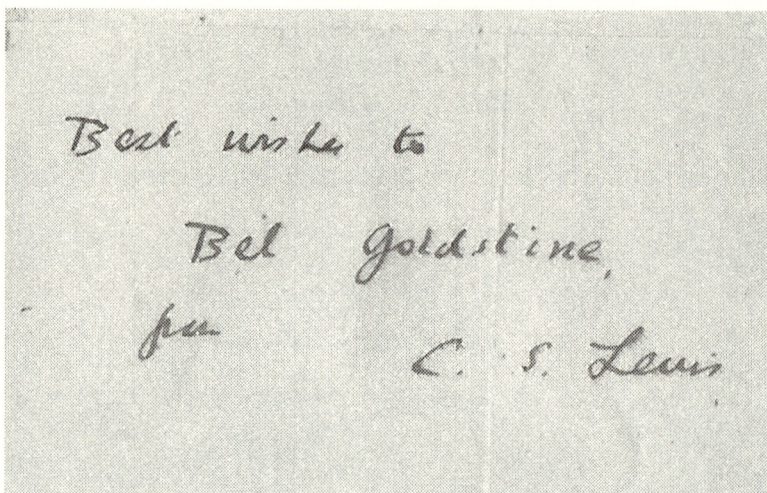

The example of Lewis's adult signature provided above is on a 2" x 3" piece of paper pasted into the front of an American first edition of Lewis's novel, *Till We Have Faces*, purchased at an eBay auction in 2003. Whoever this Bel Goldstine was, the name is Jewish, and it would seem from the warm inscription that she must have been an American known to Lewis, who had apparently written to him to request his autograph to put in her copy of his book. Other than the wife of Cecil Roth, of whom I have written earlier, the only Jewish American woman whom Lewis knew, to my knowledge, was Joy Davidman Gresham. The only important thing to me at that point was that this was a fine example of a Lewis signature.

About a year later I received a catalogue from my British friend and bookseller, Ian Blakemore, in which he offered another signed first American edition, *Surprised By Joy*, with a very interesting inscription:

To Bel with love from
Jack
C. S. Lewis
Nov. 11th *1957*

Surely this Bel was none other than Bel Goldstine – but this book was obviously signed for her in England (since he never visited the United States) – and the inscription made it clear that she was indeed very special to him. It was now essential that I learn who Bel Goldstine was, so again I turned to Google, and to my amazement and delight learned that not only was she (and still is) the well-known author of *Up the Down Staircase*, Bel Kauffman.

More importantly, I learned that from their student days at Hunter College, Bel was Joy Davidman's best friend. She had, in fact, visited Jack and Joy during Joy's final days, bringing along her copy of *Surprised By Joy* for him to sign and spending two weeks with them at The Kilns. Another amazing "coincidence", for had Ian not acquired that book for his stock, and had he not been a friend who regularly sent me his catalogues, I would probably have never gone to any length to learn the identity of Bel Goldstine (her married name). Moreover, all this was confirmed later in a telephone conversation with this charming lady of 94, whose phone number I found in the Manhattan telephone directory.

Unburied Treasure

Among the many Ohioans joining the 1849 "gold rush" to California was Daniel Brown, of Akron, a son of my great-great-great grandfather, James Brown. Old Jim had distinguished himself by making money – more than any member of the Brown family before or since – and young Dan had followed in his father's footsteps well before his 18h birthday. The problem, however, was that this was exactly what they did. They made all sorts of money – silver coins, gold coins, and paper currency, all produced in their own workshops by master craftsmen and engravers.

There was as yet no Federal currency, and among the state banks issuing same, that of the Bank of Missouri was highly favored. In California, however, the medium of exchange was limited to coinage, and since coins were heavy and thereby difficult to send home to one's family, the miners welcomed the young newcomer representing himself as the agent of the Bank of Missouri, with a large supply of crisp, new banknotes to be exchanged for raw gold.

By the time enough of this illicit currency reached the East and was found to be what it was, Dan and his stash of gold had boarded a steamer for Panama and made his way through the jungle to the Atlantic coast and home. But the journey had taken its toll, and he died only a few weeks thereafter. His gold, thought to have been buried somewhere in his 300-acre homestead, was never found, despite much digging by family and friends – which reminds me of a story:

Old John had gone through a bad winter, and dreaded the thought of trying to till the few acres he customarily planted each spring. Despondent, he wrote to his son, who had just begun serving a jail sentence for bank robbery, and told him of his plight. Back came an immediate letter: "For heaven's sake, don't do any digging, Dad! That's where I buried the money!" – and soon thereafter a large body of law-enforcement officials arrived with a warrant and proceeded to dig up the entire acreage. Needless to say, they found no money – but the field was ready for planting!

Nor is one likely to find buried treasure in his own backyard – although sometimes it may be sitting out in plain view. Such was my experience recently when Dan Hamilton alerted me to an eBay auction of a 1961 issue of *The Saturday Evening Post* containing a little-known article by Owen Barfield, "The Rediscovery of Meaning," of which I was unaware, and which should certainly have been in my Barfield collection.

The auction site featured a picture of the magazine cover – a beautiful painting of Boston's famous Park Street, with the edge of the Boston Common on its left, the gold-domed state capitol at the head of the street, and down in the lower right corner the side entrance to the Park Street Church. It was at this very side entrance in February 1952 that I first met the 18-year-old girl who was to become my wife later that year. For the past 20 years or so a copy of this magazine, acquired long ago at an Indianapolis flea market just for its cover picture, had been lying, unopened and unread, atop a cabinet in our "Eagle and Child" library alongside my Owen Barfield collection.

Of Boys and Horses

Of the myriad secondhand and antiquarian book fairs in England during the entire year, the international book fair at the Hotel Russell at Russell Square in June is one of the most outstanding. Several years ago, having arrived an hour or so before the fair opened, I noticed a large banner strung over the street half a block away – *Book Fair Here Today.* Apparently some of the lesser dealers, unable to reserve space at the Russell Hotel fair, had organized a secondary event at the nearby motel, so to kill time I wandered on down. It turned out to be the highlight of the day – indeed, of my week in London.

I had barely entered the premises when I was warmly greeted by John Joseph Flynn, a fellow Lewis collector from California, who directed me to a booth on the opposite side of the room where he had seen earlier what the dealer supposed was one of the rarest of Lewis rarities – an uncorrected proof copy of *The Horse and His Boy.* When a book is about to be published, the printer runs off a dozen or so copies and binds them in a plain paper wrapper to be given to one or more of his readers and perhaps a few others, to be examined for typographical errors. Most important, a copy also goes to the author, for any corrections he may wish to make before starting the press run. For a Lewis collector to come across an uncorrected proof of one of the most popular of Lewis books, one of the Chronicles of Narnia, is being in "hawg heaven."

Unfortunately, the dealer in question had just taken the book to the Russell Hotel, hoping one of the larger dealers might be able to offer an opinion as to its value. He had left the book with one, who would phone a more knowledgeable dealer in America with its description and a request for a price estimate. If I would return in a couple of hours, the book's owner would have it back for my examination.

I spent the next hour going over the wares of the other dealers – which, amazingly, yielded another uncorrected proof copy – not of a Narnia book, but of J. R. R. Tolkien's little book, *Smith of Wootton Major.*

The price was reasonable, so I bought it – and then had to go to Oxford the next day to buy back my copy of the first edition of the book, which I had just sold to Blackwell's, in order to have it to compare with the uncorrected proof.

By now the main fair at the Russell Hotel had opened – although my purchases there turned out to be far less exciting than what I found at the other fair. However, it provided the opportunity to greet many dealers whose shops I had frequented in the past, and to meet in person others with whom I had done business only by mail. But my primary mission was to get back to have a look at that uncorrected proof of *The Horse and His Boy*.

Handling this treasure was a delight in itself. The dealer confided that he had found it at a church jumble sale (a rummage sale, in American English), where a book dealer next door had suggested a price of 35 pence (about 50 cents in our coin of the realm) to the ladies of the church, assuming it was just a worn paperback. Suspecting it might be an uncorrected proof, my dealer had latched on to it, to bring to London for verification. Even the "big-time" dealer at the Russell wasn't absolutely sure that this is what it was, however, but since the publisher was Geoffrey Bles, and his firm didn't do paperbacks (a fact of which the dealer was unaware), I assured him that it was most certainly an uncorrected proof.

It wasn't the brightest thing I could have done as the prospective purchaser. Better I had just suggested it might be a proof copy, and we might have arrived at a price based on presumption, not fact. The expert advice I offered next, however, was even less brilliant. When I asked him what he wanted for it, he allowed as how he wasn't really sure. So what did his dealer friend at the Russell learn from his American contact? "Well, he thought it should be worth at least as much as a first edition of the book. Do you have any idea of what a first edition of that book is worth?" Eager to demonstrate my Lewis expertise, I blurted out, "Oh, I should think at least as much as a thousand dollars!" – and immediately realized the fatality of that remark. Eager to demonstrate how ready he was to turn a handsome profit, he instantly replied, "If you're willing to pay $1000 for it, it's yours!"

Hoist by my own petard, I could only feebly respond in the affirmative. Not only was it a rarity among rarities, but the book was dedicated to none other than Douglas Gresham, Lewis's stepson – with whom I was scheduled to spend the next weekend at his estate in Ireland, and whose signature (or better yet, a nice personal inscription to me) would considerably enhance its value. Moreover, a like endorsement by the illustrator, Pauline Baynes, on the title page where her work was acknowledged would be icing on the cake.

Of course, I didn't have $1000 or the sterling equivalent thereof in my pocket, and he didn't take credit cards – and since it was Sunday, I could only offer to pay him the following day after drawing funds from my sterling account at Barclays Bank. He was planning to return to his home in Cornwall that evening at the close of the fair, but the thought of a 2000-fold profit deterred him from that immediate objective. He agreed to meet me the following morning in Wimbledon at the home of my good friends, John and Angela Fields, with whom I was staying.

I got the money from the bank, and he arrived promptly at our agreed-upon meeting time. Up to that point I was still heaping abuse upon myself for having been so stupid as to cite a figure of $1000 for something that he would obviously have sold for a fraction of that price. However, when I saw the shabby station wagon he was driving, piled high with unsold books he had taken to the fair, the sun shone on our transaction. He was obviously one of those many book-dealers so common in England who love the business but whose income necessitates a very modest lifestyle. He had been astute enough to find something that could possibly be of far greater value than what he had paid for it, and now his purchase had paid off handsomely. I, in turn, while not entirely sure of what a first edition of *The Horse and His Boy* was worth in those days – and even less certain of the value of an uncorrected proof – was satisfied that the price I paid was not unreasonable.

It did seem even at that time to be a win-win situation for both of us, and I was amply rewarded a couple of years later, when again in England I visited a number of small book fairs out in the provinces. Strolling into one of them that weekend, I was greeted with a shout of warm welcome (most uncharacteristic of an Englishman!) as a nearby dealer immediately recognized me. It was, of course, my Cornish friend, whom I was able to congratulate on his astuteness and my great pleasure in owning the book – for I had indeed had it inscribed by Doug that following weekend. Moreover, upon my return to London I phoned Pauline to ask if I might take her to dinner the next evening, and upon dropping her off at her home, I sheepishly produced the book, showed her Doug's inscription, and requested her kindness in doing the same. This is what each had written:

Now you've met the boy and his horse. May this remind you of your weekend at Rathvinden. Best wishes, Doug.

(Doug kept a beautiful pair of stallions on his Irish estate.)

Pauline's inscription was even more personal:

for Ed – Pauline Baynes
and thanks for your friendship – with every best wish and love

While at Rathvinden, I'd had the opportunity to go through a first edition of *The Horse and His Boy* and found many changes made by Lewis from his original text in the uncorrected proof. Many were simply the correction of typographic errors, but others were to improve the text. The most significant revision was on page 80, with Shasta's first encounter with a cat among the tombs.

The original version:

The light was too bad for Shasta to see much of the cat except that it was very big and very friendly. It stood up on its hind legs and rubbed its head against his knees. It was purring like a dynamo and its tail stood straight up.

"Puss, puss," said Shasta. "I suppose you're not a talking *cat."*

But the cat only stared at him and purred. Then it started walking away, and of course Shasta followed it. It led him right through the tombs and out of the desert side of them. There it lay down and started having a thorough wash, and when it had washed every bit of itself it curled up and buried its nose in its tail like a cat that means to have a good sleep.

Lewis apparently felt that a more distinctive description of Aslan's first appearance to Shasta was in order, so he rewrote it thus:

The light was too bad for Shasta to see much of the cat except that it was big and very solemn. It looked as if it might have lived for long, long years among the tombs, alone. Its eyes made you think it knew secrets it would not tell.

"Puss, puss," said Shasta. "I suppose you're not a talking *cat."*

The cat stared at him harder than ever. Then it started walking away, and of course Shasta followed it. It led him right through the tombs and out of the desert side of them. There it sat down bolt upright with its tail curled round its feet and its face set toward the desert and towards Narnia and the North, as still as if it were watching for some enemy.

Through access to a rarity such as this uncorrected proof one can more fully appreciate Lewis's meticulous choice of language that made the Chronicles of Narnia such an enormous success. I assumed, of course, that this would doubtless be the only uncorrected proof of a Narnia book I would be fortunate enough to find – but I was proved wrong, for in the next few years I found two more, *The Silver Chair* and *The Magician's Nephew.* The most interesting change from the proof of *The Silver Chair* was that on page 48, where he tells the reader that the title of the next Narnia book was to be *Narnia of the North.* You won't find that in any published copy of *The Silver Chair*!

A Grief Reserved

A book that has troubled some readers is Lewis's poignant expression of the myriad feelings that overwhelmed him in the weeks following the death of his beloved Joy. Compiled from notes scribbled in a succession of notebooks – four of these "MS books" as he refers to them at the beginning of the final chapter – *A Grief Observed* traces Lewis's emotional upheaval from the days immediately following her death to the time weeks later when he at last records a sense of closure.

Theirs had been a truly idyllic marriage – that of the brilliant Oxford don and confirmed bachelor who at the age of 57 married an ex-communist former Jewish American poet and writer in a civil ceremony so that she might remain in Britain, and then truly took her as his chosen bride in a proper Christian ceremony a year later as she lay in hospital dying of cancer. She had what he regarded as a miraculous remission, and for the next three years they lived in what could rightly be described as a state of marital bliss, transforming the bleak atmosphere of the Lewis household at The Kilns into one of warmth that the Lewis brothers had never known before.

His grief was profound, and while he managed to write three more books in the next three years, it seems that the spark which ignited the enormous literary output of prior years had faded to a faint glow. Published in September 1960, just two months after Joy's death, the first British edition appeared under the pseudonym N. W. Clerk, and he refers only to her as "H." "N. W." was the pseudonym he used for his many poems published in *Punch* and other journals – "nat whilk," an Anglo-Saxon phrase meaning "I know not whom" (i.e., "anonymous"). "Clerk" was simply that – a person whose job is to record the notes of the proceedings.

As his biographer, George Sayer notes in *Jack: C. S. Lewis and his Times*, "The book is so intimate and personal that it had to be published pseudonymously or anonymously if at all. He would have found unbearable the correspondence that would have followed publication under his own name. It was published only because he thought it might help others who had suffered bereavement, a hope in my experience that was justified. ... When he gave me a copy, because he thought it might help my wife who just lost her father, he said, 'It is by a man I know.'"

The book has indeed helped many in their grief. I myself have given it to a number of friends for that purpose. My friend Jack Gamble, who with his wife Jean operates the foremost antiquarian bookstore in Northern Ireland, told me a particularly interesting story about his use of the book. In the late '70s, the son of Jack's bank manager, a promising young attorney, was gunned down by IRA assassins who mistook him for a detective on their hit list when he walked out of a police station after visiting a jailed client. Jack gave it to the bank manager, who not only found solace in it but passed it on to the teacher of his younger daughter when told by the teacher that her classmates had been unable to cope with the daughter's grief, and were simply shunning her because they didn't know how to respond. The teacher then dealt with the situation by reading portions of the book to the class, which resulted in a complete change in the children's ability to relate to the situation.

When I first met Walter Hooper he related how Jack had told him that soon after the book was published he received some five or six copies of the book from well-wishers who thought it would help Lewis in *his* grief! However, another reader wrote to say that he thought he knew the real name of the author – a comment with which Lewis was not pleased.

Although it received some favorable reviews, the book did not sell very well because it appeared to have been written by an unknown author. The American first edition was not published until February 1963, and of course it did not sell well either. With a large stock of unsold copies at the time of Lewis's death ten months later, the publisher, Seabury Press of Greenwich, Connecticut, obtained permission from the estate to reissue the dust jacket, with C. S. Lewis as author. Covering the N. W. Clerk books with the C. S. Lewis jacket, they were able to quickly dispose of their leftover stock and had to reissue the book under Lewis's name.

Thus we have some three versions of what might be considered the first American edition(s) – the 1963 N. W. Clerk book in like jacket, the Clerk book in the Lewis jacket and finally, the Lewis book in the Lewis jacket. Like the first editions of *Spirits in Bondage* and *Dymer*, published under the pseudonym of Clive Hamilton, one can't always judge a book by its cover.

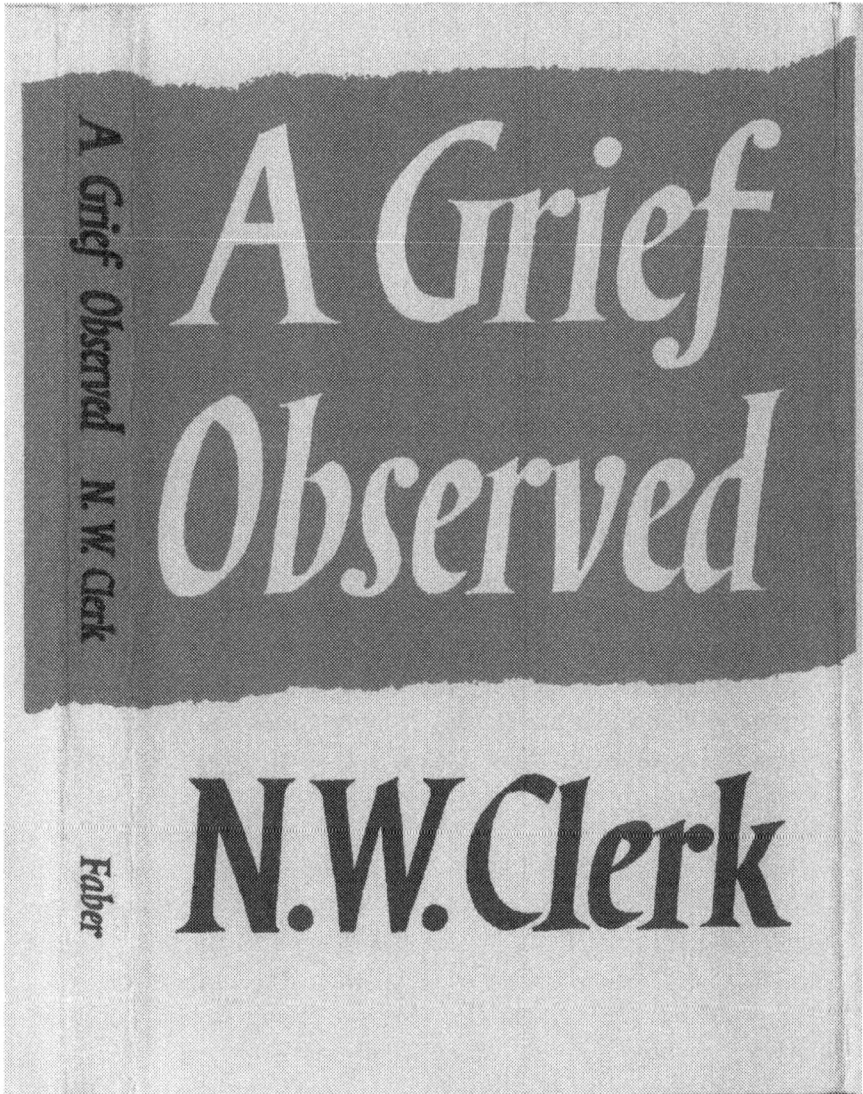

(Lewis collectors of his first editions should be aware of a somewhat similar situation, but for very different reasons, in determining which of two versions is the true first American edition of his monumental academic work, *English Literature in the Sixteenth Century*. The book was issued both in Britain and America in 1954 by Oxford University Press. The British edition can be found in two versions, identical but for having the pages trimmed one centimeter at the bottom and dyed blue on the top-edge, resulting in a slightly shorter volume. This volume was printed in England and sent unbound to their New York office, which had the book bound after having the top-edge dyed and the bottom trimmed, with a different dust jacket bearing the New York address, but otherwise identical to the British jacket. (Oxford University Press is the far-flung remnant of the British Empire, with offices in the U.S., Canada, Australia, New Zealand, India, Pakistan, Nigeria, and South Africa.) Sometime thereafter, the New York office issued the book in the same binding but with undyed top-edge, identifying it on the back of the title page as "First Published 1954" and "PRINTED IN THE UNITED STATES OF AMERICA". So if you're a collector and want to be sure you have the true American first edition, you'd better buy one of each.)

But back to *A Grief Observed* – why should some readers be troubled by it? Consider this passage, for example:

Meanwhile, where is God? This is one of the most disquieting symptoms. When you are happy, so happy that you have no sense of needing Him, so happy that you are tempted to feel His claims upon you as an interruption, if you remember yourself and turn to Him with gratitude and praise, you will be – or so it feels – welcomed with open arms. But go to Him when your need is desperate, when all other help is vain, and what do you find? A door slammed in your face, and a sound of bolting and double bolting on the inside. After that, silence. You may as well turn away. The longer you wait, the more emphatic the silence will become. There are no lights in the windows. It might be an empty house. Was it ever inhabited? It seemed so once. And that seeming was as strong as this. What can this mean? Why is He so present a commander in our time of prosperity and so very absent a help in time of need of trouble?

126

I tried to put some of these thoughts to C. this afternoon. He reminded me that the same thing seems to have happened to Christ: "Why hast thou forsaken me?" I know. Does that make it easier to understand?

Not that I am (I think) of much danger of ceasing to believe in God. The real danger is of coming to believe such dreadful things about Him. The conclusion I dread is not "So there's no God after all," but "So this is what God's really like. Deceive yourself no longer."

Methinks the only ones likely to be troubled by such a passage are those who have never known real, honest grief.

(The 1976 Bantam paperback version of *A Grief Observed* contained a wonderful 58-page reminiscence of Lewis by his friend Chad Walsh. Walter Hooper adds more insight in his 1991 essay "C. S. Lewis: The Man and His Thought." These two essays do much to dispel the modern myths concerning Jack's so-called "loss of faith.")

Last Letters and Last Words

Anyone led to believe that Lewis may have lost his faith after Joy's death (as some have also suggested after seeing *Shadowlands*, with its misleading scene near the end when Jack and young Doug Gresham are sitting together in the attic of The Kilns), need only read his last book, *Letters to Malcolm: Chiefly on Prayer*. Written shortly before his death on November 22, 1963, it was not published in Britain until January 1964 and in America in early February.

The American publisher Harcourt, Brace and World had anticipated its release with a little volume, *Beyond the Bright Blur*, printed in a limited edition of 350 copies bearing the notation:

BEYOND THE BRIGHT BLUR is taken from LETTERS TO MALCOLM: CHIEFLY ON PRAYER by C. S. Lewis, which will be published in the year 1964. This limited edition is published as a New Year's greeting to friends of the author and his publisher.

Inserted in the book was a small card: *With the Season's Greetings from Harcourt, Brace & World, Inc.*

Some years ago I came across a fine first edition of *Letters to Malcolm* in a bookshop in Banbury, near Oxford (memorialized in the nursery rhyme beginning, *Ride a cock horse to Banbury Cross, to see a fine lady upon a white horse* ...). Within it were two very important pieces of paper, apparently unnoticed by the seller (given its paltry £2 price). The first was a printed publisher's slip, "With the compliments of Mr. Jocelyn Gibb," indicating that this was an advance copy given to the owner of the book by the publisher prior to its release. (Gibb was Lewis's editor at Geoffrey Bles Ltd., who published most of his books.) This fact alone made the book worth more than an ordinary first edition – and if the recipient was someone of prominence, the value would be further increased. Gibb had crossed out the printed "Mr" and written this poignant note:

Publication of both of these will be on 27 Jan 64. I hope you will like them. Sad, oh sad, that it is CSL's last. Jock Gibb 9 Jan 64

Apparently Gibb had sent this person an advance copy of *Letters to Malcolm* and that of another book soon to be published. But what about that second piece of paper hidden therein – a neatly folded handwritten letter, dated just four days later, indicating that the recipient of the books had promptly responded with his expression of gratitude:

13 Jan 64

My dear Dr. Coggan

Thank you for your kind letter. I hope you will like "Letters to Malcolm". As usual, and to the end, Lewis doesn't pull any punches, notably over Drs. Vidler and Robinson. You ask about the identity of Malcolm. Yes, he's a fictional character, though his character was undoubtedly constructed from various friends with whom he had correspondence and conversation. Malcolm, as you will find, is the constant "objector", full of doubts and a nice sort of chap who was trying to achieve the same final objective that Lewis was.

Thank you for the charming things you say about the Lewis/Bles fellowship which, as far as I was concerned, was quite the happiest I have ever known. He was such a loyal man to work for – and with. The executors have asked me to edit a book by some five different hands, assessing the various sides of CSL and his work. This I have agreed to do and have started work on it. I hope the last chapter, marginal and yet perhaps revealing, will be called "Letters to his publisher." Yours very sincerely, Jock Gibb

And who might this Dr. Coggan have been? He was, in fact, Dr. Donald Coggan, Archbishop of York, later to become Archbishop of Canterbury, Head of the Church of England from 1974 to 1980 – whose book an unsuspecting used book dealer had sold for a fraction of its value.

Vidler and Robinson were both guilty of scandalous attacks on the fundamentals of Scripture, but Robinson's was by far the worst. John A. T. Robinson's book, *Honest to God*, shocked not only to the Church of England, of which he was Bishop of Woolwich, but the evangelical church throughout the world.

The book on which Gibb was working was *Light on C. S. Lewis*, published in 1965, with nine contributors rather than the five originally envisioned by its editor. It included a preface by Lewis's closest friend, Owen Barfield – whose own copy I was privileged to have in my collection.

Although *Letters to Malcolm* was his last book, Lewis's final work was an essay – *We Have No "Right to Happiness"* – completed just a few weeks before his death and published in America's oldest magazine, *The Saturday Evening Post*, founded by Benjamin Franklin.

(Lewis was, of course, not new to American magazines in general and the *Post* in particular, whose issue of December 19, 1959 featured *Screwtape Proposes a Toast*. This final word from that infamous senior devil was incorporated 14 months later in a new edition of the book that had made C. S. Lewis a household word, *The Screwtape Letters and Screwtape Proposes a Toast*, with a new and additional Preface dated 18 May 1960.)

A New Kind of Joy and a Sad Farewell

In 1951, after more than 30 years at Oxford University, Lewis was at last proposed for a professorship, that of Professor of Poetry. Although unsuccessful in establishing himself professionally as a poet, he nevertheless always enjoyed that literary genre, with more than a hundred of his single, short poems having been published in his lifetime in various magazines and other publications.

This Chair was to be filled by a vote of all Senior Members of the University – many of whom resented his enormous success as an author of "popular" books, especially those on Christianity. His strongest opponent was Cecil Day-Lewis, a poet and detective novelist, and despite strong opposition in some quarters, he had a good showing, with 173 votes against 194 for Day-Lewis. (Some years ago I came across a biography of Day-Lewis by his son, in which he quotes from a letter from his father, saying that the election might well have gone the other way except for the peculiar fact that in listing him among the many candidates, the printer of the ballots had erroneously placed him on the ballot as Lewis, C. D. just above Lewis, C. S. in the alphabetical listing. As a result, Day-Lewis was certain that many who voted for him did so in error either because of poor eyesight or senility, thinking they were voting for C. S.!)

In January 1954 the Council of the Senate of Cambridge University declared its need for a Professor in Medieval and Renaissance English, and for months Lewis resisted their overtures to him to accept the position because he did not want to move from Oxford. However, when they agreed to let him commute from Oxford and offered him accommodations equal to those he had at Magdalen College, he gratefully accepted. The position was not attached to a particular college, and he was delighted when he learned that his rooms would be in St. Mary Magdalene. Writing to Sister Penelope in Wantage, he said,

My address will be Magdalene, so I remain under the same Patroness. This is nice because it saves "administrative" readjustments in Heaven."

In his inaugural lecture at Cambridge, *De Descriptione Temporum*, he refers to himself and other "western" writers as dinosaurs. He was extremely happy at Cambridge, but by 1962 recurring illness had kept him from his regular schedule, and in October 1962 he gave his last lecture series of lectures, and reluctantly submitting his resignation.

Having read the lecture not long before I purchased a group of letters from a Los Angeles dealer, I was struck by the closing sentence in this one, a reply to one sent to him in early July 1963 by Karen Housel of New York City, asking for an appointment with him near the end of August. On July 18th he wrote in a very feeble hand:

Dear Miss Housel, I can give you no assurance as to what I will be doing by the end of August. After a long illness I am now suffering a relapse and at present waiting to be admitted to hospital as soon as there is a vacancy. One of my complaints is anaemia. This, tho painless, has a most debilitating effect on the mind; so that even if I were technically "well" again, you would find yourself confronted with, almost, an imbecile. Thanks for the kind things you say, but look for no help from me. I am but a fossil dinosaur now.
Yours sincerely, C. S. Lewis

Karen obviously replied immediately to express her condolences, for this one was written just 10 days later:

28 July 1963
Dear Miss Housel, Professor C. S. Lewis was very pleased to receive your cheering letter. However, Professor Lewis is seriously ill and unable to write you himself. He sends you his warmest regards.
I am, yours sincerely, Walter Hooper

In early 1964, Warnie advertised in the U. S. for copies of Jack's letters to be included in what was to become *Letters of C. S. Lewis*, published in 1966. In May, Karen saw the advertisement and wrote to ask if he would like her letter of 18 July, to which he replied on 7 May:

Dear Miss Housel, Many thanks for your letter of the 3rd. A very large number of people have responded most generously to my appeal for my brother's letters, but you are the only one so far with an evident knowledge of Boxonian history. Yes indeed, I should be very grateful for the letter you refer to, and am impatient to see it. I miss my brother dreadfully. Over the years we had collected so many shared experiences and memories which could be discussed only with him, and now there are so many things I cannot discuss with anyone.
Yours sincerely, W. H. Lewis

By the time Karen's letter from Jack arrived in early June, Warnie was already off on another binge in Ireland. Walter Hooper, who was at this time living at The Kilns with Warnie and assisting him with various matters, wrote to thank her on 24 June:

Dear Miss Housel, I am Major W. H. Lewis' friend writing to thank you for your kind letter and the C. S. Lewis enclosure. Major Lewis is, at present, on holiday but I shall make certain he sees your letter as soon as he returns. I might mention that it was a most extraordinary thing that you had a letter written by Professor Lewis on 13th July 1963. He could never have managed it on the 14th, and he went into a coma on the 15th that almost ended his life. I made his tea on Sunday morning; and even though he could hardly hold his cup, (this was on the 14th) he was so considerate and gentle as when he was in good health – one of God's most nearly perfect creatures.
With thanks and best wishes, I am, yours sincerely, Walter Hooper.

When Warnie had not yet returned two weeks later, Walter sent the letter back to her after making a copy for Warnie. Since it is apparent that Warnie eventually read Jack's letter of 18 July 1963, it did not appear in *Letters of C. S. Lewis*. When I asked Walter about this a few years ago, he was unaware of the reason for its absence. I could only assume that Warnie was so overcome by the fossil dinosaur reference that he decided not to publish it – and possibly destroyed the copy, since it did not appear in the revised and enlarged edition of *Letters of C. S. Lewis* edited by Walter in 1988.

Having received a copy of the letter from me, Walter included it in *C. S. Lewis: Collected Letters, Volume III*, published in 2006.

Walter's replies to Karen Housel served a very useful purpose on the very day I found them in Los Angeles. Having visited this bookseller on prior trips, I had swung by his shop on my way from the airport to a meeting in San Bernardino to ask if he had any Lewis first editions. He did not, but offered me these letters instead.

The meeting was one called by Dr. Stan Mattson, president of the C. S. Lewis Foundation, to respond to the charges made against Walter Hooper in *The C. S. Lewis Hoax*. He had assembled a panel of Lewis scholars and a handwriting expert to review and comment upon each of the specific charges, which included among other things the possibility that Walter may never have been close enough to either Jack or Warnie to have acted as secretary to either – a charge clearly refuted by these letters.

Other Lewis Letters

The earliest Lewis letter I acquired was also my first, a one-page handwritten letter in 1933 to his editor, R. W. Chapman, at Oxford University Press, which had just published his first academic text, *The Allegory of Love* – still a classic in its field more than 70 years later. The letter was folded in Chapman's copy of the book, with his penciled initials, RWC, on the flyleaf. On the blank endpapers in back, Chapman listed in pencil the pages on which he had found typographical errors, about which he wrote to Lewis. Lewis replied:

My dear Chapman, Thanks for both letters. After wondering whether the best reply to the "pinpricks" would not be "Ah, yes – that's the worst of depending on these local printers!", I accept them all except sheows which is Spenser's own spelling. I will also add two more, worse, p. 96 quotation l. 5 for ye read He. P. 331 5 lines before the first quotation for pictures read pictured. Yes – Cissie and Flossie do appear in Tasso and I trust it doesn't matter though I'd just as soon they didn't. But I don't mind about the lovely lay – it is just the sort of enervating Omar-Khayyam stuff you ought to find there. "Purifying complexities" – the next time you come across a real commercial pornogram in a French bookshop, read a page or two and note how it all depends on isolating one nerve in a way quite impossible in real life – in fact is just as conventional (tho' for a worse purpose) as roaring farce. Smoky rain is alright seasoned with sufficient usquebaugh see Waverly
yours, C. S. Lewis!

To this he added a postscript: *Congratulations to the "local printer" on giving us a translation of Otto's Das Heilige at 3/6 – very nice.* The "local printer" to which he humorously referred was Oxford University Press.

Jack's humor comes through in his writings, but there's a special joy that comes from reading one of his actual letters, holding it in one's hand as though it had just arrived in the mail and chuckling over an unexpected witticism.

Such a one, dated 30 November 1942, was among several I acquired years ago from the widow of D. H. Banner, who had been referred to me by my friend, Stephen Schofield:

Dear Banner, Thanks very much indeed for the picture of Webb. ... Yes, I knew him well, and also Brightman ... who used to live on my staircase ... I only wish I could come and see you, specially if it included the chance of meeting Miss Potter ... She has a secure place among the masters of English prose .... The Professor of Anglo-Saxon and I have often played with the idea of a pilgrimage to see her, and pictured what fun it would be to shoulder aside the mobs of people who wanted to show you all the Wordsworth places with the brief rejoinder, "We are looking for Miss Potter ...." I would be at Jerusalem!
With very many thanks, yours sincerely, C. S. Lewis

Banner was an artist who lived in Ambleside in the Lake District, where Beatrix Potter (Lewis's favorite as a child) and the poet, Wordworth also lived. He was an undergraduate at Oxford about the same time as Lewis and apparently had asked Lewis about some of their colleagues. The "Professor of Anglo-Saxon" was, of course, Tolkien, who also had a great respect for the excellence of Beatrix Potter's children's books. The letter was typed by Warnie and signed by Jack, who added below his signature: *I hope you noted Rabbit, Peter in the Milton book!*

I pondered the Rabbit, Peter bit until it dawned on me that "the Milton book" must be Lewis's *A Preface to 'Paradise Lost'*. Assuming the reference might be to an index listing, I turned to the "R" listings – and there it was: *Rabbit, Peter ... 70*. On page 70, where he discusses "obedience," Lewis writes: *It is, after all, the commonest of themes; even Peter Rabbit came to grief because he would go into Mr. McGregor's garden.*

Stephen Schofield, to whom I was introduced by Pauline Baynes, was an expatriate Canadian who lived near her in Surrey, where he produced *The Canadian C. S. Lewis Journal* for many years. He was a charming person but quite deaf, and after a long evening of otherwise great conversation in which my contribution had to be at a much higher decibel level than his, I was very grateful for his wife's invitation to stay for the night. I thought of my evening with Stephen when my wife begged me to get hearing aids some years ago – which I reluctantly did, much to her relief.

Jack was always full of good humor, according to those who knew him. I particularly enjoyed hearing of a time when he was walking with Tolkien when they were approached on the street by a panhandler asking him if he could spare a few shillings. He immediately dove into his pocket and gave the beggar all his change. When Tolkien admonished him, "Jack, you shouldn't have given that fellow all that money. He'll just spend it on drink," Jack replied, "Well, if I'd kept it, I would have only spent it on drink."

Jack and Warnie had been brought up to fear going into poverty, and although Jack was extremely generous in giving away more than half his earnings to needy people and causes, both brothers were extremely frugal in their habits. I've noted elsewhere Jack's habit of using the blank side of returned manuscripts for scratch paper, but many of the letters I've collected reflect Warnie's frugality.

When Warnie was at home, he was an immense help to Jack with the latter's enormous amount of correspondence, for Jack never failed to answer any of the huge volume of mail he received. He never learned to type, presumably due to a genetic peculiarity in his finger joints that made the use of a typewriter difficult – yet he wrote most of his manuscripts by hand, as well as most of his letters. Letters typed by Warnie were usually short – often only a couple of lines – so they took little room on a full sheet of paper. Using the cheapest paper available – what we used to call second sheets in the days of carbon paper – he would type two or three letters on one page, have Jack sign them, then very neatly tear them apart (as evidenced by one or both upper and lower edges not trimmed with scissors), fold them, and tuck them in their envelopes, which he addressed by hand.

This is a typical "strip letter" by Warnie:

REF.321/49.   Magdalen College,
                                                   Oxford.
                                               14th.July 1949.

Dear Mr.Kennedy,

        I am leaving Oxford tomorrow,and shall be to and fro for a bit.
Will you be here after August 15th? I should find it easier to arrange a meeting
then.

                                               yours sincerely,

                                                  C. S. Lewis

Warnie kept track of the letters he typed by assigning a sequential reference number to each in the upper left corner, in this instance REF.321/49 – the 321st letter in 1949. Dated July 14, 1949, it was the 321st letter he typed for Jack in just over six-and-a-half months.

Frugal as the brothers were, Warnie would often mail a letter in the envelope of a letter received earlier, crossing out the incoming address, filling in the new outgoing address, and affixing a fresh stamp. Apparently the Royal Mail Service had no objection, and the recipient would receive an envelope with two stamps (one American and the other British if the envelope had come from the United States), and two different postmarks. Here is one bearing an incoming postmark of November 11, 1956 and an outgoing one of December 29, 1956, with the new stamps pasted over the old stamp:

With Lewis signatures selling at a premium these days, this one came with a bonus – signed three times after two of them smudged:

REF.162/49.

Magdalen College,
Oxford.
14th. March 1949.

Dear Canon Smyth,

Whether Milton would have liked to be commemorated by a window in an Anglican church is a question! But I'll ask my Solicitor to send you a small cheque.
About Pride: *Samson Agonistes* 502-515 is the bit which, for me, shows that Milton finally saw through its subtlest form and definitely got beyond Stoicism. And thanks for the delicious Howler.

yours sincerely,

C. S. Lewis

Sorry! Sorry again   Something radically wrong with this blotting paper!

A Ghostly Encounter

I recently had the good fortune to obtain a British first edition of *Surprised By Joy* that belonged to J. B. Phillips, the Anglican (Church of England) cleric who devoted some 25 years to his scriptural translation, *The New Testament in Modern English* – my favorite of the modern translations.

When he first began his translation activities during the Second World War, he sent a sample of his work over to C. S. Lewis for criticism and suggestion. Lewis sent the sample back promptly with this cryptic comment: "It's like seeing an old picture after it's been cleaned." Lewis encouraged Phillips to plunge in and translate all the New Testament epistles, which he did. He began with the Epistles, published in 1947 as *Letters to Young Churches*, for which Lewis wrote the Introduction (later reprinted separately as the essay "Modern Translations of the Bible"). Lewis praises the work again for its clarity and fresh revealing of the old truths, saying, "It would have saved me a great deal of labour if this book had come into my hands when I first seriously began to try to discover what Christianity was."

The Phillips translation of the Gospels followed in 1952; that of the Acts of the Apostles – *The Young Church in Action* – in 1955 and *The Book of Revelation* in 1957. He also translated four prophetic books from the Old Testament, published in 1963.

In his 1967 book about the Bible, *The Ring of Truth: A Translator's Testimony* he describes a most amazing encounter with C. S. Lewis – after the latter's death:

Many of us who believe what is technically known as the Communion of Saints, must have experienced the sense of nearness, for a fairly short time, of those whom we love soon after they have died. This has certainly, happened to me several times. But the late C.S. Lewis, whom I did not know very well, and had only seen in the flesh once, but with whom I corresponded a fair amount, gave me an unusual experience. A few days after his death, while I was watching television, he "appeared" sitting in a chair within a few feet of me, and spoke a few words which were particularly relevant to the difficult circumstances through which I was passing. He was ruddier in complexion than ever, grinning all over his face and, as the old-fashioned saying has it, positively glowing with health. The interesting thing to me was that I had not been thinking about him at all. I was neither alarmed nor surprised nor, to satisfy the Bishop of Woolwich, did I look up to see the hole in the ceiling that he might have made upon arrival. He was just there – "large as life and twice as natural"! A week later, this time when I was in bed reading before going to sleep, he appeared again, even more rosily radiant than before, and repeated to me the same message, which was very important to me at the time. I was a little puzzled by this, and I mentioned it to a certain saintly Bishop who was then living in retirement here in Dorset. His reply was, "My dear J ...., this sort of thing is happening all the time."

The reason why I mention this personal and memorable experience is that although "Jack Lewis" was real in a certain sense it did not occur to me that I should reach out and touch him. It is possible that some of the appearances of the risen Jesus were of this nature, being known technically as veridical visions. But the writers of the Gospels in their naive unselfconscious way make it plain that something much more awesome and indeed authoritative characterized Christ's "infallible proofs".

On the fly leaf of his copy of *Surprised By Joy*, he had written: *J. B. Phillips, Burton in Kendal, 1956, from Elizabeth Ann.* When offered the book, I questioned whether this was *the* J. B. Phillips, since Burton in Kendal (or Burton-in-Kendal, as it's usually written) is in the Lake District in the north of England, whereas Phillips' introduction to my copy of *The New Testament in Modern English* gave his address as Swanage, Dorset, in the south of England.

Although the book was enhanced by a letter from C. S. Lewis, neatly taped to the fly leaf long ago (as evidenced by the yellowed cellotape, the British equivalent of our Scotch tape), I was reluctant to invest in it unless I could be sure. But how to find out why he might have lived for a time in Burton-in-Kendal?

A Google search turned up many web sites in which J. B. Phillips is mentioned, but none had any information about his having lived for a short time in the North. However, on one was a side-bar with the name of a London solicitor (lawyer) to whom inquiries about the estate of J. B. Phillips could be addressed. Since Phillips died in 1982, it seemed unlikely that this person would still be around 24 years later, but contacting him was worth a try. Typing his name and London address into the search page of an Internet telephone directory for Great Britain (one can find directories for most countries in the world on the Internet!), I was amazed to see that it was a current address, and when I dialed the number, he answered the phone!

Not only was he the person who had handled the estate 24 years earlier, but was a close friend of Phillips' wife, who had died only a few months earlier. He was most cordial when I explained the reason for my call, and although he confirmed that J. B. Phillips had lived most of his life in Swanage, he also knew that Phillips often spent time in the summer at the famous Keswick Convention, a Christian gathering that began in 1875 and continues to this day. Located in the city of Keswick in the beautiful Lake District of northern England, the Convention features three weeks of Bible teaching and Christian fellowship, with speakers from all over the world. As a family, we had the privilege of attending the Convention briefly in 1972 while living in England, but Keswick had already played a very important role in my life, for it was at the Canadian Keswick in Ontario, an offshoot of the British Convention, that my parents committed their lives to Christ in 1931.

My new acquaintance assumed that in 1956 Phillips was staying in Burton-in-Kendal while attending the nearby Convention, where his friend Elizabeth Ann undoubtedly gave him the book, so with that good information and the Lewis letter, I had no doubt that this was indeed *the* J. B. Phillips.

A Forger Exposed – and the Comeuppance of an "Expert"

Having had the good fortune to have seen hundreds of pages of Lewis's handwritten work and many examples of his signature, I am often called upon to either read his often illegible handwriting or to authenticate his signature. Unfortunately, it is a signature that is not very difficult to duplicate, and increasingly those of dubious origin are appearing on the market these days, on eBay in particular.

Of the signed books, letters, and other Lewis material I've owned, his adult signatures range from 1930 to shortly before his death in 1963, so I've had opportunity to see many slight variations – as well as his very different teenage signature shown elsewhere herein. Some time ago I purchased a signed copy of a first edition of *Beyond Personality* from a very reputable dealer on the West Coast, only to find when it arrived that the signature looked questionable. However, I was not as concerned about it as I should have been, and sold it to a local collector who had asked me for a signed copy.

Still uneasy about the matter, I decided to seek advice from someone who has seen more Lewis signatures than anyone – Walter Hooper – when I next visited him in Oxford. To my dismay, he opined that it was definitely not Jack's, but may well have been done by Warnie. As I've noted, Warnie typed thousands of letter for Jack, but always had Jack sign them. Usually Jack would dictate the letter, but on many occasions Warnie would compose the letter, then give it to Jack for his approval and signature. It was Walter's further opinion that this may have been an effort by Warnie to duplicate his brother's signature in the latter's absence, in this instance signing a book that had been left with him to obtain Jack's signature.

Upon my return home, I reluctantly emailed the dealer to ask what provenance of the book he might be able to provide in the hope that perhaps Walter was wrong – where the dealer had obtained it and any additional information that might account for its history. The most ideal provenance would be written evidence of its having been owned by someone who had personally had it signed by Lewis or who knew the person who had obtained the signature.

143

Such evidence is rarely available, however, for a simple signature in a book having no indication of who might have owned it, and when the book has likely passed through multiple owners.

In this instance, however, it seems that the bookseller from whom I bought it had the signature authenticated two years earlier by a recognized Lewis expert to whom he had turned for advice when he was considering its purchase for his own collection. Unfortunately, the expert was none other than myself! As he told me, he had sent me a scan of the signature at the time he bought it from an east coast dealer, asking me if I thought it was genuine – and how I let that one slip by I shall never know. Of course, I had to return the price paid to me, and I couldn't ask the seller to return my money after my having been responsible for his having bought it earlier. He did, however, very generously offer to refund his profit on the sale, so that in effect we split the difference in the loss. Oh, how the mighty sometimes fall!

Nor have I been infallible in assessing Lewis signatures I've seen on eBay. Last year I bid successfully on a signed book, for which the seller had provided a scan of just the signature. It looked fine to me, but when I received the book, I was shocked to see that the letters in the signature were twice as high as any Lewis handwriting I had ever seen. Lewis always wrote in a very cramped style, and there was no possibility that he would ever have written in so large a hand. In addition, there was not only a dot after the lower end of the "C" but another one opposite the upper end. I had assumed it was just an artifact in the somewhat fuzzy eBay scan, but it was definitely not an artifact in reality but clearly done with the same ink. The seller disclaimed any knowledge of its being a forgery, but gave me a refund – and promptly listed it again on eBay. She later sold an identical one on eBay, and my only conclusion is that the forger somehow delighted in leaving his own signature on his work – in the form of an extraneous dot.

Years ago I was offered a Lewis letter by a bookseller in England, which I bought sight unseen. Unfortunately, some child had scrawled on the front of it, but this was a minor fault, given the interesting nature of the letter.

The signature was definitely that of Lewis, as was the text, but the handwriting in the body of the two-page letter was clearly not that of Lewis. The date of the letter would have been enough to give me a clue as to the identify of the scribe, but having already had correspondence with that person many years earlier before he changed his handwriting style, I immediately recognized it as that of Walter Hooper. (See also the Karen Housel correspondence in *A New Kind of Joy and a Sad Farewell*.) Lewis had obviously dictated it to Walter, but signed it himself in his weak hand.

Walter had first met Lewis some months earlier, and Lewis had become attracted to the pleasant young American from North Carolina. They met on numerous occasions, and when Warnie was off on an alcoholic binge in Ireland, Jack asked Walter to be his personal secretary. As this letter and the letters to Karen Housel demonstrate, Walter eagerly accepted the offer, doing much more for Jack than just helping him with his correspondence. One notable task was to go to Cambridge with Douglas Gresham and bring back all of Jack's papers, books, and other personal belongings.

With Warnie's continued absence during that summer, Jack begged Walter to remain in Oxford, but because of a teaching commitment back in North Carolina that Fall, he had to leave, promising to return to Oxford immediately at the end of term. Shocked and deeply saddened to learn of Jack's death in November, he returned to Oxford in January, and was appointed by the executors of the Lewis estate to go through all of Jack's papers and to become the literary advisor to the estate, with responsibility for editing posthumous publications of Jack's work. For more than forty years he has toiled endlessly to carry out that enormous responsibility, searching out everything that Jack ever wrote or which was recorded of everything he ever spoke " whether lectures, sermons, letters to the editor, poems published in *Punch* or other magazines, prefaces to other's books, or whatever. We all owe him a great debt of gratitude!

Acquiring a Rare Narnia First Edition – and a New Friend

Early in 2005 a bookseller in Edinburgh, Scotland, offered me a first edition of *Prince Caspian*, inscribed on the title page, "To Penelope with love, from C. S. Lewis." Her bookplate showed her to be Penny Berners-Price, and since it was apparent from the inscription that she was more than a casual contact, I again searched that source of all information on the Internet, www.google.com, in hope of learning who she might have been. Of the many web sites turned up by Google, one seemed more promising because it had an email address – that of a professor of chemistry at an Australian university, Sue Berners-Price.

I wrote to Professor Berners-Price to tell her of my acquisition, and to ask if by some unlikely circumstance she might know anything about Penelope Berners-Price – and indeed she did. Not only is she the goddaughter of Penelope, she replied, but Penelope was still alive and well, living in Scotland, and, in response to a phone call to her immediately upon receiving my e-mail, she said that Penelope would very much like to hear from me. Sue also told me the fascinating story of how Penelope's parents became acquainted with C. S. Lewis, and later enjoyed a lasting friendship with him.

A woman who said she was the wife of C. S. Lewis, the famous author and Oxford don, had been living at the Court Stairs Hotel near Ramsgate, owned by Alan and Nell Berners-Price, parents of Penny. Her husband, she had assured them, would pay the bill as soon as he arrived. After many weeks, during which she told them he had been delayed for one reason or another, Nell went to Oxford and presented Lewis with a stack of unpaid bills, asking him when he was going to take care of the matter. "But I'm not married!" he replied, much to her surprise. Returning to the hotel, she had the woman arrested, and Lewis served as a witness at her trial. It turned out that her name was Mrs. Hooker, and she had been in jail several times for this same offense.

Some months after acquiring this treasure, while visiting a new friend in London who wanted me to see his C. S. Lewis collection, I was surprised to see Penny's same bookplate in a first edition of *The Horse and His Boy*, with her childish inscription above it: *Given to me by Daddy in 1955, Penelope Berners-Price, 10 years old.* He told me he had also owned a first edition of *The Silver Chair* with the same bookplate, which he had sold to a mutual friend of ours. When I later contacted that friend upon my return home, I learned that he had *three* of her books.

After many overseas telephone conversations, during one of which she told me her complete set of Narnia books had been accidentally sold in 2004, I had the pleasure of meeting Penelope in Oxford in June 2005, near to which she had recently moved from Edinburgh. She was particularly eager to see The Kilns, the Lewis home at which she had enjoyed tea with Jack and her parents on several occasions as a child some 40 years earlier. She was thrilled to see the house restored just as she remembered it, and then told me she had a surprise for me. While unpacking her things from Edinburgh a few days earlier, she was amazed to find that one of her precious Narnia books, *The Last Battle*, was among them, having somehow escaped the same fate as the other six. Moreover, it was the only other one of the seven signed by Lewis, and she graciously let me buy it. Now, with two of my own Penny Berners-Price books and the other four from the two friends who generously exchanged their copies for comparable copies of those titles, I have fond hopes of eventually tracking down that last copy and thus completing the set.

As it turned out, the Berners-Price story was told in a book given me by Walter Hooper not long before, but which I had not yet read completely – the 940 page ultimate reference book on C. S. Lewis: *C. S. Lewis: A Companion and Guide.* Had I known the story, however, I would never have come to know my charming new friend!

My fond hope is that this picture of her bookplate will jog some reader's memory and bring the lost volume home for its family reunion. If anyone knows the whereabouts of that first British edition of *The Voyage of the Dawn Treader* with this bookplate, I shall be forever grateful for an email to lewisbooks@aol.com. If the book has no dust jacket, I will happily exchange a fine copy in an equally fine jacket for it.

Ex Libris

PENNY BERNERS-PRICE

The Search Goes On

By the time my Lewis collection went to Taylor seven years ago, I had accumulated multiple copies of every Lewis title, only the finest of which was in the collection. Thus left with more than two hundred Lewis first editions, I let it be known through various means on the Internet that I had Lewis first editions for sale.

As the volume of inquiries has slowly increased in the past few years, I have continued to look for fine copies to replace titles no longer in stock, and more recently have added a number of Lewis letters to those I acquired years ago. Although Lewis wrote thousands of letters in his lifetime, most of them are in two libraries – the Bodleian Library at Oxford University, and the Marian Wade Center at Wheaton College. Lewis letters rarely appear on the market these days – no more than two or three a year on average – and I have been buying most of them. Although too costly to be affordable by most Lewis collectors, the profits from their sale, along with sales of the many surplus Lewis first editions remaining after selling my basic collection to Taylor University, have enabled us to enjoy a considerable increase in our giving to Christian ministries.

The most difficult items to find are dust jackets for the earliest editions, and these are often worth much more than the books themselves, as I may have already explained, simply because they are so much fewer in number. They are easily torn or soiled, and many are thus discarded. Only two in the collection at Taylor University were without dust jackets when they bought the collection – *Spirits in Bondage* and *The Allegory of Love*. Although it is highly unlikely that I will ever find the former in the original dust jacket, after more than twenty years of searching I was able to turn up a jacket for the latter in mid-2005. It is very shabby, falling apart at the folds, wrinkled on the edges, and with some pieces missing – but it's the real thing, as determined by a tiny date, [5/36], on the page, kindly supplied by the publisher 70 years ago!

It was much too fragile to place on the near-mint first edition *Allegory of Love* in the collection, but modern technology came to the rescue. Dan Hamilton was able to scan the tattered scraps of the first edition dust jacket, and electronically "merge" it with a scan of a much cleaner and complete third-edition jacket on hand. He painstakingly "cleaned" the grubbiness of 70 years from the scan, and produced a stunning replica of the first edition jacket as it must have looked in 1936.

Building on that success, he was able to recreate a "clean" jacket for *Spirits in Bondage* from a scan of a color copy provided by Walter Hooper from his personal copy – given to him by C. S. Lewis.

Until genuine jackets come along, the replicas will do nicely – and now there are no "naked" first editions on the shelves of the collection.

A Modern Peril of International Trade

With much of the used and rare book business being conducted on the Internet these days, as is much other business, many more orders are coming from other countries, with payment in foreign currencies. Exchange of currencies is no problem for merchants who accept credit cards, but for the small part-time dealer, this is not a viable option. Money orders or checks were thus the usual means of payment – with long waits for clearance of the latter before an order could be shipped – until the advent of services such as PayPal, through which any currency can instantly be sent from or received into one's bank account for a nominal fee.

When I recently received a very large email order for Lewis first editions from a bookseller in South Africa, I therefore immediately became suspicious when he specified that payment would be made by U. S. Postal Service money order through his agent in the United States, and that a British company would arrange for pickup and shipment of the order.

Suspicion increased further when I told him I would prefer to pay through a credit card or PayPal, to which he replied that PayPal was not available in South Africa (which I doubted) and that the use of credit cards was just making its way into that country (which I knew to be an absurd statement, having used my credit cards while traveling in South Africa more than twenty years ago). It now seemed apparent that this was a scam, but hoping that I might be instrumental in the apprehension of the perpetrators – particularly the American agent who would send the money orders – I continued the correspondence with my chatty friend, "Al Stevens."

When at last I received three money orders for $990 each ($1000 being the maximum for which a U. S. Postal Service money order can be issued), I contacted the office of the postal inspectors in Indianapolis for advice. From information provided on the USPS web site, it was apparent that these were counterfeit, and I was advised to turn them over to the superintendent of my local post office branch.

151

When the latter showed me a genuine money order with its imbedded watermarks, the counterfeit was obviously just that – for instead of having an imbedded watermark seen only when held up to the light, the watermark had been imprinted on the surface!

This particular scam, as I now learned, involves sending a merchant money orders well in excess of the purchase price of the merchandise, with some excuse that the excess is to be sent to an overseas recipient through a MoneyGram, with the merchandise being sent to that same address. No postal clerk would fail to recognize the counterfeits, but an untrained bank clerk would likely accept them as a deposit to one's business account, from which the cash would then be withdrawn to send as a MoneyGram. If the merchant then shipped the goods, the scam artist would receive his cash and the added bonus of the merchandise – and the unwary merchant would later be informed that the counterfeits had been detected by the postal service and the money deducted from his account.

In this instance, the cash – in the amount of $2765.35 – was to be sent to a warehouse company in London in payment for storage and onward shipping costs of rare books, works of art, and other goods purchased by the South African dealer. Since the three money orders were not sufficient to pay for my books and the cash transmission, I notified my friend Al that I would hold them until the others were received before depositing them in my bank account (not wanting him to know that I had already turned them over to the postal inspectors). He apologized for the oversight on the part of his American agent and instructed her to send the balance. The next day three more money orders for $990 each were delivered by DHL courier service from Dallas, Texas.

By now I hoped that the information I was able to provide the Indianapolis postal inspectors (the names and addresses on the money orders, and the DHL envelope through which the sender could easily be traced) would have spurred the Dallas office to immediate action while the sender was still oblivious to the fact that the counterfeits had not yet been detected. However, when I turned in the remaining money orders several days later I learned that the clerk handling them in the inspector's office was too busy to deal with the matter as yet! Since the cash had not yet been received by the London agent, the perpetrator in Dallas had undoubtedly become wary and moved to another location. Such is the futility of attempting to work with government bureaucrats.

In Conclusion

As the foregoing anecdotes have demonstrated, these thirty-some years of collecting the works of C. S. Lewis have been marked repeatedly by events that collectively cannot be attributed to mere chance. Such, moreover, has been the story of my life.

My mother and father were wonderful, moral individuals, but not until I was six years of age did they recognize, through the influence of a caring friend, that there was more to life than the pleasures of having a nice home, a decent income, a loving family, and all the other good things that accrue to moral, decent people. There was a lack in their life. As the great 17th century French mathematician, physicist, and philosopher, Blaise Pascal, wrote:

There is a God-shaped vacuum in the heart of every man which cannot be filled by any created thing, but only by God the Creator made known through Jesus Christ.

Through the ministry of the Randall Memorial Baptist Church in Williamsville, New York, the Buffalo suburb in which I and my brothers grew up, my parents filled that vacuum by turning their lives over to Jesus Christ. Two years later my mother died at 32 from a wound infection incurred through a minor accident, and my father had to assume sole responsibility for three small boys. Upon her death the congregation of that little church embraced us with an overwhelming love. The result was that all of my brothers and I likewise became followers of Jesus Christ in our early teens.

That faith was to sustain me through high school, military service in Europe during World War II, premedical university studies, and admission to the country's finest medical school under circumstances that I am still unable to explain, for my premedical academic record was below that required in those days for admission to any medical school.

With a Doctor of Medicine degree from Harvard Medical School, followed by a Master of Public Health degree from the Harvard School of Public Health, I was afforded entree to a series of professional opportunities in international medicine that took me throughout the world and into the presence of kings, presidents, and other world leaders, including the last emperor. And while there is some fleeting pleasure in having one's biographical sketch in such standard reference works as *Who's Who in America, Who's Who in the World,* and *Who's Who in Medicine and Healthcare,* such recognition is nothing compared to having the knowledge that one's name is written in the most important book of all, the Book of Life, spoken of by such great men as King David and the apostle Paul.

Every step of my life's journey has been marked by improbable circumstances that clearly indicated God's hand therein, including the pursuit of a hobby that has culminated in seeing the results of one's efforts now enjoyed by many. I hope you have enjoyed reading these accounts – and if they left you somewhat less than thrilled, at least you have the bibliography that follows to aid you in collecting Lewis first editions, if that brings you pleasure. But the treasure, after all, is in the eternally-true content, and not the fine bindings or interesting dust jackets. As a friend once remarked to me, "Even if they were only crayon scribbles on old paper towels, Jack's words would still lift up the world to God."

FIRST EDITIONS OF C. S. LEWIS

A descriptive bibliography

The term "first edition" has become so loosely used these days that I restrict its use herein to the first press run of any Lewis book – i.e., the first published appearance of that book. I realize that there are many disagreements about the use of the term "first edition" in the antiquarian trade, but I prefer this very restrictive definition. To list a book simply as "first edition" in the heading of a catalogue or eBay listing, for example, is used by sellers to get one's attention, but it is sure to disappoint (and certainly to annoy) the discriminating collector who then finds it to be the "third printing of the first edition" in the body of the listing, for example.

Such a later printing from the same type or plates may be shown by Lewis's publishers in different ways. A second printing of the first edition may be designated "2nd impression," "reprinted July 1942," or "2nd edition," for example.

Having limited my collecting of Lewis to the true first editions, I have limited knowledge of later editions, and have therefore not attempted to cover that large field. I have, however, provided descriptions of some of the more important later editions – particularly those of some of his earliest works – with a new preface or other important changes in the original text that make them desirable for a collector who concentrates only on first editions. Where there was no American edition at or about the same time as the British first edition, I have so noted this.

Although most Lewis first editions, both British and American, are easily identified as such, some are not. Since the rate of attrition for dust jackets is much greater than that for the books which they originally covered, dust jackets of later printings of the first edition are often used to enhance the appearance of a naked first edition. The dust jacket on a Lewis first edition will usually have no designation as such, whereas the jacket on a reprint may or may not state the printing, using one or the other of the designations noted above.

It is therefore especially important to accurately identify first edition dust jackets, whose value may exceed that of the book itself – and by a very large margin for first edition dust jackets for the very popular Chronicles of Narnia, for example. The dust jacket descriptions in this bibliography may therefore be its greatest value to collectors and booksellers alike.

Although dust jackets are often found with the price clipped from the corner of the front flap, there are a number of examples of Macmillan jackets herein in which one or both corners have apparently been clipped by the publisher, with the price intact. I have had examples of Macmillan jackets on first editions of some Narnia titles in which a tiny remnant of a price remained after clipping, but it was not possible to tell if the clipped price differed from the intact price. One might assume that the original price was incorrectly printed, so that it had to be clipped and the correct price then printed. I know almost nothing of the publishing business, so I can only report what I've seen.

As will also be noted herein, some books published by Oxford and Cambridge University presses have a British price in one corner of the front flap of the jacket and an American price in the other corner, one or the other to be clipped by the seller according to the country in which the book was to be sold. This became apparent to me when I found jackets on duplicate copies that still had both prices. In such instances, the American edition was sometimes in a very different binding from that of the British, yet in other instances identical to the British.

For the sake of brevity I have limited most descriptions to only the essential details, but have expanded on these in those instances that seemed to warrant doing so. The descriptions may seem excessive to some, but, sad to say, there are unscrupulous people who have modified less-valuable editions by "tipping" in other pages from ruined first editions and offering them as the real thing. (I have seen such a book on eBay recently – a later-printing *Lion, Witch and Wardrobe* with a pasted-in title page, advertised as the true first.) Such books often have a different "feel" to them – different paper weights or textures, different board colors – something that seems off; the extra printing and binding details here will help allay or bring into focus any suspicions extending beyond the title page.

Measurements of height and width are included in all listings, with the addition of thickness in a few instances where I have found variation in such due to differences in the thickness of the paper, rather than in a reduction in the number of pages. Measurements of width are taken from the outermost protrusion of the rounded spine in a fine copy, and are therefore subject to slight variation in more worn copies – and boards may vary slightly from copy to copy in their measurements.

In the page-by-page descriptions, the forward slash "/" indicates a line break, with the word, words, or figure that follows being on the next line. Words not in parentheses are as they actually appear; those in parentheses are descriptive, usually of a decorative device. For example, the lettering on the spine of *Spirits in Bondage* is described as:

Spirits/in/Bondage/(figure)/Clive/Hamilton/HEINEMAN

Reading from top to bottom, it appears thus:

Spirits
in
Bondage

(figure)

Clive
Hamilton

HEINEMANN

In the above example the font size as it appears on the book happens to be the same for each word. In most cases, however, the font sizes of the words differ, but I have not attempted to show these differences in the descriptions.

During some 30 years of collecting Lewis first editions, I acquired many duplicates in the course of continually upgrading the collection, thus having many opportunities to observe subtle changes in both books and dust jackets, including price changes, variations in binding, and even changes in the quality of paper within a single printing of the first edition due to wartime paper shortages in Britain. I have attempted to document all such variations, but will welcome such additional examples with which anyone may be familiar.

I must apologize if my use of any term to describe color seems to conflict with what one observes in a book he may have. One man's fuchsia may be another's purple, so I have tried to stick to variations in primary colors by the use of red-purple, purple-red, blue-yellow, etc., the second color being predominant.

The number of pages includes all pages between the endpapers, including any blank pages. With the more valuable titles, check to determine if any sheets are missing – such as the front free endpaper, which may have been removed because of an ugly inscription – or have been replaced. Since the endpapers are a continuous double sheet (one-half pasted down, the other half free), it should be relatively easy to see if the front free endpaper has been replaced.

Some books are dyed on the top-edge – the top of the closed pages – the dye being barely visible on an open page.

For those who only want a quick reference to features identifying the first edition, without all the other bibliographic detail, a **KEY TO FIRST EDITION** precedes the detailed description of the book. For the dust jacket, however, a careful review of the details is recommended.

Listings are in chronological order, but the index on the next page indicates the section number(s) assigned to each book title.

An alphabetic page index is provided at the end of the book for greater ease in locating a specific title by its page number.

In addition to the anecdotes which make up the first part of this book, from time to time you will find personal notes inserted at appropriate places in what might otherwise be rather dull bibliographical detail, which I hope will be of interest. (Some information has been duplicated between the two halves of this book. This is deliberate, and intended for the pleasures of both the casual reader and the collector.)

Finally, should any doubt remain about the authenticity of your first edition, please feel free to write (Dr. Edwin Brown, 8153 Oakland Road, IN 46240), phone (317-257-7454), or email (lewisbooks@aol.com) – and by all means, let me know of any errors or additional information you would like to call to my attention.

CHRONOLOGICAL INDEX OF FIRST EDITIONS

1. SPIRITS IN BONDAGE/A Cycle of Lyrics.
London: William Heinemann, March 20, 1919 (under the pseudonym of Clive Hamilton, a combination of Lewis's first name and his mother's maiden name).
119 pp 12.7cm x 18.8cm Medium gray-blue, coarsely-woven cloth.

<u>KEY TO FIRST EDITION</u>: Date on back of title page: 1919
(no reprints of the first edition are known)

<u>Front board</u>: (single blind-stamp rule around the edges)
<u>Spine</u>:(lettered in gold)
Spirits/in/Bondage/(figure)/Clive/Hamilton/HEINEMANN
<u>Rear board</u>: (blind-stamped Heinemann logo in a 2x2 cm ruled square: an "X" shaped figure filling the square, with the letters W and H on either side of the figure)
<u>Endpapers</u>: (blank, off-white) There is no half-title.
<u>Page (1)</u>: SPIRITS IN BONDAGE
<u>Page (2)</u>: (advertisement) Recent Verse by John Masefield, Eden Phillpotts, Siegfried Sassoon, and R. E. Vernede, in a 5.6 x 8.9 cm rectangle.
<u>Page (3)</u>: (TITLE PAGE) SPIRITS IN BONDAGE/A CYCLE OF LYRICS/BY/CLIVE HAMILTON/IN THREE PARTS/I. THE PRISON HOUSE/II. HESITATION/III. THE ESCAPE/"The land where I shall never be/The love that I shall never see"/19 (Heinemann windmill logo) 19/(8.4 cm single line)/LONDON /WILLIAM HEINEMANN (See illustration no. 1)
<u>Page (4)</u>: *London: William Heinemann, 1919*
<u>Page 5</u>: CONTENTS/ PAGE / PROLOGUE 7 / PART I: THE PRISON HOUSE/(21 lines) I. SATAN SPEAKS 11 through THE AUTUMN MORNING 53/ 5
<u>Page 6</u>: CONTENTS/ PAGE/ PART II: HESITATION/ (3 lines)XXII. L'APPRENTI SORCIER 57 through XXIV. IN PRAISE OF SOLID PEOPLE 62/PART III: THE ESCAPE/(16 lines) XXV. SONG OF THE PILGRIMS through XL: DEATH IN BATTLE/6
<u>Pages 7-8</u>: PROLOGUE
<u>Pages 9-(106)</u>: (text pages)
<u>Page (107)</u>: PRINTED AT/THE COMPLETE PRESS/WEST NORWOOD, LONDON
<u>Page (108)</u>: (blank)

Page (109): List of/Poetry (in red)/(Heinemann windmill logo)/William Heinemann/21 Bedford Street, Strand/LONDON/W.C.2.
Pages (110) through (119): (advertisements)
(110) SOLDIER POETS (upper right corner, in red) SIEGFRIED SASSOON: The Old Huntsman & other Poems; Counter-Attack and other Poems/ R. E. VERNEDE: War Poems and Other Verses/ ROBERT GRAVES: Fairies and Fusiliers/ GEORGE LEWIS: Spirits in Bondage

Although the real name of the author of *Spirits in Bondage* is shown, his first name is erroneously given as George instead of Clive, and he is referred to as "G. S. Lewis" in the brief biographical sketch of each of the soldier poets.

(111) (Excerpts from two poems of the poets on the previous page) From "Counter Attack and other Poems" by Siegried Sassoon (in red in the left margin) THE GENERAL. (with 5 lines of verse)/From "War Poems & other Verses" by R. E. Vernede (in red in the left margin) To C. H. V. (with 16 lines of poignant verse to his wife) (as noted on the previous page, he was later killed in action)
(112) SOLDIER POETS (continued) (upper right corner, in red) GEOFFREY DEARMER: Poems/NEW VOLUMES OF POETRY AUTUMN 1918 (upper right corner, in red) GEORGE ROSTREVOR (one title)/LAURENCE HOUSMAN (one title)/JOHN MASEFIELD (5 titles)
(113-114) (a long listing of poetry, plays, and fiction by Swinburne, with marginal notes in red)
(115) From "Fairies and Fusiliers" by Robert Graves (in red in left margin) NOT DEAD. (with 11 lines of verse)/ From "Escape and Fantasy" by George Rostrevor (in red in left margin) ELYSIUM. (with 12 lines of verse)
(116) The Poetical Works of/SAROJINI NAIDU (3 titles)/The Poetical Works of/ LAURENCE HOPE
(4 titles)/EDMUND GOSSE/ Collected Poems
(117) From "Lollingdon Downs and other Poems," by John Masefield (in red in the left margin) XXIX. (with 14 lines of verse)/ From "The Broken Wing," by Sarojini Naidu (in red in the left margin) THE VICTOR. (with 18 lines of verse)

(118) ARTHUR SYMONS/Poems (description of two volumes)/The Collected Works of/FIONA MACLEOD (with description of seven volumes)/The Selected Writings of/WILLIAM SHARP (with description of five volumes)/The Poems of/JOHN GALSWORTHY (one volume)
(119) MAURICE HEWLETT/The Song of the Plow/EDEN PHILPOTTS/Plain Song/ISRAEL ZANGWILL/Blind Children/ JOHN HELSTON/Aphrodite, and other Poems/GEORGE RESTON MALLOCH/Poems and Lyrics/ANTHOLOGIES (in red in the left margin) (list of four anthologies).

Dust jacket: (Gray paper, lettered in black)
Front panel: SPIRITS IN/BONDAGE/BY/CLIVE HAMILTON
Spine: SPIRITS/IN/BONDAGE/BY/CLIVE/HAMILTON/ 3/6 /NET/HEINEMANN
Back panel: (advertisements, in a single-rule border 9.3 cm x 15.7 cm) RECENT VERSE/Escape and Fancy./By George Rostrevor ... / POEMS by Siegfried Sassoon ... /POEMS by John Masefield ... /THE WORKS OF SWINBURNE .... /LONDON: WILLIAM HEINEMANN
Front flap: (publisher's note, in a single-rule border 5.1 cm x 15.9 cm): (figure)/Mr. William Heinemann/will be glad to send .... /through a bookseller./(figure)
Back flap: (blank)

At the age of 7, Lewis began writing about an imaginary "Animal Land" (published in 1985 as *BOXEN: The Imaginary World of the Young C. S. Lewis*). As a teenager, however, his first ambition was to be a poet. While under the tutelage of W. T. Kirkpatrick, to whom his father had sent him in 1914 when he was unable to tolerate the life at a private school, Lewis began voraciously studying the craft of poetry and writing verse himself during his holidays from school. At age 17 he wrote two of the romantic lyrics which later appeared in *Spirits in Bondage*. These and some 50 other poems written during the two-year period he was with Kirkpatrick were copied into a notebook which he titled *The Metrical Meditations of a Cod* ("cod" being a northern Irish term of humorous self-deprecation), 14 of which are included in *Spirits of Bondage*. The other verses in his first published book were written while on army duty in France and during recovery from his wounds.

The theme of *Spirits in Bondage* – that nature is malevolent and that any God that exists is outside the cosmic system – reflects the influence of Kirkpatrick's atheism on the young scholar, but by the time he returned to Oxford after the war, Lewis began having doubts about the validity of his views of a remote and uninvolved God. For the next ten years he would continue to modify these views as he came closer and closer to a real understanding of God.

Although the few reviews of the book appeared in such first-class papers as *The London Times* and *The Scotsman* and were quite favorable, the book did not sell well, and after a few years the publisher destroyed most of the copies. The book is extremely rare today – I have known of only a half-dozen copies to have appeared on the market in the past 15-20 years.

As with a number of Lewis's books, there was no American first edition. In 1984, however, Harcourt Brace Jovanovich issued a new edition in paperback, edited and with a Preface by Walter Hooper.

2. DYMER.
London: J. M. Dent and Sons Ltd., September 20, 1926
(under the pseudonym Clive Hamilton)
104 pp   13.5cmx19cm   Gray-blue patterned cloth.

KEY TO FIRST EDITION: *On back of title page:*
FIRST PUBLISHED . . 1926
(no reprints of the first edition are known)

Front board: (in black) (embossed figure of the leaping Dymer on a background of clouds, sunshine, rain, and lightning, oval-shaped, 4cm x 6cm; blind-stamped rule on three edges)
Spine: (lettered in gold) DYMER/*by*/ Clive Hamilton (on a sunburst background, with "*by*" on a cloud over the sun, and six stars below "Hamilton")/ (lettered in black) J.M.DENT/&SONS.LTD
Rear board: (blank)
Top edge of pages: (same gray-blue color as cloth)
Endpapers: (blank)
Page (i): DYMER
Page (ii): (quotation) Nine nights I hung upon the Tree, wounded with/the spear as an offering to Odin, myself sacrificed to myself./*Havama.*
Page (iii): (title page) Design by R. L. Knowles, as reproduced on the jacket and title page of the American first edition, but slightly reduced to leave ½" margin around decorative border, and with publisher's identification at the bottom thus: LONDON & TORONTO/J.M. DENT & SONS LTD./NEW YORK (twig and leaf design/E. P. DUTTON & CO. Hooded angelic figure in gray, rest of design and lettering in black.
Page (iv): *All rights reserved*/FIRST PUBLISHED 1926/PRINTED IN GREAT BRITAIN
Page v: CONTENTS/ PAGE/CANTO I (ten dots) 1 (through) CANTO IX (ten dots) 93 /*The title-page is a reproduction from a drawing/by R. L. Knowles*
Page (vi): (blank)
Page 1 through page (104): (text pages)
Page (105): MADE AT THE/TEMPLE PRESS/LETCHWORTH/IN/GREAT BRITAIN (with background of a daisy with two leaves, 1.5cm square)

Page (106): (blank)

Page(1): (advertisements) LETTRES,/ILLUSTRATEDBOOKS, ETC./ AUTUMN 1926/(single rule)/(single rule)/J. M. DENT & SONS LTD. . LONDON/ H

Page (2): (blank)

Page 3:Unpublished Stories and a Play/*By Count Leo Tolstoy*/ (lengthy description)/The Little Room/By Guy N. Pocock/(brief description)

Page 4: (3 titles) Blindness By Henry Green/(description)/The Minister's Daughter/By Hildur Dixelius/ (description)/ Samuel Butler and/His Family Relations By M. Garnett/(description)

Page 5: (3 titles) The Gates of Horn/ ByBernard Sleigh/ (description)/Under the Northern Lights/By Alan Sullivan/ (description)/The Pearl Lagoon/By Charles Nordhoff/(description)

Page 6: The Romances of Alexandre Dumas/(description of 48 volumes)

Page 7: (3 titles) The History of Rasselas, Prince of/Abissinia By Samuel Johnson, LL.D./(description)/The Gypsy Life of Betsy Wood/By M. Eileen Lyster/(description)/The Cromer Street Chronicles/By Norman P. Greig/(description)/

Page (8): (3 titles) The Life of Benevuto Cellini/Translated by Anne Macdonnell/(description)/The Travels of Marco Polo/Introduction by John Masefield/(description)/For Sons of Gentlemen/by Kerr Shaw/(description)/J.M.DENT & SONS LTD., 10-13 BEDFORD STREET, LONDON.

Dust jacket:

Front panel: (black type and figure, on a dark-gold background, as on the front board (see description thereof), in a gold border: fine double-rule within a heavy single-rule.)

Spine: DYMER (with sunburst above) (in black)/*by*/Clive Hamilton (on a gold sunburst, with stars below Hamilton)/JMDENT&SONS Ltd (at bottom of spine)

Back panel: (advertisements lettered in black, within a double-rule border) *Unpublished Stories and a Play* by Count Leo Tolstoy, *The Minister's Daughter* by Hilder Dexelius, *Blindness* by Henry Green, *The Gates of Horn* by Bernard Sleigh (all priced at 7s. 6d. net)

Front flap: (blank)

Back flap: (blank)

Published the year after Lewis began what was to be a 30-year career at Magdalen (pronounced *"Mawdlin"* in Oxford) College, University of Oxford, *Dymer* took the longest to write of any of his books, but was the least successful commercially, despite many favorable reviews. As his biographer, George Sayer, notes in *Jack: C. S. Lewis and His Times*, "So few copies of the first edition were sold that it is now an even rarer book than *Spirits in Bondage*. Not more than a dozen copies are known to exist." (Having personally acquired four copies of the first edition – one in a dust jacket -- and having seen five more in major libraries, I was inclined to doubt the accuracy of that statement. When I alluded to it the last time I saw George in 1997, he wasn't quite sure where he had got that information. Nonetheless, it is indeed a very rare book.)

Dymer is very much about Lewis himself – and its publication marked a significant turning point in this life. In one way or another he spent nine or ten years working on it, beginning with a basic myth that came into his mind when he was about seventeen – "the story of a man who, on some mysterious bride, begets a monster, which monster, as soon as it has killed its father, becomes a god," as he notes in the Preface to the second edition, published a quarter of a century later, in 1950. (For a synopsis, see description of the dust jacket front flap on the American edition.)

Dymer is about the relationship of fantasy to reality. Through the years he spent writing it, he was concerned about the powerful role played in his life by his productive imagination – a tendency to withdraw from life and to luxuriate in fantasies of love, cruelty, lust, or heroism. ("From at least the age of six, romantic longing – *Sehnsucht* – played an unusually central part in my experience.") As he wrote, however, he was able to work through his obsessions and succeeded in severely diminishing his excessive fantasizing – but fortunately, not so completely as to interfere with the later writing of such classics as the Chronicles of Narnia and the Space Trilogy. The poem begins, for example, with several stanzas of satire on the totalitarian state, into which he put his hatred of Malvern College (which he left to study with Kirkpatrick) and army life. It ends with Dymer redeeming himself by facing himself, and, in the process, doing something to redeem the earth. His subsequent courage in

171

facing the truth results in his death, but sets off a process of cosmic rebirth – and he becomes a god.

It was a long poem, and, unfortunately, published at a time when long poems by little-known writers were no longer being read. However, reprinted in 1950 by Dent with an explanatory preface by Lewis, it has since captured the imagination of Lewis followers and others alike. Except for many single short poems published in *Punch* and other publications in later years (and compiled posthumously in *Poems* and *Narrative Poems* by Walter Hooper), Lewis abandoned his dream of becoming a poet and turned to the prose works that made him one of the great writers of the 20th century.

3. (First American edition) **DYMER.**
New York: E. P. Dutton & Company, 1926
(Under the pseudonym Clive Hamilton)
105 pp.   13.5 x 19.7 cm   Ocher cloth (bound 2 cm into boards) and pink-purple paper (usually mottled in all copies I have seen, though this may be an aging artifact).

KEY TO FIRST EDITION: On back of title page:
Copyright 1926
(There is no acknowledgment of first edition, but I know
of no early reprints of the first American edition.)

Front board: (cream label, 6.3 x 3.3, imprinted in red) DYMER/BY CLIVE/HAMILTON
Spine: (cream label, 1.7 x 3.7 cm, imprinted in red) DYMER/BY CLIVE/HAMILTON (with head and shoulders of angelic being, as on front of jacket and title page)
Rear board: (blank)
Pages: (top-edge trimmed; fore- and bottom-edge untrimmed)
Endpapers: (blank)
Page (i): DYMER
Page (ii): (same quotation from *Havamal*)
Page (iii): (title page) (as on dust jacket – see illustration no. 3 – but slightly reduced to leave ½" margin around decorative border. Angelic being is somewhat different shade of gray than on title page of British first edition)
Page (iv): Copyright 1926/By E. P DUTTON & COMPANY/ (rule) /*All rights reserved/Printed in the United States of America*
Page v: (Contents as in British edition, without acknowledgment of Knowles drawing)
Page (vi): (blank)
Page (vii): DYMER
Page (viii): (blank)
Page 1 through 105: Text fills one more page than British edition. Pages are identical until page 40, where last 3 lines of verse 14 are carried over to page 41, resulting in a total of 105 pages. Verso of page 105 is blank, and 3 blank pages are inserted at the end, before the free endpaper. There are no advertisements.)

Dust jacket:

Front and back panels: (Knowles design, as on title page, completely fills both front and back panels, with angelic being in fuchsia)

Spine: (lettered in black, on off-white paper): DYMER/BY CLIVE/ HAMILTON/(head and shoulders of angelic being)/E. P. DUTTON/ & COMPANY

Front flap: (lettered in black): DYMER/By/CLIVE HAMILTON/ *With a decorative title page in two colors by R. L. Knowles*/ (publisher's blurb) This impressive and beautiful poem unfolds a mystical story of great poignancy. The fable is roughly of a boy brought up under a rigid system, from which his imagination suddenly drives him forth. Love wakes to him, from the far immortal plane where love is an ideal existence which visits us in the unrecapturable mood. When the mood is lost, Dymer, without knowing why it is lost, seeks it in dream life. He learns the lying nature of a dream pretending to reality in a beautiful myth that ends with his death, and the mystical resurgence of truth, through evil, in that death./(rule)/E. P. DUTTON & COMPANY/681 Fifth Avenue New York City/(F-721)

Back flap: (lettered in black) MORE SONGS/FROM LEINSTER/ By/W. M. LETTS/(summary of book)/(rule)/E. P. DUTTON & COMPANY/ 681 Fifth Avenue, New York City/(F-691)

The first American edition of *Dymer* is even rarer than the first British edition, and few copies in the dust jacket are to be found today.

4. (Second edition, British and American) **DYMER**.
London: J. M. Dent and Sons Ltd and New York: The Macmillan Company, October 19, 1950.
104 pages   12.6 cm x 18.8 cm   Orange cloth

KEY TO THIS EDITION: On back of title page:
First published 1926/Last published 1950

Reissued with a 7-page preface by Lewis, beginning: "At its original appearance in 1926, *Dymer*, like many better books, found some good reviews and almost no readers. The idea of disturbing its repose in the grave now comes from its publishers, not from me, but

I have a reason for wishing to the present at the exhumation. Nearly a quarter of a century has gone since I wrote it, and in that time things have changed both within me and round me; my old poem might be misunderstood by those who now read it for the first time."

He then goes on to explain how the thought of *Dymer* came to him when he was 17 years old, and gives a brief but poignant autobiographical sketch of his transition from his rejection of Christianity at an earlier age to his conversion over a decade later – with reference to various passages in *Dymer* that reflected his teenage rejection of God.

Both book and dust jacket were printed in Great Britain. The only difference between the British and the American dust jackets was the price of 12s. 6d. in the *upper* right corner of the front flap on the British jacket and $1.50 in the *lower* right corner of the American jacket.

Front board: (blank)
Spine: (lettered in gold) DYMER: C. S. LEWIS (horizontally)/
DENT (vertically)
Rear board: (blank)
Top-edge: Orange
Front endpapers: (blank, off-white)
Page (i): DYMER
Page (ii):(Quotation from *Havamal*, as in prior editions)
Page (iii): (title page) DYMER/by/C. S. LEWIS/LONDON: J. M.
DENT & SONS LTD./NEW YORK: THE MACMILLAN
COMPANY
Page (iv): This book is copyright. It may not be/reproduced whole or in part by any method/without written permission. Application /should be made to the publishers: /J. M. DENT & SONS LTD./ Aldine House – Bedford St. – London/Made in Great Britain/by/The Temple Press – Letchworth – Herts/and Bradford and Dickens – Drayton House – W.C.1./First published 1926/Last published 1950
Page (v): TO/MARJORIE MILNE
Although the 1926 first edition of *Dymer* has no dedicatee, Lewis dedicated the 1950 second edition to Marjorie Milne, to whom he was introduced in the 1940s by Owen Barfield. A devout Roman

Catholic, Miss Milne became such an admirer of Lewis that she thought he should head a new religious movement. By 1947, she had become so overbearing in her admiration of Lewis that he wrote to Owen Barfield, "Never communicate any troubles of mine again to M. Milne. Through no will of my own I occupy already a larger place in her thoughts than I could wish, and the degree of her sympathy is such as to make her miserable and to embarrass me." She did so much of the talking when visiting Lewis that Owen Barfield was led to comment, "She's a good creature when all's said and done: especially when all's said and done!"

Page (v)i: (blank)
Page (vii): CONTENTS/PAGE/CANTO I (ten dots) 1 (through) CANTO IX (ten dots) 93
Page (viii): (blank)
Pages ix-xv: Preface
Page (xvi): (blank)
Page 1 through page (104): (text)
Rear endpapers: (blank)

Dust jacket: Gray paper, with all lettering in orange-red
Front panel: DYMER/A Poem/by/C. S. LEWIS
Back panel: EVERYMAN'S LIBRARY (with description of types of books offered, etc., in double-rule border)
Spine: DYMER/C. S. LEWIS/DENT (as on spine of book)
Front flap: (Publisher's blurb: *This narrative poem was first published in 1926,*etc.)
Back flap: Books by/C. S. LEWIS/(line)/(list of his books through 1947)

My copy from which this description was taken is one presented by Lewis to his best friend, Owen Barfield, with the following inscription on the front free endpaper: *"Owen Barfield from Jack Lewis, Oct. 1950"*.

(At age four, Clive Staples Lewis suddenly announced to his parents that his name was "Jacksie" (later amended to "Jack"), and from thereon refused to answer to any other name. Although called Jack by friends and colleagues, he infrequently signed his name other than "C. S. Lewis," even in letters to his closest friends.) (See note following description of no. 16, *The Problem of Pain.*)

5. THE PILGRIM'S REGRESS.

London: J. M. Dent and Sons Ltd., May 25, 1933.
256 pages   13.2 x 18.9 cm   Rust brown cloth.

<u>**KEY TO FIRST EDITION:**</u> On back of title page:
First Published 1933

<u>Front and back boards</u>: (blank)
<u>Spine</u>: (lettered in reddish-brown)
THE/PILGRIM'S/REGRESS/(asterisk)/C. S. LEWIS/DENT
Top-edge: Reddish-brown
Endpapers: Double-width "MAPPA MUNDI" in reddish-brown, front and back, by R. L. Knowles (initials R.L.K. in lower right corner of free endpaper). Verso blank, front and back.
<u>Page (1)</u>: THE PILGRIM'S REGRESS
<u>Page (2)</u>: (blank)
<u>Page (3)</u>: (title page) (in double-ruled border 8.6 x 14.1 cm) THE/ PILGRIM'S REGRESS/(rule)/An Allegorical Apology/ for/ Christianity Reason and Romanticism/(rule)/BY C. S. LEWIS/(rule) /As cold waters to a thirsty soul,/so is good news from a far country. /--- Proverbs/ (rule)/(oval decoration)/(rule)/LONDON /J. M. DENT AND SONS LTD
<u>Page (4)</u>: *Printed by the Guernsey Star and Gazette/Company Ltd., in Guernsey, C.I., British Isles/for/J. M. Dent & Sons Ltd./Aldine House, Bedford St., London/ Toronto–Vancouver/Melbourne– Welling- ton/All rights reserved/First Published 1933*
<u>Page (5)</u>: To ARTHUR GREEVES

At age 16 Lewis first met Arthur Greeves, with whom he was to become a friend for life. Although the parents of both were friends and neighbors, it was not until 1914 that Lewis first visited the family when he was told that Arthur was ill and would welcome a visit. Overcoming his natural shyness, Lewis hesitatingly made the journey across the street. "I found Arthur sitting up in bed. On the table beside him lay a copy of *Myths of the Norsemen*. 'Do *you* like that?' said I. 'Do *you* like that?' said he. Next moment the book was in our hands, our heads were bent close together, we were pointing, quoting, talking, – soon almost shouting – discovering in a torrent of questions that we liked not only the same thing, but the same parts of it and in the same way; that both knew the stab of Joy and that, for both, the arrow was shot from the North. Many thousands of people have had the experience of finding the first friend, and it is none the less a wonder; as great a wonder as first love, or even greater. I had been so far from thinking such a friend possible that I had never even longed for one; no more than I longed to be King of England." Later that same year, when Lewis returned to school in England, they began a correspondence that lasted until only a few weeks before Lewis died, writing to each other weekly for many of those years. Much of this correspondence fills the 566 pages of *They Stand Together: The Letters of C. S. Lewis to Arthur Greeves (1914-1963)* (edited by Walter Hooper), London: Collins. 1979.

Page (6): (blank)
Page (7): CONTENTS/BOOK ONE/THE DATA/(followed by Chapters I to VI, pages 12-27)/BOOK TWO /THRILL/(followed by Chapters I to VIII, pages 32-48)
Page (8): CONTENTS—*Continued*/BOOK THREE/THROUGH DARKEST ZEITGEISTHEIM/(followed by Chapters I to IX, pages 52-70/BOOK FOUR/BACK TO THE ROAD/(followed by Chapters I to IV, pages 74-81/ BOOK FIVE/ THE GRAND CANYON/ (followed by Chapters I to VII, pages 88-110
.Page (9): CONTENTS—*Continued*/BOOK SIX/NORTHWARD ALONG THE CANYON/(followed by Chapters I to VII, pages 116-134/BOOK SEVEN/SOUTHWARD ALONG THE CANYON/ (followed by Chapters I to XII, pages 138-168/BOOK EIGHT/ AT BAY/ (followed by Chapters I to II, pages 174-178
Page (10): CONTENTS—*Continued*/(followed by Chapters III to X, pages 181-205)/BOOK NINE/ ACROSS THE CANYON/(followed by Chapters I to VI, pages 210-221/BOOK TEN/THE REGRESS/ (followed by Chapters I-X, pages 226-252
Page (11) and pages 12 through (256): (text)

Dust jacket: Buff paper
Front panel: (by Thomas Derrick) (lettered in red; design and "Drawn by Thomas Derrick" in black)
Spine: (lettered in black on buff paper) THE/PILGRIM'S/REGRESS/(twig and leaf in red)/C. S. LEWIS/ DENT
Back panel: (advertising) NEW NOVELS (as part of triple-ruled border top, left and bottom)/(novels are *FLO* by F. C. Boden; *THE PRODIGAL FATHER* by Richard Church; *GENTLEMEN –THE REGIMENT!* by Hugh Talbot; *YET IN MY FLESH* by M. E. Mitchell; *THE GOLD RIM* by Irene Rathbone; *TO DREAM AGAIN* by John Fisher; *ON THE HILL* by Lewis Gibbs; *FRUITS OF THE EARTH* by Frederick P. Grove/ 7/6 J. M. DENT AND SONS LTD. – BEDFORD STREET – LONDON W.C.2
Front flap: *5s. net/* (followed by synopsis of book) Though the dragon and giants of this fable ... out of the realm of controversy.
Back flap: (1 cm square design of crossed arrows)/PRINTED IN GREAT BRITAIN/AT THE TEMPLE PRESS/LETCHWORTH/ HERTS/(same design)

With the disappointing sales results of his first two books of poetry, Lewis's ambition to be a poet soon dwindled, and from that point on his contributions of poetry were limited to single poems published in *Punch* and other periodicals. By 1926, when *Dymer* was published, the young atheist Lewis had begun to believe in a nebulous power outside of himself, leading to his eventual conversion to Christianity five years later, in 1931. In August 1932, while visiting his friend Arthur Greeves in Northern Ireland, he undertook to write about his conversion – and in just two weeks completed as allegory the story of his spiritual journey, *The Pilgrim's Regress*, incorporating several religious lyrics in its final chapters.

The book was published in May 1933, and although the few reviews were mostly favorable, only 650 of the first printing of 1000 copies were sold. Some of the reviewers apparently assumed that Lewis was a Roman Catholic, and brought the book to the attention of Frank Sheed, of the Roman Catholic publishing house of Sheed and Ward. Sheed then asked Dent to print 1500 copies for himself, which Sheed and Ward had bound and issued under their own imprint, both in London and in New York.

Because of the confusion surrounding Sheed and Ward's British and American editions and some of the interesting changes made by them, I have included these and the Bles third edition.

6. (Second British edition) **THE PILGRIM'S REGRESS.**
London: Sheed and Ward, 1935.
256 pp. 13.2 x 18.9 cm   Olive-gray cloth

KEY TO THIS EDITION: Date at bottom of title page:
                         MCMXXXV

Front and back boards: (blank)
Spine: (lettered in red) THE/PILGRIM'S/REGRESS/C. S. LEWIS/SHEED&WARD
Endpapers: (double-width "MAPPA MUNDI" in reddish-brown, front and back, by R. L. Knowles, with initials R.L.K. in lower right corner of free endpaper, as in no. 5)

The pagination of this second edition is the same as that in the first edition, except that Sheed and Ward added a short "Argument" at the beginning of each of the ten books because they thought Lewis was worried about obscurity in the book. However, Lewis was not pleased, as evidenced by his hand-written comments on the front flap of the dust jacket of a copy in the Wade Center at Wheaton College, Wheaton, Illinois. In the publisher's blurb, Lewis has underlined some of the passages, followed by asterisks, and then added the following: *The suggestions* (referring to the "Arguments") *are put in by the unspeakable Sheed with no authority of mine & without my knowledge.*

In addition, Sheed and Ward made the following changes from the Dent first edition:
Title page: (at the bottom) LONDON/SHEED & WARD, INC./1935
Verso of title page: *First published by J. M. Dent & Sons Ltd., 1933*

Dust jacket: Pictorial dust jacket, in blue and brown
Front panel: (*"The Pilgrim's Regress"*, *"C. S. Lewis"*, and several decorative touches on the design are in blue; "Sheed", "Ward", and nearly all of the design are in brown.)
Spine: (lettered in brown) *PILGRIM'S REGRESS* (vertically on spine)
Back panel: (advertisement) *The Visions of Piers Plowman /by /William Langland ... 8s. 6d. net/*(review from Times Literary Supplement)
Front flap: (publisher's blurb): (First published by J. M. Dent) The/allegory obviously suggests ... / ... in which the realm of/ controversy is altogether transcended./5s.net (price in lower right corner)
Back flap: (blank)

7. (First American edition) **THE PILGRIM'S REGRESS.**
New York: Sheed and Ward, 1935.
256 pp.   13.2 x 18.9 cm   Three different bindings have been noted, without evidence of precedence: orange cloth, with brown lettering on spine; rust-brown cloth with black lettering on spine; and maroon, with silver lettering on spine.

KEY TO THIS EDITION: Date at bottom of title page: **1935**

Front and back boards: (blank)
Spine: THE/PILGRIM'S/REGRESS/*(asterisk)/SHEED&WARD
Endpapers: Double-width MAPPA MUNDI in reddish-brown, as in first and second British editions, but with addition of "Printed in England" (in light gray) at the bottom right corner of the map.

The pagination of the American edition is the same as that of the British edition, with the following change:
Title page: (at bottom) NEW YORK/SHEED & WARD, INC./1935

Dust jacket:
Identical to that on the British first edition, but with price of $2.25 at bottom right of front flap, and with price of $3.00 net for The Visions of Piers Plowman advertised on the back panel.

8. New and revised third edition (British): **THE PILGRIM'S REGRESS.**
London: Geoffrey Bles, 1943.
199 pp.   12.7 x 18.9 cm   Dark green cloth
British war-time paper shortage made this edition much thinner, due to paper thickness and size, and reduction of type size.

KEY TO THIS EDITION: On back of title page:
First published in 1933/New and revised edition 1943

Front and back boards: (blank)
Spine: Paper label 2 x 3.5 cm: (Double-rule in green)/C. S. LEWIS (in black)/(Single rule in green)/
The/Pilgrim's/Regress(all in black)/(Double-rule in green)
Endpapers: (double-width MAPPA MUNDI, as in first edition, but in black – and only on front endpaper. Rear endpaper is blank.)

Besides a valuable Preface in which Lewis explains what he meant by Romanticism, he makes his story clearer still with the occasional footnote and running headlines on every page explaining exactly what the story is about. These running headlines take the place of the "Arguments" in the second edition by Sheed and Ward.

Page (1): THE PILGRIM'S REGRESS
Page (2): (blank)
Page (3): (TITLE PAGE) THE/PILGRIM'S REGRESS/An Allegorical Apology for Chistianity/Reason and Romanticism/by/ C. S. LEWIS/As cold waters to a thirsty soul/so is good news from a far country./ --Proverbs
Page (4): *First published in 1933/New and revised edition 1943*/To/ARTHUR GREEVES/PRINTED IN GREAT BRITAIN BY ROBERT MACLEHOSE AND CO. LTD./THE UNIVERSITY PRESS/GLASGOW
Pages 5-14: PREFACE TO THIRD EDITION
Pages 15-18: (Contents)
Pages 19-199: (text)

Dust jacket:
Front panel: THE PILGRIM'S/REGRESS (lettered in red)/ (knight on horse, as on first edition)/ C. S. LEWIS/ *Author of 'The Screwtape Letters'/* GEOFFREY BLES(lettered in red)
Spine: (single rule in red)/THE/PILGRIM'S/ REGRESS/by/C. S. LEWIS (lettered in black)/(single rule in red)/BLES (lettered in black)
Back panel: (Advertisements in black and red for): THE SCREWTAPE LETTERS, 12th large impression; THE PROBLEM OF PAIN, 12th large impression; Broadcast Talks, 2nd large impression; Christian Behaviour, 3rd large impression.

Because later printing dust jackets are often put on earlier books, one can detect the substitution by checking both the advertisements and the impression of each title. As will be noted later, this can be a particular problem with the dust jackets found on *Christian Behaviour,* where the publisher made a slight, and usually unnoticed, change in the blurb on the front flap, and continued to issue the first edition in the modified jacket.

Front flap: (a long blurb lettered in black): Through the dragons and giants … a new Preface./8s. 6d. net (price lettered in red)
Back flap: (blank)

9. (Second American edition) THE PILGRIM'S REGRESS.
New York: Sheed and Ward, 1944.
256 pp   12.7 x 18.9 cm   Brown-yellow cloth.

Not a true second edition, but merely a 1944 reprinting of the Sheed and Ward 1st edition of 1935, lacking the PREFACE and the running headlines of the Bles 3rd edition, while retaining the Arguments that Lewis despised.

KEY TO THIS EDITION: Date at bottom of title page: **1944**

Front and back boards: (blank)
Spine: (lettered in brown)

<u>Endpapers</u>: (double-width MAPPA MUNDI, as in first edition, but in black – and only on front endpaper. Rear endpaper is blank.)
<u>Title page</u>: (1944 date at bottom of page, with only "PRINTED IN THE UNITED STATES OF AMERICA/BY THE POLYGRAPHIC COMPANY OF AMERICA, N.Y." on the verso)

Dust jacket: Lettered throughout in black on yellow background, except for flaps, which are off-white
<u>Front panel</u>: *Pilgrim's/*RE *– gress/"A modern 'Pilgrim's Progress' with/much of the faery charm and troubl-/ing significance of the great original/*. . . IT IS POSSIBLE THAT/'PILGRIM'S REGRESS' IS LEWIS'/MASTERPIECE."/-- Vincent Starrett in *The Chicago Tribune./C. S. Lewis*
<u>Spine</u>: LEWIS(horizontally)/PILGRIM'S RE—GRESS (vertically)/SHEED/&/WARD (all horizontally)
<u>Back panel</u>: (advertisement for THE FLOWERING TREE – price $2.00 within a double-rule border)
<u>Front flap</u>: (publisher's blurb, summarizing the story)/$1.50 (with both corners clipped at a slight angle)
<u>Back flap</u>: (advertisement for GILBERT KEITH CHESTERTON, by Maisie Ward, price $3.00, also clipped at both corners)

10. THE ALLEGORY OF LOVE.

Oxford: The Clarendon Press, May 21, 1936.

378 pp.   14.8 cm x 22.5 cm.   Very dark blue cloth

KEY TO FIRST EDITION: Date at bottom of title page: **1936**

Front and back boards: (blank)
Spine: (lettered in gold) (gold single-rule/THE/ALLEGORY/OF/LOVE/LEWIS/(Oxford University crest)/OXFORD/(gold single-rule)
Endpapers: (blank off-white – followed by a blank page)
Page (i): THE ALLEGORY/OF LOVE
Page (ii): OXFORD UNIVERSITY PRESS/AMEN HOUSE, E.C. 4/London Edinburgh Glasgow New York/Toronto Melbourne Capetown Bombay/ Calcutta Madras/ HUMPHREY MILFORD/ PUBLISHER TO THE/ UNIVERSITY
Page (iii): (TITLE PAGE) THE ALLEGORY/OF LOVE/A STUDY IN MEDIEVAL TRADITION/BY/C. S. LEWIS, M.A./FELLOW OF MAGDALEN COLLEGE/ OXFORD/(Latin quotation) /OXFORD/AT THE CLARENDON PRESS/1936
Page (iv): PRINTED IN GREAT BRITAIN
Page (v): TO/ OWEN BARFIELD/ WISEST AND BEST/ OF MY/UNOFFICIAL/TEACHERS

Owen Barfield, with whom I was privileged to develop a friendship when he was in his early 90s, was born in 1898, the same year as Lewis, but outlived him by 36 years. They first met as students at Oxford University, becoming the closest of friends for the remainder of Lewis' life. In his biography, *Surprised by Joy*, Lewis writes of him: "There is a sense in which Arthur and Barfield are the types of every man's First Friend and Second Friend. The first is the *alter ego*, the man who first reveals to you that you are not alone in the world by turning out (beyond hope) to share all your most secret delights. There is nothing to be overcome in making him your friend; he and you join like raindrops on a window. But the Second Friend is the man who disagrees with you about everything. He is not so much the *alter ego* as the anti-self. Of course he shares your interests; otherwise he would not become your friend at all. But he has approached them all at a different angle. He has read all the right books but has got the wrong thing out of every one. It is as if he spoke your language but mispronounced it. How can he be so nearly right and yet, invariably, just not right? He is as fascinating (and infuriating) as a woman. When you set out to correct his heresies, you find he forsooth has decided to correct yours! And then you go at it, hammer and tongs, far into the night, night after night, or walking through fine country that neither gives a glance to, each learning the weight of the other's punches, and often more like mutually respectful enemies than friends. Actually (though it never seems so at the moment) you modify one another's thought; out of this perpetual dogfight a community of mind and a deep affection emerge. But I think he changed me a good deal more than I him. Much of the thought which he afterward put into *Poetic Diction* had already become mine before that important little book appeared. It would be strange if it had not. He was of course not so learned then as he has since become; but the genius was already there."

For a fascinating read, see *Owen Barfield on C. S. Lewis*, Wesleyan University Press, Middletown, Connecticut, 1989 (edited by G. B. Tennyson).

Page (vi): (blank)
Page (vii): PREFACE/It is to be hoped ... The
Page viii: PREFACE (cont'd))/untiring intellect of Mr. H. Dyson. ... C.S.L.
Page (ix): CONTENTS/I. COURTLY LOVE ... I/ ... INDEX ... 367
Page (x): (blank)

The copy from which this description was taken was that of R. W. Chapman, Lewis' editor at Oxford University Press, whose penciled initials, *RWC*, are on the front free endpaper. On the back pasted-down endpaper Chapman has listed, in pencil, pages on which typographical errors appear. Laid in at the back is an extensive review from *The Times Literary Supplement* of Saturday June 6, 1936, at the top of which is written in pencil: *Put in my copy – RWC.*

Also laid in is a one-page holograph letter from Lewis, in response to a letter from Chapman pointing out the typographical errors:

My dear Chapman, Thanks for both letters. After wondering whether the best reply to the "pinpricks" would not be "Ah, yes – that's the worst of depending on these local printers!", I accept them all except sheows which is Spenser's own spelling. I will also add two more, worse, p. 96 quotation l. 5 for ye read He. P. 331 5 lines before the first quotation for pictures read pictured. Yes – Cissie and Flossie do appear in Tasso and I trust it doesn't matter though I'd just as soon they didn't. But I don't mind about the lovely lay – it is just the sort of enervating Omar-Khayyam stuff you ought to find there. "Purifying complexities" – the next time you come across a real commercial pornogram in a French bookshop, read a page or two and note how it all depends on isolating one nerve in a way quite impossible in real life – in fact is just as conventional (tho' for a worse purpose) as roaring farce. Smoky rain is alright seasoned with sufficient usquebaugh see Waverly. yours, C. S. Lewis!

And a postscript: *Congratulations to the "local printer" on giving us a translation of Otto's Das Heilige at 3/6 – very nice.*

In 1938, Oxford University Press reprinted the first edition, with corrections.

Dust jacket:
The original dust jacket for this book is so rare that not until 2005, after more than 20 years of searching, was I able to find a copy in its original jacket. The key to the original jacket is the tiny date in brackets at the bottom of the back panel: **[5/36]** Early reprint jackets are of identical design, but may be identified as of later issue by reviews, later book advertisements, etc.

All lettering is in blue on cream-colored paper:

Front panel: THE ALLEGORY/OF LOVE/*A STUDY IN/MEDIEVAL TRADITION*/BY/C. S. LEWIS/(diamond decorative figure comprising 36 tiny filigrees)/OXFORD/AT THE CLARENDON PRESS
Spine: (decorative triangle comprising 22 filigrees) /THE /ALLEGORY/OF/LOVE/(tiny arrow-like figure)/LEWIS
The bottom of the spine is missing in the only example I have

ever seen. It undoubtedly had the name of the publisher.

Back panel: OXFORD BOOKS/(seven titles, from *THE ART OF POETRY* to *MODERN PROSE STYLE*)/OXFORD UNIVERSITY PRESS/[5/36] (The book was published on May 21, 1936.)

Front flap: (Publisher's blurb)

The *Romance of the Rose,* its ancestors and descendants, are here studied not as an obstacle to be surmounted on our way to Chaucer, but as a true expression of the ages which produced them. The allegorical form is found to be at once an imaginative bridge from mythical to reflective consciousness and a principal origin of romanticism; and the formalities of medieval love are seen in their true relation both to the Nineteenth Century theory of marriage and to our present discontents. Such an approach enables the author in his last chapter to restore *The Faerie Queene* to a position which it has not held since the age of Milton.

Back flap: OXFORD/UNIVERSITY PRESS/(ten international addresses/ HUMPHREY MILFORD/AMEN HOUSE/E.C.4

Since later dust jackets are often used to cover earlier editions, one should carefully examine suspect jackets for clues that may indicate their later state. Advertisements for books issued after the issue date of the book on which the jacket is found provide clear evidence of a replacement dust jacket, as do prices on unclipped jackets that are higher than the original issue price.

11. THE ALLEGORY OF LOVE.

London: Oxford University Press, 1938. The first edition, reprinted with corrections.

KEY TO THIS EDITION: On back of the half-title:
First published **1936**/*Reprinted, with corrections,* **1938**

The book is identical to the 1936 edition, with the following exceptions:

- Page (ii) (verso of the title page) has the following entry at the bottom of the page: *First published 1936/Reprinted, with corrections, 1938*
- Page (iii) (TITLE PAGE): The publisher is shown as: OXFORD UNIVERSITY PRESS/LONDON: HUMPHREY MILFORD and the 1936 date has been removed.
- Page (379) (identification of the printer): *Reprinted photographically in Great Britain in 1938/by LOWE & BRYDONE, PRINTERS, LONDON, from sheets/of the first edition*

12. OUT OF THE SILENT PLANET.
London: John Lane The Bodley Head, September 23, 1938.
264 pp + 4 pp of advertisements   13 cm x 19 cm   Mauve cloth.

KEY TO FIRST EDITION: On back of title page:
First published in 1938
and bound in purple-maroon cloth, with gold lettering on the spine
and the top-edge dyed the same color. (See my later note regarding
the reissued cheap edition.)

Front board: (blank)
Spine: (lettered in gold) OUT OF/THE SILENT/PLANET/ C. S.
LEWIS/THE/BODLEY/HEAD
Rear board: (blank)
Top edge of pages: (dyed mauve, same color as cloth)
Endpapers: (blank, off-white)
Page (i): (blank)
Page (ii): (blank)
Page (iii): OUT OF THE SILENT PLANET
Page (iv): (blank)
Page (v): (TITLE PAGE) OUT OF THE SILENT/PLANET/*by*/C. S.
LEWIS/LONDON/JOHN LANE THE BODLEY HEAD
Page (vi): *First published in 1938*/ Made and Printed in Great
Britain by/Butler & Tanner Ltd., Frome and London
Page (vii): TO MY BROTHER/W. H. L./a life-long critic of
the/space-and-time story

Warren Hamilton Lewis – 1895-1973 – "Warnie" to his younger
brother Jack. The two brothers became and remained the rest of their
lives the best of friends. He served in France, as did Jack, during the
First World War, and remained in the Royal Army Service Corps,
serving in Sierra Leone, West Africa, and in China. In 1930, when
standing before the Great Buddha of Kamakura, he became
convinced of the truth of Christianity. In his diary on May 13, 1931
he wrote: "I started to say my prayers again after having
discontinued doing so for more years than I care to remember. ...
The wheel has now made the full revolution – indifference,
scepticism, atheism, agnosticism, and back again to Christianity."

(*Brothers and Friends: The Diaries of Major Warren Hamilton Lewis,* 1982)

Recalled to active duty during World War II, he was sent to France again in 1939 but was evacuated at Dunkirk the following year and transferred to the Reserves. The brothers lived together at The Kilns in Headington Quarry, Oxford, where in 1943 Warnie became Jack's secretary. Jack was by then receiving large quantities of mail from his admirers as the result of the success of *The Screwtape Letters*, but he never learned to use the typewriter, so Warnie typed most of his letters. The brothers were so frugal that many of these letters were typed on the thin paper used for carbon copies – as many as 3 or 4 brief replies to a page, which was then torn into strips for mailing. Along with a number of such letters in my collection, I also have several envelopes that further reflect their frugality – from incoming mail, on which their name and address was crossed out and the new recipient's name and address written in, and a new stamp affixed.

(Warnie was a successful writer in his own right, with a number of volumes on French history.)

Page (viii): (blank)
Page ix: NOTE/*Certain slighting references ... his debt to them* /*C.S.L.*
Page (x): (blank)
Page (xi): OUT OF THE SILENT PLANET (a second half-title)
Page (xii): (blank)
Pages 1 through 264: (text)
Pages (265-268): (4 pages of advertisements) a selection from/THE BODLEY HEAD/*fiction list*/(solid rule, thicker in the middle)/MARJORIE BOWEN (4 titles) ... BEN TRAVERS (6 titles)/*John Lane The Bodley Head Ltd/8 Bury Place London WC1*

Dust jacket: The most striking (and one of the rarest) of all Lewis first edition dust jackets, by Harold Jones.
<u>Front panel and spine</u>: (See illustration on page 45)
<u>Back panel</u>: (Lettered in black in a double-rule rectangle, 8 cm x 11.7) *New and Forthcoming/ FICTION/* (6 books) PROMENADE/G. B. Lancaster ... DOWN MANGEL STREET /Mabel Constanduros/ THE BODLEY HEAD
<u>Front flap</u>: (lettered in black) THIS is the story of a voyage to another planet ... Mr. Lewis, in a word, has written a remarkable first novel./(lettered in purple) *Jacket by Harold Jones*/(in large black letters) 7s 6d net
<u>Back flap</u>: (blank)

With the publication of *Out of the Silent Planet* Lewis found that he could incorporate Christian theology in fiction in a way that might almost be described as subliminal. His biographer, George Sayer, wrote: "*Out of the Silent Planet* initially received about sixty reviews, quite a large number for a book by a little-known writer. Only two reviewers showed any awareness of the book's Christian theology. It was typically regarded as just science fiction. ... The reviewers' failure to see the point of the book gave Jack the idea that would be basic to all his children's stories: 'If there was only someone with a richer talent and more leisure I think that this great ignorance might be a help to the evangelisation of England; any amount of theology can now be smuggled into people's minds under cover of romance without their knowing it.'"

The book did not sell well, but was re-issued in 1940 as "The First Cheap Edition" in a different binding with a price of 3s 6d. The binding was rose-red cloth instead of mauve, with the same style lettering on the spine as the first edition, but in black instead of gold. I recently learned from an old Blackwell employee that the cheaper edition was printed in 1940 by Basil Blackwell from Lane plates, something done commonly by Blackwell during the war, but with the top-edge not dyed.

The original Harold Jones jacket was used, with the original price of 7s. 6d. clipped by the publisher, removing a large triangular piece from the lower right corner. Overprinted in red, immediately below the publisher's blurb on the front flap, is: RECOMMENDED BY/THE BOOK SOCIETY. Also overprinted in red, below the original last line on the flap, *Jacket by Harold Jones*, is: FIRST CHEAP EDITION/3s 6d net.

In 1943, the book was again reissued, in light blue cloth and black lettering on the spine, with *Reprinted* 1943 added beneath *First published in* 1938 on the verso of the title page.

13. (First American edition) **OUT OF THE SILENT PLANET.**
New York: Macmillan, September 28, 1943.
174 pp   14.4 cm x 20.8 cm   Medium bright blue cloth

KEY TO FIRST EDITION: Date at bottom of title page: **1943** (see note at end of description)

Front board: (blank)
Spine: (lettered in yellow) OUT OF/THE SILENT/PLANET/C. S. LEWIS/MACMILLAN/ (dash-dot-dash) (see below)
Rear board: (blank)
Endpapers: (blank, off-white)
Page (i): OUT OF THE/SILENT PLANET
Page (ii): (Macmillan logo and locations world-wide)
Page (iii): (TITLE PAGE) OUT OF THE/SILENT PLANET/By C. S. LEWIS/NEW YORK/THE MACMILLAN COMPANY/1943
Page (iv): *All rights reserved*/PRINTED IN THE UNITED STATES OF AMERICA
Page (v): *To*/MY BROTHER W.H.L./*a life-long critic of the time-and-space story*
Page (vi): NOTE: Certain slighting references ... his debt to them./C.S.L.
Page (vii): OUT OF THE SILENT PLANET (a second half title)
Page (viii): (blank)
Pages 1 through 174: (text pages)
Pages (175-176): (blank)

Dust jacket:
Front panel: (purple background, with greenish-blue ¼" band top and bottom) (greenish blue planet, with ring, surrounded by 6 white stars)/*Out of/the Silent/Planet* (lettered in white)/A NOVEL by/C. S. LEWIS (lettered in greenish-blue)
Spine: (lettered in purple on greenish-blue background) C.S. LEWIS /*Out of the Silent Planet*/ MACMILLAN (all parallel to spine)
Back panel: *Also by C. S. Lewis*/THE SCREWTAPE LETTERS/"This admirable ... bleak sky of satire" – LEONARD BACON in the *Saturday Review of Literature*
Front flap: (lettered in purple on white) (price of $2.00 in upper right corner) (publisher's blurb): OUT OF THE/SILENT PLANET /... from the Malacandran point of view.
Back flap: (formal full-face photograph of Lewis in purple, 5 cm x 5.3 cm/C. S. LEWIS/(short biographical sketch) (This was the first photo of Lewis to appear on a dust jacket.)

The only indication that this is the first American edition of *Out of the Silent Planet* is the 1943 date on the title page, with only *Copyright 1943* on the verso. The 1944 reprint, identical to the first edition except for the 1944 date on the title page, is frequently offered as a first edition by uninformed dealers. With the publication of *Perelandra* in 1944, Macmillan added the words *First printing* to the verso of its title page. While all copies I have seen are lettered in yellow on the spine, I have recently seen a copy with the 1943 date lettered in white, with a single round dot beneath "Macmillan" on the spine; all the other copies I've seen (all lettered in yellow) have a dash-dot-dash embellishment below the name, with a square dot. I have always assumed that those with yellow lettering were the first printing of the first edition. Whether those with the white lettering on the spine preceded or followed it, I am not prepared to say, nor have I a clue as to the significance of the single white dot – and would welcome any input!

14. REHABILITATIONS *AND OTHER ESSAYS.*

London: Oxford University Press, March 23, 1939.
197 pp.   14.7 cm x 22 cm   Black cloth.

<u>KEY TO FIRST EDITION</u>: Date at bottom of title page: **1939**

<u>Front board</u>: (blank)
<u>Spine</u>: (lettered in gold) LEWIS (parallel to top of
spine)/REHABILITATIONS *AND OTHER ESSAYS/* OXFORD
(parallel to bottom of spine)
<u>Rear board</u>: (blank)
<u>Endpapers</u>: (blank, off-white)
<u>Page (0)</u>: (blank)
<u>Page (0)</u>: (blank)
<u>Page (i)</u>: REHABILITATIONS/*and other Essays*
<u>Page (ii)</u>: *By the same Author*/CRITICAL/*THE ALLEGORY OF
LOVE/* Clarendon Press, 15s./ IMAGINATIVE/*THE PILGRIM'S
REGRESS/*
Sheed and Ward, 5s./*OUT OF THE SILENT PLANET*/John Lane,
The Bodley Head, 7s. 6d.
<u>Page (iii)</u>: (title page)REHABILITATIONS/*AND OTHER ESSAYS/*
BY/ C. S. LEWIS/ FELLOW OF MAGDALEN COLLEGE/
OXFORD/OXFORD UNIVERSITY PRESS/*LONDON NEW YORK
TORONTO*/1939
<u>Page (iv)</u>: OXFORD UNIVERSITY PRESS/AMEN HOUSE, E.C.
4/*London   Edinburgh   Glasgow   New   York*/*Toronto   Melbourne
Capetown   Bombay*/ *Calcutta   Madras*/HUMPHREY   MILFORD
/PUBLISHER TO THE UNIVERSITY/ PRINTED IN GREAT
BRITAIN
<u>Page (v)</u>: *To*/HUGO DYSON

Hugo Dyson was Lecturer and Tutor in English at Reading
University from 1921-1925, and a Fellow of Merton College,
Oxford from 1945-1963. He was instrumental in Lewis's conversion
to Christianity, and later an active member of the Inklings – the
group of Oxford friends, centered on Lewis, who met regularly from
1930 to 1963 to talk and to read aloud what they were writing. For a
fascinating account of these friends, see *The Inklings* by Humphrey
Carpenter, 1978.

Page (vi): (blank)
Page (vii): PREFACE/A MAN is seldom ... In spite of the/(footnote)
Page viii: (PREFACE continued)
Page (ix): CONTENTS/I ... IX ...
Page (x): (blank)
Pages (1) through 197: (text pages) (first page of text has printer's letter B at the bottom)
Page (198): PRINTED IN/GREAT BRITAIN/AT THE / UNIVERSITY PRESS/OXFORD/BY/JOHN JOHNSON /PRINTER/TO THE/UNIVERSITY
Dust jacket:
Front panel: (lettered in black on tan paper) C. S. LEWIS/(double rule)/ REHABILITATIONS/*and other Essays* (at an angle from lower left to upper right)/(double rule)/OXFORD UNIVERSITY PRESS
Spine: (vertically, from bottom to top) REHABILITATIONS : LEWIS
Back panel: *BY THE SAME AUTHOR*/THE ALLEGORY OF LOVE/ 15s. net/(3 reviews)/(double rule)/ *OTHER OXFORD BOOKS*/(3 titles)/ *OXFORD UNIVERSITY PRESS*
Front flap: (publisher's blurb) MR. LEWIS'S name will be will be remembered ... should attract many readers./(dotted slanted line for price-clipping)/Price/7s. 6d. net
Back flap: (blank)
The copy from which the above description was taken is from the library of English poet Ruth Pitter, CBE, the first woman to receive the Queen's Gold Medal for Poetry. She became a Christian through listening to Lewis' BBC talks on theology during World War II, and later wrote to him to ask if they could meet. He had already become fond of her poetry, and was therefore pleased to make her acquaintance. They became friends, and she visited often at The Kilns, the Lewis brothers' home in Headington. After one such visit, Lewis remarked that if he were not a confirmed bachelor, Ruth Pitter would be his choice for a wife.

On the front free endpaper she has written:
Moderate, just & lively
Values
Talked about. Effects.

Mr E = N. E consc. Bones.
C. S's suggestions.
Other kinds than lyric
Canon F's own

The essays include "Shelley, Dryden, and Mr. Eliot," "William Morris," "The Idea of an 'English School,'" "Our English Syllabus," "High and Low Brows," "The Alliterative Metre," "Bluspels and Flalansferes: A Semantic Nightmare," "Variation in Shakespeare and Others," and "Christianity and Literature."

There was no American first edition.

15. THE PERSONAL HERESY: A CONTROVERSY.

(With E. M. W. Tillyard)
London: Oxford University Press, April 27, 1939
150 pp.   14.6 cm x 22 cm   Dark green cloth

KEY TO FIRST EDITION: Date on the title page: **1939**

Front board: (blank)
Spine: (lettered horizontally in gold) TILLYARD — THE
PERSONAL HERESY: A CONTROVERSY – LEWIS
Rear board: (blank)
Endpapers: (blank, off-white)
Page (i): THE/PERSONAL HERESY/*A CONTROVERSY*
Page (ii): (blank)
Page (iii): (title page) THE/PERSONAL HERESY/*A
CONTROVERSY*/BY/E. M. W. TILLYARD/*Fellow of Jesus
College, Cambridge*/AND/C. S. LEWIS/*Fellow of Magdalen
College, Oxford*/
OXFORD UNIVERSITY PRESS/LONDON NEW YORK
TORONTO/1939
Page (iv): OXFORD UNIVERSITY PRESS/AMEN HOUSE, E.C.
4/London Edinburgh Glasgow New York/Toronto Melbourne
Capetown Bombay/Calcutta Madras/HUMPHREY MILFORD
/PUBLISHER TO THE UNIVERSITY/PRINTED IN GREAT
BRITAIN
Page (v): PREFACE/The authors would like … The readers of this
book cannot
Page vi: PREFACE(continued)/fall into that error … of *Essays and
Studies*/E.M.W.T./C.S.L.
Page (vii): CONTENTS/THE PERSONAL HERESY /I ...VI ...
/NOTE: *By* C.S.L.
Page (viii): (blank)
Pages (1) through 150: (text pages)
Page (151): PRINTED IN/GREAT BRITAIN/AT THE
/UNIVERSITY PRESS/OXFORD/BY/JOHN JOHNSON
/PRINTER/TO THE/UNIVERSITY

Dust jacket:

Front panel: E. M. W. TILLYARD/(single rule)/ THE/PERSONAL/
HERESY/(single rule)/C. S. LEWIS
Spine: THE/PERSONAL/HERESY/(single rule)/TILLYARD
/AND/LEWIS
Back panel: RECENT OXFORD BOOKS/ (five titles, from
MODERN POETRY to THE TRIPLE THINKERS/OXFORD
UNIVERSITY PRESS
Front flap: (publisher's blurb) It is seldom ... for having done so.
Back flap: (blank)

In his book, *Milton*, Tillyard complained that such matters as style
"have concerned the critics far more than what the poem is really
about, the true state of Milton's mind when he wrote it." Lewis
dubbed such criticism "The Personal Heresy." In this book Tillyard
and Lewis dispute the matter of the relation of the poet to his work.

There was no American first edition.

16. THE PROBLEM OF PAIN.

London: The Centenary Press, October 18, 1940.
148 pp   12.7 cm x 19 cm   Black cloth

KEY TO FIRST EDITION: Date at bottom of title page: MCMXL

Front board: (blank)
Spine: (on white paper label, 2 cm x 4.5 cm, lettered in black):
(triple rule in green)/*The/Christian/Challenge/Series*/(short single-rule in green)/THE/PROBLEM/OF/PAIN /(short single-rule in green)/C. S. LEWIS/(triple-rule in green)
Rear board: (blank)
Endpapers: (blank, off-white)
Page (i): *The Christian Challenge Series*/THE PROBLEM OF PAIN
Page (ii): *By the same Author*/THE PILGRIM'S REGRESS/OUT OF THE SILENT PLANET
Page (iii): (title page) THE PROBLEM OF PAIN/*by*/C. S. LEWIS, M.A./ *Fellow of Magdalen College, Oxford*/THE CENTENARY PRESS/37 ESSEX STREET, STRAND, LONDON/MCMXL
Page (iv): (George MacDonald quotation)/PRINTED IN GREAT BRITAIN BY THE WHITEFRIARS PRESS LTD./LONDON AND TONBRIDGE
Page (v): TO/THE INKLINGS
Page (vi): (blank)
Page vii and viii: PREFACE
Page ix: CONTENTS
Page (x): (blank)
Pages 1 through 145: (text pages)
Page (146): (blank)
Pages 147-148: (index)

Dust jacket:
Front panel: (red lettering on off-white background) THE PROBLEM/ OF PAIN/C. S. LEWIS. M.A./(off-white lettering on red background) THE/CHRISTIAN/CHALLENGE/SERIES
Spine: (red lettering on off-white background) THE/PROBLEM/OF PAIN/C. S. LEWIS/M.A./(off-white lettering on red background) THE/CHRISTIAN/CHALLENGE/SERIES/(red lettering on off-white background)/THE/CENTENARY/PRESS

: THE OPINIONS OF THREE EMINENT PEOPLE
/(reviews of three people and one newspaper)
Front flap: (publisher's blurb) (Price of *3s. 6d. net* in lower right
corner, with a faint red slanted dotted line for price-clipping)
Back flap: *Christian Challenge Series*/(list of 23 titles and authors in
the series)

In a first edition of *The Problem of Pain,* acquired from Owen
Barfield some years ago, is the following letter, on Magdalen
College stationery, that accompanied the book sent to him two days
before its release on October 18, 1940: *Oct 16ᵗʰ 1940 My dear
Barfield, A book on this subject from me at Oxford (wh. continues to
be Gideon's fleece) to you in the front line seems rather impertinent.
When wd. you like a few quiet nights here? Do come and spend one
or two. You are daily in my thoughts. Yours, C. S. Lewis* (This was
during the Battle of Britain, when London was being bombed
nightly by the Germans.)

Barfield had pasted the letter to the front pasted-down endpaper, but
only at the bottom of the letter, rather than the top, so that the
following notes written by him on the back of the letter could be
read:
*Either redemption is better than innocence or the Parable of the
Prodigal Son is sentimental bilge. Obedience, as an element in
response, varies directly with the extent to which the response is
either (a) mechanical or (b) contrary to inclination and first
judgment. Therefore, (i) never an end in itself (ii) an unsatisfactory
trope for the unique response of created to creator.*

Barfield's penciled notes appear throughout the book.

17. (First American edition) **THE PROBLEM OF PAIN.**
New York:Macmillan, October 26, 1943.
148 pp. 13.5 cm x 19.5 cm Green cloth

KEY TO FIRST EDITION: On title page: **1943**
(with no copyright date on the back)

Front board: (blank)
Spine: (double rule)/(vertical from top to bottom) LEWIS THE
PROBLEM OF PAIN/MACMILLAN/(double rule)
Rear board: (blank)
Endpapers: (blank, off-white)
Page (i): *The Problem of Pain*
Page (ii): *By the same author*/The Pilgrim's Regress/Out of the
Silent Planet/The Screwtape Letters
Page (iii): (title page) THE PROBLEM OF PAIN/by/C. S. LEWIS,
M.A./ *Fellow of Magdalen College*/NEW YORK/THE
MACMILLAN COMPANY/ 1943
Page (iv): *All Rights Reserved*/PRINTED IN THE UNITED
STATES OF AMERICA
Page (v): TO/THE INKLINGS
Page (vi): (a George MacDonald quotation)
Pages (vii)and (viii): PREFACE
Page (ix): CONTENTS/(chapters I through X, plus Appendix)
Page (x): (blank)
Pages 1 through 148): (text pages plus index plus one blank sheet)

Dust jacket: (lettered in dark green on very light green throughout)
Front panel: *THE*/PROBLEM/OF PAIN/*By*/C. S. LEWIS/*Fellow of
Magdalen College Oxford*/Author of "The Screwtape Letters"/(in a
box) "This book cannot fail to be a landmark in the lives of many."
The Hibbert Journal
Spine: THE/PROB-/LEM/OF/PAIN/Lewis/MACMILLAN
Back panel: THE PROBLEM OF PAIN/by/ C. S. LEWIS/ (four
reviews)/ THE MACMILLAN COMPANY Publishers
Front flap: (publisher's blurb)/$1.50 (on right edge)

<u>Back flap</u>: C. S. LEWIS/(diamond)/Clive Staples Lewis is the author of a number of books: "Out of the Silent Planet." "The Screwtape Letters," "The Problem of Pain," "The Case for Christianity," and many others. Mr. Lewis was a Second Lieutenant with the Somerset Light Infantry during the First World War. He was lecturer at University College, Oxford, 1924; Gollancz Memorial Prizeman, 1937; and he is at present Fellow and Tutor of Maddalen College, Oxford./(star figure)

18. THE SCREWTAPE LETTERS.
London: Geoffrey Bles, February 9, 1942
160 pp   12.8 cm x 19 cm   Black cloth

KEY TO FIRST EDITION: On back of title page:
FIRST PUBLISHED 1942

Front board: (blank)Spine: (on white paper label, 1.5 cm x 3.2 cm, lettered in black): (double-rule in green)/C. S. LEWIS/(single-rule in green)/*The/Screwtape/Letters/*(double-rule in green)
Rear board: (blank)
Endpapers: (blank, off-white)
Page (1): THE SCREWTAPE LETTERS
Page (2): *BY THE SAME AUTHOR*/THE PILGRIM'S REGRESS /OUT OF THE SILENT PLANET/THE PROBLEM OF PAIN
Page (3): (title page) THE/SCREWTAPE LETTERS/*by*/C. S. LEWIS/ *Fellow of Magdalen College, Oxford*/GEOFFREY BLES, 37 ESSEX STREET, STRAND,/LONDON
Page (4): *Reprinted with some alterations by kind/permission of "The Guardian"*/ALL RIGHTS RESERVED/FIRST PUBLISHED 1942/PRINTED IN GREAT BRITAIN/BY UNWIN BROTHERS LIMITED/WOKING
Page (5): TO/J. R. R. TOLKIEN
Page (6): (blank)
Page (7): (quotations from Luther and Thomas More)
Page (8): (blank)
Pages 9 and 10: PREFACE
Pages 11 to 160: (text)

Dust jacket:
The cheap papers used for dust jackets in England during World War II were subject to marked color change over the years. Very rarely does one see a Screwtape dust jacket these days in its original white color. Twenty years ago, after acquiring a number of first editions of this book in dust jackets, I assumed the original color of the paper was light tan or cream, until I came across a mint copy in a very white jacket at the home of Peter Jolliffe, from whom many of my Lewis first editions were acquired – and I have not seen one like it since that time.

The jacket is lettered in black throughout.

Front panel: (entire panel is within a red double-ruled border) *THE/SCREWTAPE LETTERS*/By/C. S. LEWIS/Fellow of Magdalen College, Oxford/(within a single-rule red border) A new book by the author of "THE PROBLEM OF PAIN" one of the most widely read and discussed books of recent years./GEOFFREY BLES : THE CENTENARY PRESS

Spine: THE/SCREW-/TAPE/LETTERS/C. S. LEWIS /THE /CENTENARY/PRESS

Back panel: THE CHRISTIAN CHALLENGE SERIES/Edited by ASHLEY SAMPSON/(single rule)/(advertisement for two books – THE PROBLEM OF PAIN – Sixth large edition – 3s. 6d. net and THE MASTERY OF EVIL by Roger Lloyd – 3s. 6d. net)/(single rule)/GEOFFREY BLES : THE CENTENARY PRESS/37 Essex Street, Strand, London

Front flap: (publisher's blurb) THE SCREWTAPE LETTERS/A new book ...

some practical hints about strategy./(in lower right corner, with diagonal dash line for price clipping) 5s. net

Back flap: (blank)

The Screwtape Letters, originally published serially in *The Guardian*, a religious magazine, comprise 31 letters on temptation from Screwtape, an elderly devil in Hell's civil service, to his nephew Wormwood, whose "patient" is a young Englishman recently converted to Christianity. Because of war-time limitation on paper usage and the enormous popularity of the book, it was reprinted many times – 8 times in 1942 alone. Like *The Problem of Pain*. the publisher has carefully identified every reprinting by month and year on the verso of the title page, and by the number of the edition at the top of the front flap of the jacket, in red: e.g., *Tenth Edition.*

One of my most unusual acquisitions was a copy of the first edition presented by Lewis to John Arlott, a former police detective who in 1946 joined the staff of the BBC, where as a cricket commentator on radio and television he became one of the country's most recognizable voices. This is possibly the most unusual presentation copy given by Lewis of any of his books, given the amount of Lewis handwriting appearing on both front and back endpapers. Filling the entire front pasted-down endpaper is the complete handwritten text of a Lewis poem, *Experiment,* published earlier in *The Spectator* of December 9, 1938, but titled herein, *Metrical Experiment,* with the initials *C.S.L.* at the end. Opposite, on the free endpaper, is Lewis' signature, followed by an asterisk, with the footnote, *I never could develop a nice grown-up "signature" so I just have to write my name like any other word.* Between the signature and footnote is a short four-line poem: *This first edition*

> *Is full of printer's errors:*
> *Aptly it mirrors*
> *Man's first condition.*

Opposite page 160, on the free endpaper, Lewis wrote: *I tried v. hard to get hold of the letters on the other side – from the archangel to the guardian angel. But the only bit that ever came through didn't make much sense. It was "The children continued instructing their Bears in the bend of the great river."* I have yet to find a Lewis scholar who can interpret that cryptic sentence!

19. (First American edition) **THE SCREWTAPE LETTERS.**
New York: Macmillan, February 16, 1943
160 pp.   14 cm x 21 cm   Red cloth

KEY TO FIRST EDITION: On title page: **1943**

Front board: (blank)
Spine: (black lettering) THE/SCREW-/TAPE/LETTERS/(double rule)/LEWIS/MACMILLAN
Rear board: (blank)
Endpapers: (blank, off-white)
Page (1): THE SCREWTAPE LETTERS
Page (2): *BY THE SAME AUTHOR*/THE PILGRIM'S REGRESS /OUT OF THE SILENT PLANET/THE PROBLEM OF PAIN
Page (3): (title page)THE/SCREWTAPE LETTERS/by/C. S. LEWIS/ Fellow of Magdalen College, Oxford/NEW YORK/THE MACMILLAN COMPANY/1943

Page (4): *Reprinted with some alterations by kind/permission of "The Guardian"*/ALL RIGHTS RESERVED/PRINTED IN THE UNITED STATES OF AMERICA
Page (5): TO/J. R. R. TOLKIEN
Page (6): (blank)
Page (7): (quotations from Martin Luther and Thomas More)
Page (8): (blank)
Pages 9 & 10: PREFACE
Page (x):
Pages 11 through 160: (text)

Dust jacket: (Black lettering on gray background – which may be darkened by age so that it looks tan – with all borders in red)
Front panel: *THE*/ SCREWTAPE LETTERS/*By*/ C. S. LEWIS/ *Fellow of Magdalen College, Oxford*/(in single rule border) These brilliant, challenging letters from an elder devil in hell to his junior on earth are the most vital and original restatement of religious truths produced in our times – a profound, hard-hitting, provoking, yet truly reverent book.
Spine: (double-rule)/THE/SCREW-/TAPE/LETTERS/C. S. LEWIS/MACMILLAN
Back panel: (in double-rule border) *THE*/SCREWTAPE LETTERS/*By* C. S. LEWIS/*Fellow of Magdalen College, Oxford; author of*/"*The Problem of Pain," "The Pilgrim's Regress,"*/"*Out of the Silent Planet," and other books.*/This extraordinary book … should become a classic.
Front flap: Comments/on/THE SCREWTAPE LETTERS /(comments by Dr. George A. Buttrick, *Expository Times*, and W. J. Turner in *The Spectator*) (Price of $1.50 on front edge of lower part of flap, corners of which are clipped top and bottom.)
Back flap:(comments from *Times Literary Supplement, Glasgow Herald*, and *Huddersfield Examiner*)

20. A PREFACE TO PARADISE LOST.
London: Oxford University Press, October 8, 1942
139 pp. 13 cm x 18.3 cm Dark green cloth

KEY TO FIRST EDITION: Bottom of title page: **1942**

Front board: (blank)
Spine: (lettered in gold) LEWIS (parallel to top of spine)/A
PREFACE TO PARADISE LOST (horizontally)/OXFORD (parallel
to bottom of spine)
Rear board: (blank)
Endpapers: (blank, off-white)
Page (i): A PREFACE TO PARADISE LOST
Page (ii): (blank)
Page (iii): (title page) A PREFACE TO/PARADISE LOST/(single
rule)/*Being the Ballard Matthews Lectures/Delivered at University
College, North Wales, 1941/by* C. S. LEWIS, M.A./*Fellow of
Magdalen College, Oxford*/OXFORD UNIVERSITY
PRESS/LONDON : NEW YORK : TORONTO/1942
Page (iv): OXFORD UNIVERSITY PRESS/AMEN HOUSE, E.C.
4/London Edinburgh Glasgow New York/Toronto Melbourne
Capetown Bombay/ Calcutta Madras/HUMPHREY
MILFORD/Publisher to the University/ *Printed in Great Britain*
Page v: DEDICATION/*To* CHARLES WILLIAMS/Dear
Williams,/When I remember ... /... to trust my own (continued on
next page)/(footnote): *The Poetical Works of Milton.* The World's
Classics, 1940.
Page vi: ... eyes. Apparently, the door ... can all come out ./Yours,
/C. S. LEWIS
Page vii: CONTENTS/(Dedication + 9 chapters + Appendix +
Index)
Page viii: (2 quotations, from Tasso and Browne)
Pages 1 through 136: (text)
Pages 137-139: (index)
(Note Lewis's humorous entry under R: *Rabbit, Peter*)
Page (140): THIS BOOK IS PRODUCED IN COMPLETE
CONFORMITY/ WITH THE AUTHORIZED ECONOMY
/STANDARDS/PRINTED AT THE BROADWATER PRESS
/WELWYN/HERTS

Two different printings of the first edition have been found, but are not so identified by the publisher. The boards are identical, but one of these printings is 0.9 cm thick (including the boards), whereas the other is 1.3 cm thick, the difference being due to the use of cheaper, thinner paper in the former. It may therefore be presumed that the thinner one is the earlier wartime edition, since the jacket on the thicker printing has on its back panel an advertisement for *ARTHURIAN TORSO*, which was not published until 1948. The jacket on the earlier printing is that described as follows, with additional notes indicating differences that appear on the later jacket.

Dust jacket:
Front panel: (in a white-and-olive green double-rule border) (white lettering on an olive-green background) A/PREFACE/TO /PARADISE /LOST/(olive-green lettering on white background) *by* C. S. LEWIS/ Author of *The Problem of Pain* and *The Screwtape Letters*/OXFORD UNIVERSITY PRESS
Spine: (in a horizontal line from bottom to top, in white lettering on an olive-green background, except for OXFORD, which is olive-green lettering on a white background, and is parallel to the bottom of the spine) *Lewis*   OXFORD   A PREFACE TO PARADISE LOST
Back panel: (olive-green lettering on white background, in a double-rule box) JOHN MILTON/(single rule)/ THE POEMS OF JOHN MILTON/ (followed by three other Milton titles)/(single rule) /OXFORD UNIVERSITY PRESS
(The later jacket, however, lists three Lewis titles – THE ALLEGORY OF LOVE, REHABILITATIONS, and ARTHURIAN TORSO – this last title having been published in 1948.)
Front flap: (publisher's blurb in 18 lines in olive-green lettering on white background): This book is called a Preface because its main purpose is to remove those obstacles to the enjoyment of *Paradise Lost* which have recently been accumulating. It is therefore much concerned with preliminaries – with the possibility of criticism, the nature of epic, the theology and pneumatology of the poem, and above all, the Hierarchical Principal. As regards the content of *Paradise Lost*, the author has found it his chief duty to encourage

simplicity and restore the belief that Milton may, after all, have hated what he displays as hateful. The defence of its form resolves itself into a plea that ritual, and splendour, and joy itself, have a right to exist.

The price is bottom right, in olive-green lettering, with large "7" and "6": Price/7*s*. 6*d*. *net*. The price on the later jacket is also bottom right and the same 7s. 6d. net, but is printed diagonally in small print. Above the price, under a slanted dotted line for price-cutting, the title and author are also shown.)

Back flap: *By the same Author*/THE ALLEGORY OF LOVE/15*s*. *net*/ (followed by REHABILITATIONS at 7s. 6d. net and THE PERSONAL HERESY at 6s. net)

There was no American first edition.

21. BROADCAST TALKS.

London: Geoffrey Bles: The Centenary Press, July 13, 1942
62 pp. 13 cm x 18.8 cm Coarsely-woven off-white cloth

KEY TO FIRST EDITION: Back of title page:
First Published July 1942

Front board: (lettered in red): (single-rule)/BROADCAST TALKS
/by/C. S. LEWIS/(single-rule)
Spine: (blank)
Rear board: (blank)
Endpapers: The off-white pasted-down endpapers are blank, and due to wartime paper shortage, the book was bound without free endpapers and a half-title. Because the title page and the last page were directly in contact with the pasted-down endpapers, most copies of the first edition have a strip of browning (usually referred to as "offsetting" by British dealers) on these two pages – a condition frequently seen on the free endpapers of other British books – presumably due to chemical reaction with the adhesive use on the endpapers. Because the flaps of the dust jacket interfere with this reaction, the browned areas are usually limited to the portion of the page that was not protected by the dust jacket flap. If the flap was price-clipped, the browning outlines the clipped edge.

Because of the very low-quality paper used in the first edition of *Broadcast Talks*, this condition is found in most copies of the book. Moreover, the browning often extends into the first and last several pages. Only rarely, therefore, does one see a truly fine first edition of this book.

Page (3): (title page) BROADCAST TALKS/Reprinted with some alterations from two series/of Broadcast Talks (*Right and Wrong: A Clue to/the Meaning of the Universe* and *What Christians/Believe*) given in 1941 and 1942/by/C. S. LEWIS/Fellow of Magdalen College, Oxford/GEOFFREY BLES: THE CENTENARY PRESS/37 ESSEX STREET, STRAND, LONDON

It appears that the publisher decided to eliminate the free endpapers and the half-title *after* the book was printed, so that there is no page 1 or 2.

Page (4): *First Published July 1942/*PRINTED IN GREAT BRITAIN BY J. AND J. GRAY, EDINBURGH

Page 5): (single-rule) Preface (single-rule)/I GAVE these talks … what might be called philosophy./C. S. LEWIS/MAGDALEN COLLEGE,/6*TH* April 1942.

Page (6): (single-rule) *Contents* (single-rule)/PART I ... PART II ...

Page (7): (single-rule) *Part I* (single-rule)/RIGHT AND WRONG AS A CLUE TO/THE MEANING OF THE UNIVERSE

Page (8): (blank)

Pages 9 through 62: (text)

Dust jacket: (lettered in red)

Front panel: (double-rule)/BROADCAST TALKS/Reprinted with alterations from two series:/*Right and Wrong: A Clue to the Meaning of the Universe/*and/*What Christians Believe/*by/C. S. LEWIS/*author of 'The Problem of Pain'* & *'The Screwtape Letters'/*(double-rule)

Spine: BROADCAST TALKS by C. S. LEWIS

Back panel: (advertisements) THE PROBLEM OF PAIN ... Seventh large edition. 3s. 6d. net/THE SCREWTAPE LETTERS ... Fifth large edition. 5s. net

Front flap: (Publisher's blurb)/2s. 6d. net

Back flap: (blank)

22. (First American edition of *Broadcast Talks*)
THE CASE FOR CHRISTIANITY.
New York: Macmillan, September 7, 1943
56 pp. 13 cm x 18.5 cm

Two different bindings have been noted – one in tan cloth with red lettering on the spine; the other in olive-green cloth also with red lettering on the spine. Although precedence of one over the other is not clear, the latter one may be a later printing, the copy seen having had a later dust jacket, identical to that described as follows, but printed in blue on gray and with a price of $1.25, rather than $1.00.

KEY TO FIRST EDITION: Back of title page: **First Printing**

Front board: (blank)
Spine: (lettered in red, vertically from top to bottom) LEWIS   THE
CASE FOR CHRISTIANITY   Macmillan
Rear board: (blank)
Endpapers: (blank, off-white)
Page (i): THE CASE FOR CHRISTIANITY
Page (ii): (Macmillan logo)/ THE MACMILLAN COMPANY
/NEW YORK BOSTON CHICAGO DALLAS/ATLANTA SAN
FRANCISCO
Page (iii): (title page) THE CASE/FOR CHRISTIANITY/BY C. S.
LEWIS/ FELLOW OF MAGDALEN COLLEGE, OXFORD
/*Published in England under the title/ "Broadcast Talks"/New York-
1943/*THE MACMILLAN COMPANY
Page (iv): *All rights reserved*/Printed in the United States of America
Page (v): *Preface.......*
Page (vi): (blank)
Page (vii): *Contents*
Page (1): *Part 1*
Page (2): (blank)
Pages 3 -56: (text)
Pages 1 through (104): (text)

Dust jacket: (lettered in red)
Front panel: (within a double-rule red border) *Another Brilliant
Book/by the Author of "the Screwtape Letters"/*THE CASE/FOR/
CHRISTIANITY/*By*/C. S. LEWIS/*Fellow of Magdalen College,
Oxford/* "We have never read arguments/better marshalled or
handled so/that they can be remembered, or/any book more useful to
the Chris-/tian, in the Army or elsewhere."/--*The Tablet*
Spine: (horizontally from top to bottom)
LEWIS   THE CASE FOR CHRISTIANITY   MACMILLAN
Back panel: THE SCREWTAPE LETTERS/*by*/C. S.
LEWIS/(excerpts from 8 reviews)
Front flap: (price in upper right corner) $1.00/THE CASE
FOR/CHRISTIANITY/*By* C. S. LEWIS/(publisher's blurb)
Back flap: *C. S. Lewis*/(small diamond)/Clive Staples Lewis is the
author of ... and many others/ Mr. Lewis was a Second Lieutenant

with the Somerset Light Infantry during the First World War. He was lecturer at University College, Oxford, 1924; Gollancz Memorial Prizeman, 1937; and he is at present Fellow and Tutor of Maddalen College, Oxford.

23. CHRISTIAN BEHAVIOUR.
London: Geoffrey Bles: The Centenary Press, April 19, 1943
64 pp.   13 cm x 18.8 cm   Orange cloth

KEY TO FIRST EDITION: On back of title page:
First published 1943

Front board: (lettered in black)(single-rule)/CHRISTIAN BEHAVIOUR/by/C. S. LEWIS/(single-rule)
Spine: (lettered in black) CHRISTIAN BEHAVIOUR by C. S. LEWIS
Rear board: (blank)
Endpapers: (blank, off-white)
Page (1): CHRISTIAN BEHAVIOUR
Page (2): *BY THE SAME AUTHOR*/THE SCREWTAPE LETTERS ... /THE PROBLEM OF PAIN ... /BROADCAST TALKS ...
Page (3): (title page) CHRISTIAN BEHAVIOUR/A further series of Broadcast Talks/by/C. S. LEWIS/Fellow of Magdalen College, Oxford/GEOFFREY BLES: THE CENTENARY PRESS/37 ESSEX STREET, STRAND, LONDON
Page (4): *First published 1943*/PRINTED IN GREAT BRITAIN BY J. AND J. GRAY, EDINBURGH
Page 5: *NOTE.— Eight B.B.C. Talks are here printed ...* C.S.L.
Page (6): (blank)
Pages 7 through (64): (text)

Dust jacket: Buff paper
Front panel: (lettered in buff on dark green background) CHRISTIAN/BEHAVIOUR/(symbol of a cross)/C. S. LEWIS/ *Author of 'The Screwtape Letters'/and 'The Problem of Pain'/* GEOFFREY BLES
Spine: (lettered in dark green on buff paper) CHRISTIAN BEHAVIOUR *by C. S. LEWIS/*BLES (parallel to bottom of spine)

: (advertisements):
THE SCREWTAPE LETTERS ... Ninth large impression 5s. net
THE PROBLEM OF PAIN ... 10TH large impression 3s. 6d. net
BROADCAST TALKS ... 2nd large impression 2s. 6d. net
Front flap: (lettered in dark green on buff paper) CHRISTIAN
BEHAVIOUR/In this book ... autumn of 1942./2s. 6d. net
Back flap: THE AUTHOR/(biographical sketch)

Dust jackets of the 2nd and subsequent editions, which often appear
on first editions offered for sale, are readily detected by the addition
of reviews on the front flap, and changes in advertisements on the
back panel, even if the stated edition in the upper right corner of the
front flap (e.g., *3rd Edition*) has been clipped.

Lewis was noted for his frugality, as the result of which few
manuscripts of his works exist. When manuscripts were returned to
him by the publishers, he would customarily tear the sheets in half
horizontally to make a stack of "scratch paper" on which to make
notes. When he needed to light the gas fire in his study, he would
retrieve one such piece of paper from the waste basket, fold it into a
"stick," light it with a match, and then poke it into the grate. Only
one such piece of scrap paper is known to exist, now in my
collection.

It is the lower half of a page from the "fair copy" (final draft sent to
the publisher) of the manuscript of *Christian Behaviour*, containing
a passage appearing on pages 38-39, and used to light a fire, as
evidenced by its multiple folds and burned left edge. It was retrieved
from the waste basket by a teen-age girl who was sent from London
to live with the Lewis brothers during the German bombing, as were
many London children during the war. The girl, Jill Flewett, later
became Lady Jill Freud, a British actress married to Sir Clement
Freud, member of parliament and grandson of Sigmund Freud.

What is most notable about it, however, are the penciled notes on the
other side – which proved to be notes for his next book, *Beyond
Personality*. In them he refers to a "Wing Commander Snooks", who
was "quite right in thinking experience more 'real.'" On the first
page of the book, Lewis refers to a talk he gave to a group of R.A.F.

officers, one of whom, identified only as "an old hard-bitten officer," declared that he didn't believe all the "neat little dogmas and formulas" about God, because he had "met the real thing" when "alone in the desert at night."

24. (First American edition) **CHRISTIAN BEHAVIOUR.**
New York: Macmillan, January 18, 1944.
13.1 cm x 19.3 cm 70pp. Green cloth

KEY TO FIRST EDITION: On back of title page: *First Printing*

Front board: (blank)
Spine: (lettered in black) (horizontally) CHRISTIAN BEHAVIOUR *by C. S. LEWIS* MACMILLAN
Rear board: (blank)
Endpapers: (blank, off-white)
Page (i): CHRISTIAN BEHAVIOUR
Page (ii): BY C. S. LEWIS/The Screwtape Letters/The Case for Christianity/The Problem of Pain/Christian Behaviour
Page (iii): (title page) CHRISTIAN BEHAVIOUR/By/C. S. LEWIS/ *Fellow of Magdalen College, Oxford/A Further Series of Broadcast Talks/NEW YORK/*THE MACMILLAN COMPANY/1943
Page (iv): © 1943 *First Printing*
Page (v): CONTENTS
Page (vi): (blank)
Pages 1 through 70: (text pages)

Dust jacket:
Front panel: (lettered in tan on green background) CHRISTIAN/BEHAVIOUR/(cross symbol)/C. S. LEWIS/*Author of 'The Screwtape Letters'/and 'The Problem of Pain'*
Spine: (Lettered horizontally from top to bottom in green on tan background) CHRISTIAN BEHAVIOUR *by C. S. LEWIS* MACMILLAN
Back panel: (lettered in green on tan background within a green double-rule border) THE/SCREWTAPE LETTERS/by/C. S. LEWIS/ (excerpts from four reviews)

<u>Front flap</u>: CHRISTIAN BEHAVIOUR/by C. S. LEWIS/*Author of "The Screwtape Letters*/(publisher's blurbl)/$1.00(lower right corner)

<u>Back flap</u>: (a very formal "police lineup" type of photo of Lewis, with publisher's blurb – a pity they didn't use one of his many interesting informal photos!)

25. PERELANDRA.

London: John Lane The Bodley Head, April 20, 1943.

256 pp.   13 cm x 19 cm   Coarsely-woven light blue cloth

KEY TO FIRST EDITION: On back of title page:
First Published 1943

Front board: (blank)
Spine: (lettered in gold – see note below*) PERELANDRA
/C. S./LEWIS/THE/BODLEY/HEAD
Rear board: (blank)
Endpapers: (blank, off-white)
Page (1): PERELANDRA
Page (2): *by the same author*/OUT OF THE SILENT PLANET/
THE SCREWTAPE LETTERS/THE PROBLEM OF PAIN
Page (3): (title page) PERELANDRA/*a novel by*/C. S.
LEWIS/*London*/John Lane The Bodley Head
Page (4): *First Published 1943*/(in open book design with lion on
top) BOOK/PRODUCTION/WAR ECONOMY / STANDARD
/(statement of conformity standards beneath)/ Printed in Great
Britain by/ MORRISON AND GIBB LTD., LONDON AND
EDINBURGH/ for JOHN LANE THE BODLEY HEAD
LIMITED/8 BURY PLACE, LONDON W.C.1
Page (5): To/SOME LADIES/at/WANTAGE
Page 6: PREFACE/This story ... is allegorical/C. S. L.
Pages 7 through 256: (text)

I have a variant copy of the first edition that is identical in every way
to that described above, except that the lettering on the spine is
black. Whether this is an anomaly, occasioned by a temporary
shortage of gold lettering material, or a specific print run, I am
unable to say. In any case, this is the only such copy I have ever
seen.

Dust jacket: Pictorial jacket by B. Cowell, in orange, gray-blue,
white, and black, on a gray-blue background, including the spine.
Front panel: PERELANDRA/(dragon-like figure surrounded by 3
stars)/*A NOVEL BY*/C. S. LEWIS

Spine: PERELANDRA/(surrealist figure on a five-point star)/C. S. LEWIS/THE/BODLEY/HEAD

Back panel: (lettered in black on white decorative background) (advertisements for 3 Rex Warner novels: The Aerodrome ,,, 7s. 6d.; The Wild Goose Chase ... 8s.6d.; The Professor ... 7s. 6d.)

Front flap: (on white background) PERELANDRA (lettered in yellow)/ (publisher's blurb, lettered in blue): The distinguished author ... and Thoughtful Wishing./*8s. 6d. net* (lettered in black and clipped at the lower corner just beyond the price)

A variant dust jacket has been noted, in which the corner has not been clipped and the price not imprinted. Instead, the price is shown on a brown and buff label, 1.8 cm x 2.3 cm, with the same lion-on-open-book design as on page (4), with price of 8/6 net in black on the open pages. This jacket was perhaps intended for books exported to other countries, with appropriate price label to be affixed upon import. It is clearly a first edition jacket, being identical in every respect to that described above.

A caution is to be noted with regard to the jacket. The colored ink used on the front panel and spine is extremely fragile and easily scratched. An otherwise perfect jacket was once offered to me by one of England's leading antiquarian bookstores as "fine indeed", when in point of fact it had a large series of curved, parallel scratches across the entire front panel, which the seller thought was part of the design – and, indeed, it appeared to be. To someone unfamiliar with the jacket design, small scratches on the front panel or the spine can easily appear to be part of the design.

Inexperienced sellers or buyers are cautioned to check the dust jacket carefully on first editions offered to them. Although jackets on the second, third, and possibly later editions are imprinted at the bottom of the front flap with, for example, THIRD IMPRESSION, the type is so small and the yellow color so faint that it is easily overlooked – or may have been roughly trimmed to look like a chipped area. These later jackets, however, have reviews on the lower half of the front flap, as well as advertisements on the back flap, which clearly identify them as later issues.

(on white background, lettered in blue) *Printed in Great Britain for/John Lane The Bodley Head Ltd.*

The "ladies at Wantage", to whom the book is dedicated, were Anglican nuns at the Convent of St. Mary the Virgin at Wantage, near Oxford. (The dedication of the Portuguese translation of *Perelandra* translates back into English as "Some wanton ladies"!)

One of the nuns, Sister Penelope, had developed a friendship with Lewis that was to last through his lifetime, first through correspondence and later when he was invited by the Mother Superior to address the nuns. In October 1941, Lewis sent the manuscript of *The Screwtape Letters* to Sister Penelope, asking her to keep it in case the one sent to the publisher in London should be destroyed by German bombers. Fifteen years later she wrote to him to ask if he wanted it returned. His reply: "If you can persuade any 'sucker' (as the Americans say) to buy the MS of *Screwtape*, pray do, and use the money for any pious or charitable object you like." Knowing that he would have probably destroyed the manuscript (see note under no. 24, *Christian Behaviour*), she eventually sold the manuscript to raise funds for renovating the convent's chapel, and it is now in the Berg Collection of the New York Public Library.

26. (First American edition) **PERELANDRA.**
New York: Macmillan, April 11, 1944.
238 pp.   14.5 cm x 20.7 cm   Light brown cloth.

KEY TO FIRST EDITION: On back of title page: *First printing.*

Front board: (blank)
Spine: (lettered in green) C. S. Lewis/PERELANDRA/MACMILLAN
Rear board: (blank)
Top edge of pages: Light brown
Endpapers: (blank, off-white)
Page (i): PERELANDRA

Page (ii): *By the Same Author*/OUT OF THE SILENT PLANET/THE SCREWTAPE LETTERS/CHRISTIAN BEHAVIOR/THE PROBLEM OF PAIN
Page (iii): (TITLE PAGE) PERELANDRA/*A NOVEL*/BY C. S. LEWIS/NEW YORK/THE MACMILLAN COMPANY/1944
Page (iv): *Copyright, 1944,by*/CLIVE STAPLES LEWIS./(single-rule)/All rights reserved. .... magazine or newspaper/*First printing.*/ (emblem of eagle and book)/A WARTIME BOOK ... / SET UP BY BROWN BROTHERS LITHOTYPERS/PRINTED IN THE UNITED STATES OF AMERICA / *To* / SOME LADIES / *at* / WANTAGE
Page (v): (blank)
Page (vi): PREFACE/This story ... is allegorical./C.S.L.
Page (vii): (blank)
Page (viii: PERELANDRA
Page (ix): (blank)
Page (x):
Pages 1 through 238: (text)

Dust jacket: Pictorial jacket in yellow and white on a green background, including the spine.
Front panel: Perelandra (in yellow)/A NOVEL (in white)/(design, with a castle-like structure and waves, in green and white, against a yellow sphere containing a planet and surrounded by white stars/*C. S Lewis* (in yellow script)/*Author of* THE SCREWTAPE LETTERS/and OUT OF THE SILENT PLANET
Spine: (on a green background) *Lewis* (in yellow)/PERELANDRA (in white)/*Macmillan* (in yellow)
Back panel: (lettered in green) The Books of C. S. Lewis/(single-rule)/THE SCREWTAPE LETTERS ... /OUT OF THE SILENT PLANET .... / THE CASE FOR CHRISTIANITY ... /THE PROBLEM OF PAIN ... / CHRISTIAN BEHAVIOUR (British spelling cf. American spelling on page (ii) above!)
Front flap: Perelandra/A Novel by C. S. Lewis/ ... In this tale ... both sides of the Atlantic./$2.00 (parallel to front edge of flap) (top and bottom corners clipped)
Back flap: C. S. LEWIS/(biographical sketch, mostly in Lewis' own words)

27. THE ABOLITION OF MAN. (The Riddell Memorial
Lectures) London: Oxford University Press, January 6, 1943
52 pp.   Wrappers: 14.8 cm x 23 cm (see note below)

KEY TO FIRST EDITION: Date on title page: **1943**
(Reprint edition is identified thus on the back of the title page)

Although the 1943 publication date is given in *C. S. Lewis: A
Companion and Guide* (1996) by Walter Hooper, the lectures were
given February 22-25, 1943. Moreover, this same reference refers to
a letter from Owen Barfield, dated January 22, 1944, praising the
book, which would suggest a publication date of January 6, 1944 –
which is consistent with the 1943 date on the title page.

Lewis traveled to the University of Durham with his brother Warnie,
arriving there on February 24, 1943. They then journeyed a few
miles north to Newcastle-upon-Tyne for the lectures each evening
on February 24, 25, and 26.

In these lectures Lewis analyzes the fallacies in much of the modern
trend of education in its debunking of all sentiment as propaganda
and in its fortifying of youth against emotion. He emphasizes the
necessity of teaching "the doctrine of objective value, the belief that
certain attitudes are really true, and others really false." Humanity, if
it is to survive and progress, must obey the traditional morality
common to its conception in all forms, Platonic, Aristotelian, Stoic,
Christian, and Oriental; for that is "the Way in which things
everlastingly emerge, stilly and tranquilly, into space and time." It is
the Way by which a regenerate science can "conquer Nature without
being at the same time conquered by her and buy knowledge at
lower cost than that of life."

One who seemed to understand the book best was Chad Walsh who
wrote in the New York Herald Tribune Book Review (13 April
1947), p. 5: 'This quiet little book is uniquely calculated to infuriate
John Dewey's disciples and all other moralists who want to pick and
choose from among the scraps of universal morality, who want to
have their cake and eat it too. The final chapter will horrify the
people who share Mr Lewis's views, for it presents an all-too-

plausible picture of man's destiny after the concept of absolute values has gone out the window ... In 1947 we still believe our "realism" is directed toward some desirable goal. Unless humanity makes an abrupt about-face, it seems likely that our grandchildren will have no goals. They will love or hate, caress or kill, as irrational nature dictates, and no one will use the words "good" or "bad", social" or "anti-social", or even "expedient" or "inexpedient".'

Two versions exist, differing only in the wrappers – both of which overlap the text pages by 1/8" and are printed in black on the front panel only:

(1) Orange-brown wrappers: THE ABOLITION OF MAN/OR/ REFLECTION ON EDUCATION WITH SPECIAL/REFERENCE TO THE TEACHING OF ENGLISH/IN THE UPPER FORMS OF SCHOOLS/BY/C. S. LEWIS/(*The Riddell Lectures,* 1943) /OXFORD UNIVERSITY PRESS/LONDON: HUMPHREY MILFORD/PRICE 2S. 6D. NET

(2) Olive-green wrappers: The front of the wrapper is identical to the title page, as below, except for substitution of "PRICE 2S. 6D. NET" in place of the Confucian quotation on the title page.)

Title page: UNIVERSITY(Seal of the University of Durham) OF DURHAM/ RIDDELL MEMORIAL LECTURES/ ON EDUCATION WITH SPECIAL / REFERENCE TO THE TEACHING OF ENGLISH/IN THE UPPER FORMS OF SCHOOLS/BY/C. S. LEWIS/(Quotation from Confucius)/ OXFORD UNIVERSITY PRESS/LONDON:HUMPHREY MILFORD/1943
Verso of title page: CONTENTS/I. MEN WITHOUT CHESTS/ II. THE WAY/ THE ABOLITION OF MAN/APPENDIX ... /NOTES....
Pages 1-40: (text pages)
Pages (41)-48: APPENDIX/ILLUSTRATIONS OF THE *TAO* ...
Pages (49)-52: NOTES ...

Although a number of copies of version #1 have been appeared on the market in recent years, few copies of version #2 have been seen. This version may have been specially printed for sale at the University of Durham.

28. (First American edition) **THE ABOLITION OF MAN.**
New York: Macmillan, April 8, 1947
61 pp   13.3 cm x 19 cm   Dark blue cloth

KEY TO FIRST EDITION: On back of title page: *First Printing*

Front board: (blank)
Spine: (lettered in white)
C. S. LEWIS   THE ABOLITION OF MAN   MACMILLAN
Rear board: (blank)
Endpapers: (blank, off-white)
Page (i): THE ABOLITION OF MAN
Page (ii): UNIVERSITY OF DURHAM/RIDDELL MEMORIAL
LECTURES/*Fifteenth Series*
Page(iii):   (title   page)   THE/ABOLITION   OF   MAN/OR
/REFLECTIONS   ON   EDUCATION   WITH   SPECIAL
/REFERENCE TO THE TEACHING OF ENGLISH/IN THE
UPPER FORMS OF SCHOOLS/BY/C. S. LEWIS/ (quotation from
Confucius)/NEW YORK/THE MACMILLAN COMPANY/ 1947
Page (iv): Copyright, 1947 by/THE MACMILLAN COMPANY/All
rights reserved ... for inclusion in magazine or newspaper./(single
rule)/*First Printing*/PRINTED IN THE UNITED STATES OF
AMERICA/BY   THE   VAIL-BALLOU   PRESS,   INC.,
BINGHAMTON, N. Y.
Page (v): CONTENTS (as in British edition)
Page (vi): (blank)
Pages 1 through 61: (text)

Dust jacket:
Front panel: (off-white on gray-blue background) THE/Abolition OF
Man/(gray-blue on off-white) *Author of "The Screwtape
Letters"*/(off-white on gray-blue) C. S. LEWIS

Spine: (gray-blue on off-white) LEWIS   THE ABOLITION OF
MAN   MACMILLAN
Back panel: (lettered in gray-blue) *Books by C. S. Lewis*/(nine
titles)/THE MACMILLAN COMPANY (dot) Publishers
Front flap: (lettered in gray-blue)THE ABOLITION OF MAN/
By/C. S. LEWIS/ (publisher's blurb)
Back flap: (brief biographical sketch lettered in gray-blue))

29. BEYOND PERSONALITY.

London: Geoffrey Bles: The Centenary Press, October 9, 1944
64 pp.   12.8 cm x 18.6 cm   Yellow cloth

KEY TO FIRST EDITION: On back of title page:
First published **1944**

Front board: (blank)
Spine: (lettered in blue) BEYOND PERSONALITY/*by*/C. S.
LEWIS
Rear board: (blank)
Endpapers: (blank, off-white)
Page (1): BEYOND PERSONALITY/THE CHRISTIAN IDEA OF
GOD
Page (2): *By the same author*/(five-pointed star)/(7 titles)
Page (3): (title page) BEYOND PERSONALITY/*The Christian Idea
of God*/by/C. S. LEWIS/*Fellow of Magdalen College, Oxford*
/GEOFFREY BLES: THE CENTENARY PRESS/52 DOUGHTY
STREET/LONDON
Page (4): *First published* 1944
Page 5: PREFACE/THESE Talks attempt ... thinks his own
Page 6: beliefs are true ... *April* 15*th*, 1944 C. S. LEWIS
Page 7: CONTENTS/I ... XI ...
Page (8): (blank)
Page 9-(64): (text pages)

Dust jacket: Front panel: (lettered in white on blue background)
Beyond Personality/BY/C. S. LEWIS/*Author of*/The Screwtape
Letters/GEOFFREY BLES

Spine: (lettered in blue on white background) *BEYOND PERSONALITY by C. S. LEWIS*/BLES (parallel to the bottom of the spine)

Back panel: (lettered in blue on white) (his handwritten signature) *C. S Lewis/ ...THE SCREWTAPE LETTERS/*...13th large impression.../ *THE PROBLEM OF PAIN/*...13th large impression.../*BROADCAST TALKS/*...4TH large impression.../*CHRISTIAN BEHAVIOUR/*...4th large impression.../(single-rule)/GEOFFREY BLES LTD.: THE CENTENARY PRESS/52 DOUGHTY STREET, LONDON

Front flap: BEYOND PERSONALITY/(short single rule) This book contains the addresses/ which Mr. C. S. Lewis delivered/on the Wireless in the Spring of/1944, with several additional/chapters./2*s.* 6*d. net*

Back flap: (blank)

Note: The first edition is often found with a later dust jacket which differs only as follows:

- Insertion of "on Theology" in the front flap blurb: ...This book contains the addresses/on Theology which Mr. C. S./Lewis delivered on the wireless in/the Spring of 1944, with several/additional chapters.
- On the back panel The Screwtape Letters is the 14th large impression, not the 13th.

30. (First American edition) **BEYOND PERSONALITY.**
New York: Macmillan, March 20, 1945
68 pp   13 cm x 19.2 cm   Green cloth

KEY TO FIRST EDITION: On back of title page: *First Printing*

Front board: (blank)
Spine: (lettered in white) C. S. LEWIS BEYOND PERSONALITY MACMILLAN
Rear board: (blank)
Endpapers: (blank, off-white)
Page (i): BEYOND PERSONALITY/*The Christian Idea of God*

Page (ii): *By the same author*/(7 titles) THE PROBLEM OF PAIN
.... PERELANDRA
Page (iii): (title page) BEYOND PERSONALITY/*The Christian
Idea of God*/by/C. S. LEWIS/*Fellow of Magdalen College,
Oxford*/NEW YORK/THE MACMILLAN COMPANY/1945
Page (iv): Copyright, 1945, by/THE MACMILLAN
COMPANY/All rights reserved ... /(single rule)/*First Printing*/(A
WARTIME BOOK logo)/PRINTED IN THE UNITED STATES OF
AMERICA/BY THE VAIL-BALLOU PRESS, INC.,
BINGHAMTON, N.Y.
Pages v and (vi): PREFACE
Page vii: CONTENTS /I ... XI
Page (viii): (blank)
Pages 1 through 68: (text)

Dust jacket:
Front panel: (lettered in off-white on brownish maroon background)
Beyond/Personality (with a large "P" circling "Beyond"/C. S. *Lewis*/
(brownish maroon on off-white) *Author of "The Screwtape Letters"*
Spine: (horizontally) (lettered in off-white on brownish maroon)
Beyond Personality – C. S. Lewis (brownish maroon on off-white)
MACMILLAN
Back panel: (lettered in brownish maroon on off-white) *What
Reviewers Say of C. S. Lewis's Books*/(reviews of *The Screwtape
Letters, The Problem of Pain, The Case for Christianity,* and
Christian Behaviour)/ THE MACMILLAN COMPANY –
Publishers
Front flap: *Beyond Personality/By C. S. Lewis/Author of ... and other
books/*(publisher's blurb)
Back flap: (formal bust picture with biographical sketch)

31. THAT HIDEOUS STRENGTH.
London: John Lane The Bodley Head, August 16, 1945
476 pp.   13.4 cm x 19 cm   Black cloth

KEY TO FIRST EDITION: On back of title page:
First Published 1945
Front board: (blank)
Spine: (lettered in gold) THAT/HIDEOUS/STRENGTH/
BY/C.S./LEWIS/THE/BODLEY/HEAD
Rear board: (blank)
Endpapers: (blank, off-white)
Page (1): THAT HIDEOUS STRENGTH
Page (2): BY THE SAME AUTHOR/(14 titles, from *Out of the
Silent Planet* to *The Abolition of Man*)/To/J. McNeill
("J. McNeill" was Jane Agnes "Janie" McNeill, Lewis's life-long
friend in Belfast. Janie hated the book, however, and expressed the
wish that he had dedicated any other book to her.)
Page (3): (title page) THAT/HIDEOUS/STRENGTH/*a modern
fairy-tale for grown-ups/by*/C. S. LEWIS/*London*/JOHN LANE
THE BODLEY HEAD
Page (4): *First Published 1945/*(in open book design with lion on
top) BOOK/PRODUCTION/WAR ECONOMY/STANDARD/
(statement of conformity standards beneath)/Printed in Great Britain
by/MORRISON AND GIBB LTD., LONDON AND EDINBURGH/
for JOHN LANE THE BODLEY HEAD LIMITED/8 BURY
PLACE, LONDON W.C.1
Page 5: CONTENTS/*Preface.../*(Chapters I through XVII...
Page (6): The Shadow of that hyddeous strength/Sax myle and more
it is of length./SIR DAVID LINDSAY: from/*Ane Dialog* (describing
the/Tower of Babel)
Pages 7-8: PREFACE
Pages 9 through (476): (text)

My friend, fellow collector, and British bookseller, Ian Blakemore,
had a copy of this book that was identical in every way to that
described above, except that the lettering on the spine was blue. Of
the many copies I have handled over the years, all were lettered in
gold – and the copy in the Bodleian Library is lettered in gold.

Dust jacket:
Front panel: (Pictorial dust jacket extending over spine, in yellow lettering over a blue forest, on a black background) *That/Hideous/Strength/C. S. LEWIS* (see illustration)
Spine: *That Hideous Strength   C. S. LEWIS* (logo of The Bodley Head, with initials J L)
Back panel: (blue star) *have you read the two preceding titles/which complete the trilogy of which* THAT/HIDEOUS STRENGTH *is the third and last?* (lettered in black)/OUT OF THE SILENT PLANET (lettered in blue) ... *3ʳᵈ impression 5s. net/*(black single rule)/ PERELANDRA (lettered in blue)/ ... *4ᵗʰ impression 8s. 6d./both titles are published by/*JOHN LANE THE BODLEY HEAD (lettered in black)/(blue star)
Front flap: THAT HIDEOUS STRENGTH (lettered in blue)/In this volume ... author's *Abolition of Man* (lettered in black)/*9s. 6d. net* (lettered in blue)
Back flap: (at bottom) *Printed in Great Britain for/John Lane The Bodley Head Ltd*

32. (First American edition) **THAT HIDEOUS STRENGTH.**
New York: Macmillan, May 21, 1946
459 pp.   14.3 cm x 20.8 cm   Gray cloth

KEY TO FIRST EDITION: On back of title page: *First Printing*

Front board: (blank)
Spine: (in black) (double-rule)/That/Hideous/Strength /(decoration)/LEWIS/(double-rule)/MACMILLAN
Rear board: (blank)
Endpapers: (blank, off-white)
Page (i): That Hideous Strength
Page (ii): By the same Author/(13 titles as on British edition)
Page (iii): (title page) (lettered in black, in double-rule border with decorative line top and bottom) That/Hideous Strength/A MODERN FAIRY-TALE FOR GROWN-UPS/By C, S, LEWIS/(quote as on page [6] of British edition)/New York THE MACMILLAN COMPANY 1946

<u>Page (iv):</u> Copyright, 1946/CLIVE STAPLES LEWIS/*All rights reserved ... in magazine or newspaper./First Printing/*PRINTED IN THE UNITED STATES OF AMERICA/BY J. J. KITTLE & IVES COMPANY, NEW YORK
<u>Page (v):</u> *To/*J. McNEILL
<u>Page (vi):</u> (blank)
<u>Page vii:</u> PREFACE/I have called ... a scientific colleague,
<u>Page viii:</u> PREFACE/some time before ... on its own./C. S. LEWIS/*Magdalen College,/Oxford/Christmas Eve, 1943.*
<u>Page (ix):</u> CONTENTS/PREFACE .../(Chapters I through VII)
<u>Page (x):</u> (blank)
<u>Page (xi):</u> (blank)
<u>Page (xii):</u> That Hideous Strength
<u>Page (xiii):</u> (blank)
<u>Pages 1 through 459:</u> (text)

This American edition differs in a number of ways from the British edition. (See *C. S. Lewis: Companion and Guide*, pp. 240-242)

Dust jacket:
<u>Front panel:</u> (edged in black top and bottom; black cathedral spires at top; all on red background) (white lettering) That/Hideous/Strength/(black lettering) A NOVEL BY/C. S. LEWIS
<u>Spine:</u> (horizontally) (white lettering on black) LEWIS That Hideous Strength MACMILLAN
<u>Back panel:</u> The Books of C. S. Lewis/(single rule) (six titles) THE SCREWTAPE LETTERS ... CHRISTIAN BEHAVIOUR
<u>Front flap:</u> (clipped 45 degrees upper corner and 30 degrees lower corner, with price of $3.00 parallel to edge in lower corner) That Hideous Strength/By C. S. LEWIS/*Author of ... /*(publisher's blurb)
<u>Back flap:</u> Photo of Lewis, with an interesting autobiographical sketch

33. THE TORTURED PLANET.
New York: Avon Publications, Inc., 1946
254 pp. + 2 pp of advertisements   11 cm x 16.2 cm   Paperback

<u>**KEY TO FIRST EDITION**</u>**:** On upper left corner of front and bottom of spine: price of **35c** and book code **T-211**

An abridged edition of *That Hideous Strength* specially prepared by Lewis from the British edition. The story is about one-third shorter. In the Preface, Lewis says, "In reducing the original story to a length suitable for this edition, I believe I have altered nothing but the *tempo* and the manner."

Front panel of wrappers: (on a multi-colored pictorial background of planets and shapes): AVON/(single-rule)/35c/(single-rule)/T-211 (then, in yellow lettering): C. S. LEWIS'/SCIENCE-FICTION MASTER- PIECE OF/A SUPER RACE DEDICATED TO EVIL!/ (in white) THE/Tortured Planet/ (in yellow) (THAT HIDEOUS STRENGTH)/ *Specially abridged/by the Author*

Spine: (on a green background) C. S. Lewis (in white) THE TORTURED PLANET (in yellow) AVON (in black, in a black ball)/35C (in yellow)/T-211 (in black)

Back panel: SCIENCE ON THE RAMPAGE (in yellow, on a pictorial background of a space ship and planets)/(review from *The New Yorker*)

Page (1): THE MASTER PLAN/(summary of the story, and a quote from the *Saturday Review*

Page (2): Other Avon books by/C. S. LEWIS/Perelandra/Out of the Silent Planet

Page (3): (TITLE PAGE) The Tortured Planet/Original title: *That Hideous Strength*/C. S. LEWIS/*Specially abridged by the author* /AVON PUBLICATIONS, INC./575 Madison Avenue New York 22, N.Y.

Page (4): Published by The Macmillan Company under the title *That/Hideous Strength*. Copyright, 1946, by Clive Staples Lewis./ Published by arrangement with The Macmillan Company,/Printed in the U.S.A.

Page (5): Preface/This is a 'tall story' about devilry ... also an improvement./*C.S.L.*

Page (6): (blank)

Pages 7 through 254: (text)

Pages (255-256): (advertisements)

34. THE GREAT DIVORCE.
London: Geoffrey Bles: The Centenary Press, January 14, 1946
126 pp.   13 cm x 19 cm   Yellow cloth

KEY TO FIRST EDITION: On back of title page:
First Published November 1945
(This was a printer's error. The book was actually published in
January 1946.)

Front board: (blank)
Spine: (in a reddish-orange design, 1.5 cm x 3.5 cm, lettered in
black) The/Great/Divorce/(design)/
C.S./LEWIS/(in black) BLES
Rear board: (blank)
Endpapers: (blank)
Page (1): THE GREAT DIVORCE/(Y in an oval, in lower right
corner)
Page (2): *BY THE SAME AUTHOR/*(15 titles, including *HAMLET:
THE PRINCE OR THE POEM?*, which is not a book, but a lecture
published in *The Proceedings of the British Academy*)
Page (3): (title page) THE/GREAT DIVORCE/A Dream/by/C. S.
LEWIS/*Fellow of Magdalen College, Oxford/*(quote from George
MacDonald)/LONDON/GEOFFREY BLES: THE CENTENARY
PRESS
Page (4): *Printed in Great Britain by/Robert MacLebose and
Company Ltd/The University Press Glasgow/for Geoffrey Bles
Ltd/52 Doughty Street London W.C.1/First Published November
1945*
(This publication date was a printer's error. The book was actually
published January 14, 1946. The book had originally been published
serially in *The Guardian*, as had *The Screwtape Letters*.)
Page (5): TO/BARBARA WALL/Best and most long-suffering of
scribes

Although brother Warnie typed some of the manuscripts of Jack's
books, he was not always available. During the war, when Warnie
was in the Army and Jack was looking for someone who could type
for him, Colin Hardie introduced him to his sister-in-law, Barbara
Wall, who was living in Oxford. Barbara was the sister of Christian

Hardie, wife of Colin Hardie, Inkling and colleague of Lewis at Magdalen College. She typed *That Hideous Strength, The Great Divorce,* and *Miracles.*

Page (vi): (blank)
Pages 7-9: PREFACE
Page (10): (blank)
Page (11): (another half title, identical to page (1)
Page (12): (blank)
Pages 13 through 118: (text)
Pages (119-120): (blank)

Dust jacket:
Front panel: (on greenish-tan background) *The Great/Divorce* (in white)/(all lettered in dark red): *by/*C. S. LEWIS/*Author of/'The Screwtape Letters'/*(same Y-in-oval as on half-title in book) /GEOFFREY BLES
Spine: (on tan background, lettered in dark red) THE/GREAT/DIVORCE/C.S./LEWIS/BLES
Back panel: (lettered in dark red in buff background) (his handwritten signature) *C. S Lewis / ... THE SCREWTAPE LETTERS/* ... 16th large impression ... */THE PROBLEM OF PAIN/* ... 15th large impression ... */BROADCAST TALKS/* ...5TH large impression... */CHRISTIAN BEHAVIOUR/* ... 5th large impression ... /(single-rule)/GEOFFREY BLES LTD.: THE CENTENARY PRESS/52 Doughty Street, London
Front flap: (lettered in dark red on buff background) THE GREAT DIVORCE/It is not generally ... a little Hell in it."/*7s. 6d. net*
Back flap: *In the Christian Challenge Series/*THE/MASTERY OF EVIL ... THE RESURRECTION OF CHRIST ... (10 titles by various authors)

35. (First American edition) **THE GREAT DIVORCE.**
New York: Macmillan, February 26, 1946
133 pp.   13 cm x 19 cm   Dark blue cloth

KEY TO FIRST EDITION: On the back of the title page:
First Printing

Front board: (blank)
Spine: (lettered in gold) Printed horizontally: LEWIS *The Great Divorce* MACMILLAN
Rear board: (blank)
Endpapers: (blank, off-white)
Page (i): THE GREAT DIVORCE
Page (ii): *BY THE SAME AUTHOR*/(8 titles: THE SCREWTAPE LETTERS ... PERELANDRA)
Page (iii): (TITLE PAGE) THE/GREAT DIVORCE/*by*/C. S. LEWIS/*Fellow of Magdalen College*/NEW YORK/THE MACMILLAN COMPANY/1946
Page (iv): Copyright, 1946, *by*/THE MACMILLAN COMPANY/ (short single-rule)/All rights reserved ... magazine or newspaper./(short single-rule)/*First Printing*/PRINTED IN THE UNITED STATES OF AMERICA/BY THE VAIL-BALLOU PRESS, INC., BINGHAMTON, NEW YORK
Page v through viii: PREFACE/Blake wrote ... of the after-world./ C. S. LEWIS/*April,* 1945
Page (ix): THE GREAT DIVORCE
Page (x): (blank)
Pages 1 through 133: (text pages)

Dust jacket:
Front panel: (on purple and purplish-red background) The/Great/Divorce/C. S. LEWIS/Author of 'The Screwtape Letters
Spine: (on same background) C. S. LEWIS (in purple)/The Great Divorce (in white)/*Macmillan* (in purple)
Back panel: (lettered in dark blue, on off-white background) C. S. LEWIS/(brief reviews of 7 titles: BEYOND PERSONALITY ....CHRISTIAN BEHAVIOUR)/THE MACMILLAN COMPANY (dot) *Publishers*
Front flap: (lettered in dark blue) (price in upper right corner: $1.50) THE GREAT/DIVORCE/(publisher's blurb)
Back flap: (formal full-face photograph of Lewis in dark blue, 6.3 x 7.4 cm)/C. S. LEWIS/(bio sketch)

36. GEORGE MACDONALD: An Anthology. (Edited by C S. Lewis) London: Geoffrey Bles: The Centenary Press, 1946. 128 pp.   13 cm x 19 cm   Yellow cloth

KEY TO FIRST EDITION: On back of title page:
First Published 1946

\Front board: (blank)
Spine: (lettered in black, on green background with decorative ends)
GEORGE MACDONALD:
Anthology/BLES
Rear board: (blank)
Endpapers: (blank, off-white)
Page (1): GEORGE MACDONALD/*An Anthology*
Page (2): BOOKS BY C. S. LEWIS/*Theology*/(7 titles) THE
PROBLEM OF PAIN ... THE GREAT DIVORCE/*Social
Philosophy*/THE ABOLITION OF MAN/*Romances*/(*published
by John Lane, The Bodley Head*)/OUT OF THE SILENT PLANET/
PERELANDRA/THAT HIDEOUS STRENGTH/*Literary
Criticism/published by The Oxford University Press*/THE
ALLEGORY OF LOVE/REHABILITATIONS/A PREFACE
TO 'PARADISE LOST'/HAMLET: THE PRINCE OR THE
POEM?/THE PERSONAL HERESY/(*in collaboration with E. M.
W. Tillyard*)
Page 3: GEORGE MACDONALD: *An Anthology*/by/C. S.
LEWIS/*Fellow of Magdalen College, Oxford*/ LONDON
/GEOFFREY BLES: THE CENTENARY PRESS/MCMXLVI
Page (4): *Printed in Great Britain by/Robert MacLehose and
Company Ltd/The University Press Glasgow/for Geoffrey Bles
Ltd/52 Doughty Street London W.C. I/First Published
1946*/TO/MARY NEYLAN

Mary Neylan was a pupil and friend of Lewis. In *Letters of C. S. Lewis,* his letters to her appear throughout the book as "To a former Pupil" and "To a Lady." Two years after becoming his pupil in 1931, she saw the first edition of *The Pilgrim's Regress* in the window of Blackwell's bookshop in Oxford. She later wrote to a friend, "I immediately purchased it. It was a book which chimed in with my own experience and eventually influenced me to become a

235

convert to Christianity." She and Lewis carried on an extensive correspondence from 1931 until his death in 1963; this collection of letters from Lewis is now at Taylor University.

With the collection of letters from Lewis is the dedicatory copy of the MacDonald anthology, inscribed by Lewis:
*With affectionate compliments and congratulations
from C. S. Lewis 1946*
Lewis was responsible for leading her to become a Christian and was godfather to her first daughter, Sarah. Also with the collection at Taylor is a pencil sketch of Lewis done by Mary shortly before his death. It has never been published, having been made for herself. Her first daughter (for whom Lewis was godfather) is Sarah Neylan Tisdall, from whom I purchased her mother's collection of Lewis letters for Taylor. As was her mother, she is also an artist, now living in Mexico City.

Pages 5-9: CONTENTS (365 entries)
Pages 10-22: PREFACE (by Lewis)
Pages 23-128: (text)

Dust jacket:

Front panel: (lettered in green on yellow background) *George /MacDonald/Anthology/*With an Introduction by/C. S. Lewis /(figure)/GEOFFREY BLES/(artist's name along bottom right edge) *GEO. MANSELL*
Spine: (lettered horizontally from bottom to top in green on off-white background) BLES (parallel to bottom) *GEORGE MACDONALD ANTHOLOGY* (star) *C. S. LEWIS*
Back panel: (signature in green bold type) *C. S. Lewis/*(review quote and advertisements for Screwtape Letters – 18th imp.; Problem of Pain – 16th imp.; Broadcast Talks – 6th imp.; Christian Behaviour – 5th imp.; Beyond Personality – 4th imp.)
Front flap: (title and quotation from the Introduction) (price in lower right corner has been clipped from the jacket in the Brown Collection)
Back flap: (blank)

37. (First American edition) **GEORGE MACDONALD: An Anthology** (Edited by C. S. Lewis)
New York: Macmillan, 1947
128 pp. 13.2 cm x 19.5 cm Light olive green cloth

KEY TO FIRST EDITION: Bottom of title page: **1947**

Front board: (blank)
Spine: (lettered horizontally in green, on light green background with decorative ends) *LEWIS* GEORGE MACDONALD *MACMILLAN*
Rear board: (blank)
Endpapers: (blank, off-white)
Page (1): GEORGE MACDONALD/*An Anthology*
Page (2): BOOKS BY C. S. LEWIS/*Theology*/(9 titles) THE SCREWTAPE LETTERS ... THE GREAT DIVORCE
Page 3: GEORGE MACDONALD/ *An* Anthology/by/C. S. LEWIS/ *Fellow of Magdalen College, Oxford*/NEW YORK/THE MACMILLAN COMPANY/1947
Page (4): (Copyright date 1947 and warning) To/MARY NEYLAN
Pages 5-9: CONTENTS (365 entries)
Pages 10-22: PREFACE (by Lewis)
Pages 23-128: (text)

Dust jacket:

Front panel: (lettered in off-white on green) By the author of "The Screwtape Letters"/ George/Macdonald/(green lettering on off white) AN ANTHOLOGY/C. S. LEWIS
Spine: (lettered horizontally in offwhite on green) George Macdonald LEWIS   MACMILLAN
Back panel: (lettered in green on offwhite) C. S. LEWIS (followed by three review quotations and THE MACMILLAN COMPANY – Publishers)
Front flap: (upper corner clipped, with price of $1.50 just below, parallel to edge) (bottom corner clipped twice – along right edge and along bottom edge) (title and publisher's blurb)
Back flap: (biographical sketch of MacDonald)

38. MIRACLES.
London: Geoffrey Bles: The Centenary Press, May 12, 1947
220 pp.   14 cm x 22.2 cm   Green cloth

KEY TO FIRST EDITION: On back of title page:
First Published 1947
Front board: (blank)
Spine: (lettered in gold) MIRACLES/(short single-rule)/C. S.
LEWIS/BLES
Rear board: (blank)
Endpapers: (blank, off-white)
Page (1): MIRACLES/(Y in an oval)
Page (2): *BY THE SAME AUTHOR*/(15 titles:) THE PILGRIM'S
REGRESS ... THAT HIDEOUS STRENGTH
Page 3: MIRACLES/*A Preliminary Study*/by/C. S. LEWIS
/FELLOW OF MAGDALEN COLLEGE, OXFORD/GEOFFREY
BLES/(dot)/THE CENTENARY PRESS/52 DOUGHTY STREET,
LONDON/MCMXLVII
Page (4): *Printed in Great Britain by/Robert MacLehose and
Company Ltd/The University Press Glasgow/for Geoffrey Bles
Ltd/52 Doughty Street London W.C. I/First Published 1947*
Page (5): To/CECIL AND DAPHNE HARWOOD
Page (6): (blank)
Page 7: CONTENTS/I ... XVII ... Appendix A ... Appendix B ...
Page (8): (blank)
Page (9): (poem) *Among the hills ... the golden shower.*
/C. S. L./(Reprinted by permission of *Time and Tide*)
Page (x): (blank)
Pages 11 through 216: (text pages)
Pages 217 through 220: (index)

Dust jacket:
Front panel: (green double-rule border, 12.7 cm x 20 cm) (lettered
in black) MIRACLES/*A Preliminary Study*/by /C. S. LEWIS/
GEOFFREY BLES
Spine: (green double-rule)/MIRACLES/by/C. S. LEWIS/
GEOFFREY/BLES/(green double-rule)
Back panel: (in green script) C. S. Lewis/ "C. S. Lewis
has ... fascinating quest."/ -- *The Times Literary Supplement*/

C. S. Lewis has ... thinkers of our time."/ -- *The Expository Times* /(advertisements) The Screwtape Letters/20th impression – 5s. net/The Great Divorce/2nd impression (50,000 copies) – 7s. 6d. net/The Problem of Pain/17th impression – 5s. net/Broadcast Talks/ 6th impression – 2s. 6d. net/Christian Behaviour/5th impression – 2s. 6d. net/Beyond Personality/5th impression – 2s. 6d. net/ The Pilgrim's Regress/4th impression – 8s. 6d. net/George MacDonald – Anthology/2nd impression – 5s. net/The Abolition of Man/2nd impression – 3s. 6d. net/(green single-rule)/GEOFFREY BLES LTD./52 DOUGHTY STREET, LONDON, W.C. I
Front flap: (publisher's blurb) This book ... have no significance. /10s. 6d. net
Back flap: (blank)

39. (First American edition) **MIRACLES.**
New York: Macmillan, April 11, 1944
220pp 14.0 cm x 20.7 cm Blue cloth

KEY TO FIRST EDITION: On back of title page: **First Printing**

Front board: (blank)
Spine: (lettered in gold) (single- plus double-rule) *Miracles* (double-rule) LEWIS (double- plus single-rule) (single-rule) *Macmillan* (double-rule)
Rear board: (blank)
Endpapers: (blank, off-white)
Page (1): MIRACLES
Page (2): *BY THE SAME AUTHOR*/(15 titles:) THE PILGRIM'S REGRESS ... THAT HIDEOUS STRENGTH
Page (3): miracles/*a Preliminary Study*/by/C. S. LEWIS/FELLOW OF MAGDALEN COLLEGE, OXFORD/ NEW YORK/THE MACMILLAN COMPANY/1947
Page (4): COPYRIGHT, 1947, BY THE MACMILLAN COMPANY/(single-rule) All rights reserved ... in magazine or newspaper./First Printing/LITHOGRAPHED IN THE UNITED STATES OF AMERICA
Page (5): To/CECIL AND DAPHNE HARWOOD
Page (6): (blank)

Page 7: CONTENTS/I ... XVII ... APPENDIX A ... APPENDIX B
Page (8): (blank)
Page 9: (poem) *Among the hills ... the golden shower./*C. S. L.
/(Reprinted by permission of *Time and Tide*)
Page (x): (blank)
Pages 11 through 216: (text pages)
Pages 217-220: (index)
Pages 221-222: (blank)

Dust jacket:
Front panel: (lettered in off-white, with title on gray background, enclosed in four ruled boxes) MIRACLES (in off-white on brownish maroon background) By *C. S. Lewis*
Spine: (lettered horizontally in off-white on brownish maroon) MIRACLES – *C. S. Lewis – Macmillan*
Back panel: (titles of 11 Lewis books in brownish maroon on off-white, followed by THE MACMILLAN COMPANY Publishers)
Front flap: (title, author, and publisher's blurb) (same clipping as described for #38, with price of $2.50)
Back flap: (brief Lewis biographical sketch)

40. ARTHURIAN TORSO.

London: Oxford University Press, October 21, 1948

200pp.   14 cm x 22 cm   Dark rose-red cloth

KEY TO FIRST EDITION: 1948 on title page

Front board: (blank)
Spine: (lettered in gold) *Charles Williams*/ARTHURIAN TORSO
/*C. S. Lewis*/*Oxford*
Rear board: (blank)
Top-edge: Dark rose-red
Endpapers: (blank)
Page (i): ARTHURIAN TORSO
Page (ii): (blank)
Page (iii): ARTHURIAN TORSO/CONTAINING THE
POSTHUMOUS FRAGMENT OF/THE FIGURE OF ARTHUR
/*by*/CHARLES WILLIAMS/AND/A COMMENTARY ON/THE
ARTHURIAN POEMS OF/CHARLES WILLIAMS/*by*/C. S.
LEWIS/*Fellow of Magdalen College, Oxford*/*Geoffrey Cumberlege*
/OXFORD UNIVERSITY PRESS/*London New York Toronto*/1948
Page (iv): *Oxford University Press, Amen House, London,*
E.C.4/*Printed in Great Britain*
Page (v): *To*/MICHAL WILLIAMS/*without whose permission this*
book could not/*have been made*/(Latin quotation) HEU QUIIS TE
CASUS DETECTAM CONIUIGE TANTO/EXCIPIT AUT QUAE
DIGNA SATIS FORTUNA REVISIT,/HECTORIS
ANDROMACHE?
Page (vi): (blank)
Page (vii): CONTENTS/INTRODUCTORY/*by C. S. Lewis* ...
I/THE FIGURE OF ARTHUR/*by Charles Williams*/I. THE
BEGINNINGS ... 5 ... V. THE COMING OF THE GRAIL ...
60/WILLIAMS AND THE ARTHURIAD/*by C. S. Lewis*/I.
Preliminary ... 93 ... VI. *Conclusions* ... 187
Page (viii): ACKNOWLEDGEMENTS/ The quotations from
Charles Williams's poems in *The*/*Region of the Summer Stars* and
from his novel *The Greater Trumps* are included by permission of
the respective/publishers, Editions Poetry London, and Victor
Gollancz/Ltd. *Taliessin through Logres* is published by the Oxford/
University Press. My thanks are also due to Mrs. Hadfield/ for her

241

kindness in putting her typed copy of the MS. of/*The Figure of Arthur* at my disposal --- C.S.L.

Page 1-2: INTRODUCTORY

Page (3): THE FIGURE OF ARTHUR/*BY Charles Williams*

Pages (4): (blank)

Pages 5-(200): (text pages) (final page at bottom:) Printed in Great Britain by Butler and Tanner Ltd, Frome and London

Dust jacket:

Front panel: (lettered in brown on tan) ARTHURIAN TORSO/ (black on tan) CONTAINING THE/POSTHUMOUS FRAGMENT/ OF *THE FIGURE OF ARTHUR*/BY CHARLES WILLIAMS/AND A COMMENTARY ON/THE ARTHURIAN POEMS/OF CHARLES WILLIAMS/BY C. S. LEWIS/(wavy decorative line)/OXFORD UNIVERSITY PRESS

Spine: (lettered vertically in brown on tan) ARTHURIAN/TORSO/(figure)/(black on tan)/Williams /and/Lewis/OXFORD

Back panel: (brown on tan)(logo of Oxford Books)/(advertisements for four titles of Williams, Vinaver, Loomis, and Lewis)/(single rule)/OXFORD UNIVERSITY PRESS

Front flap: (short publisher's blurb)/(45 degree dotted line in lower right corner for clipping, under which at same angle) *Williams and Lewis*/ARTHURIAN TORSO/OXFORD/12*s.* 6d./*net*

Back flap: (blank)

There was no American first edition as such. In 1974 *Arthurian Torso* was published by Eerdmans as a paperback under the title *Taliessin Through Logres/The Region of the Summer* Stars/*by Charles Williams/ and Arthurian Torso/ by Charles Williams/ and C. S. Lewis* with an introduction by Mary McDermott Shideler.

As Lewis explains in his *Introductory*, Charles Williams left two works unfinished when he died suddenly in 1945. One was a long lyric cycle on the Arthurian legend of which he had already published two installments, the first in 1938 as *Taliessin Through Logres* and the second in 1944 as *The Region of the Summer Stars*. The other unfinished work was one of prose on the history of the legend, which he was to have entitled *The Figure of Arthur*.

He then goes on to tell how the first two chapters of *The Figure of Arthur* had been read by Williams to Lewis and Tolkien some years earlier, describing that event thus: "It may help the reader to imagine the scene; or at least it is to me both great pleasure and great pain to recall. Picture to yourself, then, an upstairs sitting-room with windows looking north into the 'grove' of Magdalen College on a sunshiny Monday Morning in vacation at about ten o'clock. The Professor and I, both on the chesterfield, lit our pipes and stretched out our legs. Williams in the arm-chair opposite to us threw his cigarette into the grate, took up a pile of the extremely small, loose sheets on which he habitually wrote – they came, I think, from a twopenny pad for memoranda, and began as follow: –"

Thus ends the introduction, with *The Figure of Arthur* beginning thereafter.

Williams and Lewis "discovered" each other's writings simultaneously in 1936, when Williams wrote to Lewis to praise the manuscript of *The Allegory of Love* he had reviewed as an editor at Oxford University Press, and Lewis at the same time wrote to Williams to praise his book, *The Place of the Lion*. The two quickly became friends, and when Oxford University Press moved its office from London to Oxford at the beginning of World War II, Lewis was elated. With the end of the war, Williams was preparing to move back to London when he suddenly became ill and died. Five days later, in a letter to a former pupil, Mary Neylan (which I recently acquired), Lewis wrote: "I also have become acquainted with grief now through the death of my great friend, Charles Williams, my friend of friends, the comforter of all our little set, the most angelic man. The odd thing is that his death has made my faith stronger than it was a week ago. And I find that all that talk about 'feeling that he is closer to us than before' isn't just talk. It's just what it feels like – I can't put it into words. One seems at moments to be living in a new world. Lots, lots of pain, but not a particle of depression or resentment."

There was no American first edition.

41. TRANSPOSITION AND OTHER ADDRESSES.
London: Geoffrey Bles, 1949
64 pp.   12.5 cm x 18.5 cm   In wrappers.

KEY TO FIRST EDITION: On back of title page:
First published in 1949

Front of wrapper: (white lettering on bright red background) C. S. LEWIS/*Tranposition/and other/Addresses/*("y" in an oval) /GEOFFREY BLES
Spine of wrapper: (red lettering on white background) TRANSPOSITION AND OTHER ADDRESSES (star) C. S. LEWIS
Rear of wrapper: (red lettering on white background) *C. S. Lewis* (his signature)/(two review excerpts, *The Times Literary Supplement* and *The Expository Times* followed by list of seven books: The Screwtape Letters/20th impression – 5s. net ... The Abolition of Man/2nd impression – 3s. 6d. net/(long single-rule)/GEOFFREY BLES LTD/52, DOUGHTY STREET, LONDON, W.C.1
Page (1): TRANSPOSITION AND OTHER ADDRESSES/("y" in an oval)
Page (2): *BY THE SAME AUTHOR*/(15 titles) MIRACLES ... THAT HIDEOUS STRENGTH
Page (3): TRANSPOSITION/*//And other Addresses*/by/C. S. LEWIS/FELLOW OF MAGDALEN COLLEGE, OXFORD /GEOFFREY BLES/52 DOUGHTY STREET, LONDON
Page (4): *Printed in Great Britain by/Butler and Tanner Ltd., Frome and London/for Geoffrey Bles Ltd./52 Doughty Street, London, W.C.1/All Rights Reserved/First published in 1949*
Page 5: PREFACE/This book contains a selection ... has appeared in the *Rivista* of Milan./C.S.L.
Page (6): (blank)
Page 7: CONTENTS/PAGE/I TRANSPOSITION ... 9 ... V THE INNER RING ... 55
Page (8): (blank)
Pages 9-64: (text pages)

Dust jacket:
Front panel: (identical to front of wrapper)
Spine: (identical to spine of wrapper)
Back panel: (identical to rear of wrapper)
Front flap: TRANSPOSITION/and other Addresses/by C. S.
LEWIS/This book contains a selection of the/addresses given by Dr.
Lewis in recent/years./It includes *Transposition, Learning in War-*
/Time, Membership, The Inner Ring, and/*The Weight of Glory*, a
famous sermon/preached in the Church of St. Mary the/Virgin,
Oxford/(price in lower right corner) 2*s.* 6*d. net*
Back flap: (blank)

42. (First American edition) Published as a hardback under the title:
THE WEIGHT OF GLORY And Other Addresses.
New York: Macmillan, September 13, 1949
66 pp   19.2 cm x 13 cm   Navy blue cloth

KEY TO FIRST EDITION: On back of title page: *First Printing*

Front board: (in gold) THE WEIGHT OF/GLORY/(design as
extension of the "Y")
Back board: (blank)
Spine: (lettered horizontally in gold) C. S. LEWIS/(design—4
dots)/*The Weight of Glory*/(design)/MACMILLAN
Endpapers: (blank)
Page (i): *The Weight of Glory*/AND/OTHER ADDRESSES
Page (ii): *BY THE SAME AUTHOR*/(list of 16 Lewis books, from
Miracles to *That Hideous Strength*
Page (iii): THE/WEIGHT OF/GLORY/*And Other/Addresses*/by/C.
S. LEWIS/FELLOW OF MAGDALEN COLLEGE/OXFORD/*The
Macmillan Company*/NEW YORK/*1949*
Page (iv): COPYRIGHT, 1949, BY THE MACMILLAN
COMPANY/*All rights reserved ... /First Printing/Published in
England under the title,*/TRANSPOSITION AND OTHER
ADDRESSES/Printed ...
Page (v): PREFACE ... C. S. L.
Page (vi): (blank)
Page (vii): CONTENTS/I ... V

Page (viii): (blank)
Pages 1 through 66: (text)
Pages (67-68): (blank)

Dust jacket:
Front panel: (lettered in white on maroon background)
THE/WEIGHT OF/GLORY (with decorative tail of the G)/AND
OTHER/ADDRESSES /C. S. LEWIS
Spine: (lettered horizontally in white on maroon)
LEWIS/(design)/*The WEIGHT of GLORY and Other Addresses*
/(design)/MACMILLAN
Back panel: (lettered in maroon on white background) *Books by C.
S. Lewis*/(13 titles, from THE WEIGHT OF GLORY to GEORGE
MACDONALD: An Anthology
Front flap: (publisher's blurb, lettered in maroon on white
background) (price of $1.25 parallel to front edge of flap, 3 cm
from top) (both corners clipped)
Back flap: (lettered in maroon on white background) C. S. LEWIS
/Clive Staples Lewis was born ... *The Screwtape Letters* has been
particularly popular.

43. THE LION, THE WITCH AND THE WARDROBE.
London: Geoffrey Bles, October 16, 1950
173 pp   14cm x 20.3cm   Light greenish-blue cloth

KEY TO FIRST EDITION: On back of title page:
First published 1950

Front board: (blank)
Spine: (lettered in silver) THE/LION/THE/WITCH/AND THE
/WARDROBE/ curlicue/C.S.LEWIS/GEOFFREY/BLES
Rear board: (blank)
Endpapers: (blank)
Page (1): THE LION, THE WITCH/AND THE WARDROBE
Page (2): (blank) Inserted color frontispiece of Aslan playing with
Lucy and Susan, on slick paper
Page (3): THE LION, THE WITCH/and/THE WARDROBE/*A Story*
*for Children/by/*C. S. LEWIS/ILLUSTRATIONS BY PAULINE
BAYNES/LONDON/GEOFFREY BLES
Page (4): *Printed in Great Britain by/Butler & Tanner Ltd*
Frome/for Geoffrey Bles Ltd/52 Doughty Street London W C1
Page 5: TO LUCY BARFIELD/MY DEAR LUCY,/I wrote this
story for you, but when I began it I had/not realised that girls grow
quicker than books. As a/ result you are already too old for fairy
tales, and by the/ time it is printed and bound you will be older still.
But/some day you will be old enough to start reading fairy/ tales
again. You can then take it down from some upper shelf, dust it, and
tell me what you think of it. I shall/ probably be too deaf to hear, and
too old to understand,/ a word you say, but I shall still be/your
affectionate Godfather,/C. S. LEWIS
Page (6): (blank)
Page 7: CONTENTS/(chapters I-XVII, pages 9 – 164)
Page (8): (blank)
Page 9 through (173): (text)
Page (174): (blank)
Pages (175-176): (blank)

Dust jacket: (Later impression Narnia jackets are so noted at the top of the front flap)
Front panel: (pictorial dust jacket extending over the spine, with black lettering on gray, in the center of which is an oval picture of Peter and Lucy riding on Aslan, surrounded by two fawns and a bird, under trees, in green, tan and black) THE LION, THE WITCH/and /THE WARDROBE/(illustration) /*A Story for Children*/by/C. S. LEWIS
Spine: (lettered vertically in black on gray) THE LION/THE /WITCH,/AND THE/WARDROBE/C. S. LEWIS/(illustration of a fawn carrying an umbrella, in black and green on off-white)/BLES
Back panel: (blank)
Front flap: THE LION, THE WITCH/AND THE WARDROBE/*A Story for Children*/by/C. S. LEWIS/(in lower right corner) *8s. 6d.*/NET
Back flap: (blank)

44. (First American edition)
THE LION, THE WITCH AND THE WARDROBE.
New York: Macmillan, November 7, 1950
154pp   14cm x 21cm   Light grayish-blue cloth

KEY TO FIRST EDITION: On back of title page:
                    FIRST PRINTING

Front board: (Circular illustration of a deer, in yellow on dark blue backgroud, surrounded by yellow and blue trees)
Spine: (horizontally) (dark blue) C. S. LEWIS (dark blue on yellow background, 13.3mm x 1.6mm) (filigree) *The Lion, the Witch and the Wardrobe* (filigree) (dark blue) MACMILLAN
Rear board: (blank)
Endpapers: (blank)
Page (i): THE LION, THE WITCH/and/THE WARDROBE/*A Story for Children*/BY C. S. LEWIS/*Illustrated by Pauline Baynes* /(illustration: tree trunks with a beaver's head protruding)/THE MACMILLAN COMPANY/*New York: 1950*)

Page (ii): COPYRIGHT, 1950 BY THE MACMILLAN COMPANY/*All rights reserved, etc.*/FIRST PRINTING/PRINTED IN THE UNITED STATES OF AMERICA
Page (iii): *To Lucy Barfield/*(same dedication as in British edition)
Page (iv): (blank)
Page (v): CONTENTS/(chapters I - XVII, pages 1 – 145)
Page (6): (blank)
Pages 1 through 154: (text)

Dust jacket:
Front panel: (pictorial dust jacket extending over the spine, with black lettering on gray, in the center of which is an oval picture of Peter and Lucy riding on Aslan, surrounded by two fawns and a bird, under trees, in green, tan and black)
Spine: (horizontal black lettering) C S LEWIS (space) THE LION, THE WITCH AND THE WARDROBE (space) Macmillan
Back panel: (illustration in center, 6cm high, of the back of a fawn with umbrella)
Front flap: (top corner is clipped in all seven American dust jackets) (lettered in black on off-white background) THE LION, THE WITCH/AND THE WARDROBE/*By C. S. Lewis/*This delightfully fanciful story … he crowns them Kings and Queens of Narnia. */Illustrated by Pauline Baynes/Ages 8-12/$2.50* (in lower right corner)
Back flap: (in black on off-white background) (illustration and text from page 60 of the children in the Beavers' house) *"… in a very few minutes … to enjoy themselves."*

45. PRINCE CASPIAN.

London: Geoffrey Bles, October 15, 1951
196 pp.   14cm x 20.3cm   Dark (navy) blue cloth

KEY TO FIRST EDITION: On back of page (195):
First published 1951

Front board: (blank)
Spine: (lettered in silver)
PRINCE/CASPIAN/curlicue/C.S.LEWIS/GEOFFREY/BLES
Rear board: (blank)
Top edge of pages: (no color)
Endpapers: (front only: full-spread map of Narnia in black on off-white)
Page (1): PRINCE CASPIAN
Page (2): *BY THE SAME AUTHOR*/20 titles, from THE LION, THE WITCH AND THE WARDROBE through THE PERSONAL HERESY /(*in collaboration with E. M. W. Tillyard*)
Inserted color frontispiece of dancing children, on slick paper
Page (3): PRINCE CASPIAN/*The Return to Narnia*/by/C. S. LEWIS/ILLUSTRATED BY PAULINE BAYNES/LONDON /GEOFFREY BLES
Page (4): TO/MARY CLARE HAVARD

(Mary Clare Havard was the daughter of Dr. Robert Havard, Lewis's personal physician, close friend, and one of the most faithful attenders of the Inklings weekly meetings. Another Inkling, Hugo Dyson, gave him the nickname "Humphrey", and Lewis named the doctor in *Perelandra* "Humphrey" as a tribute to him.)

Page 5: CONTENTS/chapters I.-XV (pages 7 – 180)
Page 6: (blank)
Pages 7-(195): (text)
Page (196): *Printed in Great Britain by/Butler & Tanner Ltd Frome /for Geoffrey Bles Ltd/52 Doughty Street London W C1/First published 1951*

Dust jacket: (Later impression Narnia jackets are so noted at the top of the front flap)

Front panel: (pictorial dust jacket extending through the spine, with off-white lettering on dark blue, in the center of which is a 10cm circular picture in blue and green of Edmund, Lucy, two women and a tree, dancing within a circle of grapevine.)

Spine: (off-white lettering on dark blue) PRINCE CASPIAN/*The Return/to Narnia/by/*C. S. LEWIS/picture of Reepicheep holding a cluster of grapes/BLES

Back panel: (advertisement and reviews for *The Lion, the Witch and the Wardrobe*)

Front flap: PRINCE CASPIAN/*The Return to Narnia/*This is a sequel to Dr C. S. LEWIS'/famous Children's Book, "The/Lion, the Witch and the Ward-/robe," of which reviews are given/on the back of this cover./(price in lower right corner) *10s 6d net* Back flap: (blank)

46. (First American edition) **PRINCE CASPIAN.**
New York: Macmillan, October 15, 1951.
192 pp. 14cm x 21cm Yellow-green cloth

KEY TO FIRST EDITION: On back of title page: **First Printing**

Front board: (in black silhouette in center, approximately 11.5cm x 5.5cm) (Prince Caspian and 5 Narnians dancing)
Spine: C. S. LEWIS (figure) PRINCE CASPIAN (figure) MACMILLAN
Back board: (blank)
Endpapers: (blank)
Page (i): (half-title) PRINCE CASPIAN
Page (ii): (blank)
Page (iii): PRINCE CASPIAN/*The Return to Narnia/*BY C. S. LEWIS/(illustration of 4 children in front of an old doorway)
Page (iv): *To/Mary Clare Havard/*(copyright information)/First Printing/PRINTED IN THE UNITED STATES OF AMERICA
Page (v): CONTENTS/chapters I through XV)
Page (vi): (blank)
Pages 1 through 186: (text)

Dust jacket: (all on pink background)

Front panel: (text in black) PRINCE CASPIAN/*The Return to Narnia*/(colored illustration of tree, 2 children, and 2 adults dancing, surrounded by grapevine wreath)/*A Story for Children*/*by*/C. S. LEWIS

Spine: (horizontally, with text in black) C. S. LEWIS (colored apple twig) PRINCE CASPIAN (colored apple twig) Macmillan

Back panel: (colored illustration of Reepicheep on white background)

Front flap: PRINCE CASPIAN/*By C. S. Lewis*/(publisher's blurb)/*Illustrated by Pauline Baynes*/*8-12* $2.50

Back flap: THE LION, THE WITCH/AND THE WARDROBE/*By C. S. Lewis*/(publisher's blurb)/*Illustrated by Pauline Baynes*

47. MERE CHRISTIANITY/*A revised and amplified edition, with a new introduction, of the three books, "Broadcast Talks", "Christian Behaviour", and "Beyond Personality."*
London: Geoffrey Bles, July 7, 1952
178 pp   20.4cm x 14.5cm   Light blue cloth

KEY TO FIRST EDITION: On back of title page:
First Published **1952**

Front board: (blank)
Spine: (in silver) BLES (at bottom) (then horizontally) *MERE CHRISTIANITY* (star) *C. S. LEWIS*
Rear board: (blank)
Endpapers: (blank)
Page (i): MERE CHRISTIANITY/("Y" in an oval, in lower right corner)
Page (ii): *BY THE SAME AUTHOR*/(21 titles)
Page (iii): MERE CHRISTIANITY/A revised and amplified edition, with a/new introduction, of the three books/*Broadcast Talks, Christian Behaviour/and Beyond Personality*/by/C. S. LEWIS /GEOFFREY BLES/LONDON
Page (IV): *Printed in Great Britain by/The Garden City Press Ltd/for Geoffrey Bles Ltd/52 Dou9ghty Street London WC1*
Page v through xii: PREFACE/The contents of this book were first given on the air ... That is one of the rules common to the whole house.
Page xiii-xiv: CONTENTS/(Preface and Books I through IV)
Page (1): *BOOK I*/RIGHT AND WRONG AS A CLUE TO/THE MEANING OF THE UNIVERSE
Page (2): (blank)
Pages 3 through 25: (text)
Page 26: (blank)
Page (27): *BOOK II*/WHAT CHRISTIANS BELIEVE
Page (28): (blank)
Pages 29 through 52: (text)
Page (53): *BOOK III*/CHRISTIAN BEHAVIOUR
Page (54): (blank)
Pages 55 through 118: (text)

Page (119): *BOOK IV*/BEYOND PERSONALITY: OR FIRST STEPS/IN THE DOCTRINE OF THE TRINITY
Page (120): (blank)
Pages 121 through (177): (text)
Page (178): (blank)

Dust jacket:
Front panel: (off-white lettering on dark red background) MERE CHRISTIANITY/A revised and amplified edition, with/a new Introduction, of the three books/*Broadcast Talks/Christian Behaviour*/by/C. S. LEWIS/GEOFFREY BLES
Spine: (off-white lettering on dark red background) BLES (at bottom) (then horizontally) *MERE CHRISTIANITY* (star) C. S. LEWIS
Back panel: (red lettering on off-white background) (signature of C. S. Lewis)/(brief comments on Lewis from *The Times Literary Supplement* and *The Expository Times*, followed by listing of eleven books: The Screwtape Letters, 22nd impression, 7s. 6d. net, through The Abolition of Man, 2nd impression, 3s. 6d. net)/(single rule) /GEOFFREY BLES LTD/52 DOUGHTY STREET, LONDON, W.C.1
Front flap: (red lettering on off-white background) Some years ago Dr. C. S. Lewis/gave on the radio three series of/Addresses which were subsequently/published in three small books -- ... For this new edition the original/Addresses have been completely/revised, and in many cases amplified,/by the author, who has also written/a new and most interesting Preface./*These volumes can still be obtained separately.*/(in lower right corner) *8s. 6d. net*
Back flap: (blank)

48. (First American edition) **MERE CHRISTIANITY.**
New York: Macmillan, November 11, 1952
189 pp   14.5cm x 21cm   Bright blue cloth

KEY TO FIRST EDITION: On the back of the title page:
First Printing

<u>Front board</u>: (in white) MERE CHRISTIANITY
<u>Spine</u>: (horizontally in white) *Lewis* MERE CHRISTIANITY
Macmillan
<u>Rear board</u>: (blank)
<u>Endpapers</u>: (blank)
<u>Page (i)</u>: (half-title)
<u>Page (ii)</u>: (list of Lewis books)
<u>Page (iii)</u>: (in single-rule box) MERE CHRISTIANITY/A revised
and enlarged edition,/with a new introduction, of the/three books
The Case for Christ-/ianity, Christian Behaviour, and/*Beyond
Personality*/by/C. S. LEWIS/THE MACMILLAN COMPANY/*New
York, 1952*
<u>Page (iv)</u>: (copyright information)/*First Printing*/PRINTED IN THE
UNITED STATES OF AMERICA
<u>Page v through xii</u>: PREFACE
<u>Pages xiii--xiv</u>: CONTENTS
<u>Pages 1 through 175</u>: (text) (followed by one blank sheet)

Dust jacket: (decorative jacket by Ursula Suess, with repeated dark
blue lines in the background)
<u>Front panel</u>: (lettered in white in three boxes with dark blue
background) (top box) C. S. LEWIS (middle box) *Mere/Christianity*
(bottom box) *A revised and enlarged edition, with/a new
introduction, of* THE CASE FOR/CHRISTIANITY, CHRISTIAN
BEHAVIOUR,/*and* BEYOND PERSONALITY
<u>Spine</u>: (in white on dark blue background in three boxes) C. S.
LEWIS/*Mere Christianity*/MACMILLAN
<u>Back panel</u>: (three reviews, from *New York Times, Time Magazine,*
and *New York Herald Tribune*)
<u>Front flap</u>: (publisher's blurb)/*Jacket design by Ursula Suess*/$2.75
<u>Back flap</u>: (continuation of publisher's blurb)

49. THE VOYAGE OF THE *DAWN TREADER*.

London: Geoffrey Bles, September 15, 1952
223pp   14cm x 20.3cm   Light blue cloth

KEY TO FIRST EDITION: On back of page 223:
First published 1952

Front board: (blank)
Spine: (lettered in silver) THE/VOYAGE/OF THE/*DAWN*/
TREADER/(filigree)/C. S. LEWIS/GEOFFREY/BLES
Rear board: (blank)
Endpapers: (front only: full-spread map of Narnia, in blue on off-
white)
Page (1): THE VOYAGE OF THE/*DAWN TREADER*
Page (2): *THE CHRONICLES OF NARNIA*/(first three titles)
Page (3): (blank)
Page (4): (frontispiece in black) Plan of the *Dawn Treader*
Page (5): THE VOYAGE OF THE/*DAWN TREADER*/by/C. S.
LEWIS/WITH ILLUSTRATIONS BY /PAULINE BAYNES
/LONDON/GEOFFREY BLES
Page (6): TO/GEOFFREY CORBETT (Geoffrey Corbett was the
foster son of Owen Barfield. In 1969 he changed his name to Jeffrey
Barfield.)
Page (7): CONTENTS/(chapters I through XVI)
Page (8): (blank)
Pages 9 through 223: (text)
Page (224): *Printed in Great Britain by/Butler & Tanner Ltd
Frome/for Geoffrey Bles Ltd/52 Doughty Street London W C1/First
published 1952*

Dust jacket: (Later impression Narnia jackets are so noted at the top
of the front flap)
Front panel: (pictorial dust jacket extending through the spine, with
white lettering on dark red background, in the center of which is a
picture of the Dawn Treader in an oval 13cm x 9cm.)
Spine: (white lettering on dark red background) The/Voyage/of
the/*Dawn Treader*/by/C. S. LEWIS/(picture of Reepicheep with
paddle and tub)/BLES

Back panel: (reviews of The Lion, the Witch and the Wardrobe and Prince Caspian, with prices of 8s 6d net and 10s 6d net)
Front flap: (publisher's blurb in black with title in red, and price of *10s 6d net*)
Back flap: (blank)

50. (First American edition)
THE VOYAGE OF THE *DAWN TREADER*
New York: Macmillan, September 30, 1952
218 pp. 14 x 21cm   Gray-blue cloth

KEY TO FIRST EDITION: On back of title page: **First Printing**

Front board: (dark blue illustration of dragon head ship's prow in lower right corner)
Spine: (printed horizontally in dark blue) C. S. LEWIS (figure)
THE VOYAGE OF THE *DAWN TREADER* (figure)
MACMILLAN
Rear board: (blank)
Endpapers: (blank, followed by a blank sheet)
Page (i): (half-title) THE VOYAGE OF THE *DAWN TREADER*
Page (ii): (frontispiece) (the *Dawn Treader*)
Page (iii): THE VOYAGE OF THE/*DAWN TREADER*/By C. S. *Lewis*/ILLUSTRATIONS/BY PAULINE BAYNES/THE MACMILLAN COMPANY – NEW YORK/1952
Page (iv): (copyright information) /First Printing/PRINTED IN THE UNITED STATES OF AMERICA
Page (v): *To*/*Geoffrey Barfield*
Page (vi): (blank)
Page vii: CONTENTS/(chapters I through XVI
Pages 1 through 210: (text)

Dust jacket: (all on light gray-blue background)
Front panel: (text in black)THE VOYAGE OF THE/*DAWN TREADER*/(in 13cm x 9cm oval in center) (red ship on blue sea within wreath of seaweed and aquatic creatures on white background)/*A Story for Children*/by/C. S. LEWIS

<u>Spine</u>: (printed horizontally in black) C. S. LEWIS (figure) THE VOYAGE OF THE *DAWN TREADER* (figure) Macmillan

<u>Back panel</u>: (red and gray-blue illustration in center oval 4.5cm x 7.5cm) (mouse with paddle in a floating tub)

<u>Front flap</u>: (right upper corner clipped) (title, author, and publisher's blurb) (in lower right corner: 8-12/$2.75) (In the Taylor University collection there is also a rare variant jacket without the upper right corner clipped and with no price at the bottom, but otherwise identical to the foregoing – possibly a proof jacket.)

<u>Back flap</u>: (publisher's blurb for first two Narnia books)

51. THE SILVER CHAIR.
London: Geoffrey Bles, September 7, 1953.
220pp   14cm x 20.3cm   Dark blue cloth

KEY TO FIRST EDITION: On back of title page:
First published 1953

Front board: (blank)
Spine: (lettered in silver)
THE/SILVER/CHAIR/(filigree)/C.S.LEWIS/GEOFFREY/BLES
Rear board: (blank)
Endpapers: (front only: full-spread map of Narnia, in black on off-white)
Page (1): THE/SILVER/CHAIR
Page (2): *THE CHRONICLES OF NARNIA/*(4 titles)
Page (3): (blank)
Page (4): (frontispiece in black – two children in a forest)
Page (5): THE SILVER CHAIR/by/C. S. LEWIS/WITH ILLUSTRATIONS BY PAULINE BAYNES/LONDON /GEOFFREY BLES
Page (6): *Printed in Great Britain by/Butler & Tanner Ltd Frome /for Geoffrey Bles Ltd/52 Doughty Street London W C1/First published 1953*
Page (7): TO/NICHOLAS HARDIE
(Nicholas Hardie was the son of Colin Hardie, a colleague of Lewis' at Oxford and fellow Inkling.)
Page (8): (blank)
Page (9): CONTENTS/(chapters I though XVI)
Page (10): (blank)
Pages 11 through 217: (text)
Pages (218) through (220): (blank)

Dust jacket: (Later impression Narnia jackets are so noted at the top of the front flap)
Front panel: (pictorial dust jacket extending through the spine, with the title in off-white lettering on green, in the center of which is an oval picture in black of the silver chair surrounded by Earthmen.)

Spine: (lettered in black) THE/SILVER/CHAIR/(illustration of a Marshwiggle, in black on white background/BLES
Back panel: (advertisements and reviews of 3 previous titles, with titles in green and reviews in black, on off-white background)
Front flap: THE SILVER CHAIR/When Jill Pole was carried off … the task which the Great Lion, Aslan, had set them./(in right bottom corner) 10*s*. 6*d*. net
Back flap: (at bottom) APT/A529

52. (First American edition) **THE SILVER CHAIR.**
New York: Macmillan, 1953
216pp   14cm x 21cm   Very dark blue cloth

KEY TO FIRST EDITION: On back of title page: **First Printing**

Front board: (illustration of a seated Marshwiggle in lower right corner, in red)
Spine: (lettered horizontally in red) C. S. LEWIS (filigree) THE SILVER CHAIR (filigree) MACMILLAN
Rear board: (blank)
Endpapers: (blank)
Page (i): *THE SILVER CHAIR*
Page (ii): (frontispiece in black – two children in a forest)
Page (iii): *THE SILVER CHAIR/by C. S. Lewis/*ILLUSTRATIONS BY PAULINE BAYNES/THE MACMILLAN COMPANY (dot) NEW YORK
Page (iv): Copyright, 1953, by/THE MACMILLAN COMPANY /All rights reserved, etc./First Printing/PRINTED IN THE UNITED STATES OF AMERICA
Page (v): *To/Nicholas Hardie*
Page (vi): (blank)
Page vii: CONTENTS/(chapters I through XVI)
Page (viii): (blank)
Pages 1 through 208: (text)

Dust jacket:
Front panel: (pictorial dust jacket extending through the spine, with the title in off-white lettering on orange, in the center of which is an oval picture in black of the silver chair surrounded by Earthmen.)
Spine: (lettered horizontally) (black lettering) C. S. LEWIS (white lettering) THE SILVER CHAIR (black lettering) Macmillan
Back panel: (illustration of walking Marchwiggle, in black on off-white background, in 8.3cm x 5cm oval)
Front flap: (top corner clipped) THE/SILVER CHAIR/*By C. S. LEWIS*/Eustace and Jill ran right into ... to assist the children in their mission./*Illustrated by Pauline Baynes*/Ages 10-14/(lower right corner) $2.75
Back flap: *STORIES FOR CHILDREN*/By *C. S. Lewis*/The imaginative land of Narnia, etc./(first three titles)

53. THE HORSE AND HIS BOY.

London: Geoffrey Bles,

September 6, 1954   200pp   14cm x 20.3cm   Gray cloth

KEY TO FIRST EDITION: On back of title page:
First published 1954

Front board: (blank)

Spine: (in silver) THE/HORSE/AND/HIS BOY/(filgree)/GEOFFREY/BLES

Rear board: (blank)

Endpapers: (front only: full-spread map of the Desert, in black on off-white)

Page (1): THE HORSE AND HIS BOY

Page (2): *THE CHRONICLES OF NARNIA*/(5 titles)

Inserted color frontispiece of princes of Narnia surrounded by a crowd in Tashbaan , on slick paper

Page (3): THE HORSE AND HIS BOY/by/C. S. LEWIS/*WITH ILLUSTRATIONS BY*/PAULINE BAYNES/LONDON/GEOFFREY BLES

Page (4): *Printed in Great Britain by/Butler & Tanner Ltd Frome /for Geoffrey Bles Ltd/52 Doughty Street London W C1/First published 1954*

Page (5): TO/DAVID AND DOUGLAS GRESHAM

Page (6): (blank)

Page 7: CONTENTS/(chapters I through XV)

Page (8): (illustration: Shasta mending his father's nets)

Pages 9 through 199: (text)

Page (200): (blank)

Dust jacket: (Later impression Narnia jackets are so noted at the top of the front flap)

Front panel: (pictorial dust jacket extending through the spine, with the title in off-white lettering on dark red, in the center of which is an oval picture in black of the horse, Bree, looking at Shasta sleeping under a tree.)

Spine: (lettered in white) THE/HORSE/AND/HIS BOY/C. S. LEWIS/(illustration in black of Shasta riding on Bree)/(lettered in black) BLES

Back panel: *TALES OF NARNIA*/(advertisements, with reviews, of the previous four titles)
Front flap: THE HORSE AND/HIS BOY/When someone said that the boy Shasta ... to Narnia itself./*Pictures by Pauline Baynes*/(in lower right corner) 10*s*. 6*d. net*
Back flap: (blank)

54. (First American edition) **THE HORSE AND HIS BOY**
New York: Macmillan, October 5, 1954
201 pp. 14cm x 21 cm Pink-brown cloth

KEY TO FIRST EDITION: On the back of the title page:
FIRST PRINTING

Front board: (in dark brown, in a 7cm x 5cm oval) (figure)/The Horse and/His Boy
Spine: (lettered horizontally in dark brown) C. S. LEWIS The Horse and His Boy Macmillan
Rear board: (blank)
Endpapers: (blank)
Page (i): (half-title) The Horse and His Boy
Page (ii): (first five titles of The Chronicles of Narnia)
Page (iii): The Horse and/His Boy/*By C. S. LEWIS*(figure)/WITH ILLUSTRATIONS BY/PAULINE BAYNES/THE MACMILLAN COMPANY/New York
Page (iv): (copyright information) FIRST PRINTING/PRINTED IN THE UNITED STATES OF AMERICA
Page (v): *To David and Douglas Gresham*
Page (vi): (blank)
Page (vii): CONTENTS (chapters I through XV)
Page (viii): (blank)
Page (ix): (another half title) The Horse and His Boy
Page (x): (illustration of a boy with fishing net)
Pages 1 through 191: (text plus two blank sheets before the endpaper)

Dust jacket: (all except flaps on dark brown background)

Front panel: (in white type) The Horse and/His Boy/(illustration of horse, with boy sleeping under a tree, in black with light green sky on white background, in a 12cm x 9.5cm oval)

Spine: (horizontally in white lettering) C. S. LEWIS/The Horse and His Boy/Macmillan

Back panel: (boy on horse in 5cm x 8.5 cm oval, in black with light green and white background)

Front flap: (title, author, and publisher's blurb)/(Ages 10-14)/$2.75 in lower right corner

The upper right corner of the flap is clipped, but a tiny remnant of something, probably a price, can still be seen, which suggests that all of the American first edition jackets had a price here (perhaps Canadian) as well as on the bottom. (In the Taylor University collection there is also a rare variant jacket with a larger clipping of the upper corner, which confirms my suspicion that a price was clipped. However, this variant is also clipped at the bottom corner, with the $2.75 price showing, but there is the remnant of a dollar sign and what looks like the bottom of a "3" still showing. Your guess is as good as mine as to what this price may have been!)

Back flap: (list of the first four Narnia books)

55. ENGLISH LITERATURE IN THE SIXTEENTH CENTURY EXCLUDING DRAMA.

OXFORD: At the Clarendon Press, September 16, 1954
696 pp   15.5cm x 22.5cm (see note below)   Dark blue (navy) cloth

When first asked in 1937 to write Volume III of the Oxford History of English Literature (OHEL), Lewis wrote to one of the editors, "My dear Wilson, ... The O HELL lies like a nightmare on my chest ever since I got your specimen bibliography: I shant try to desert – anyway, I suppose the exit is thronged with dreadful faces and fiery arms – but I have a growing doubt if I ought to be doing this ... Do you think there's any chance of the world ending before the O HELL appears? Yours, in deep depression, C. S. Lewis." For nine years Lewis labored over this monumental work, which he always referred to as the "O HELL," by trying to read every book written in the 16th century and writing an essay on each one! He finally completed it in 1953 – having written 11 other books during this period, including the first four volumes of the Chronicles of Narnia.

KEY TO FIRST EDITION: At bottom of title page:
OXFORD/AT THE CLARENDON PRESS/1954

(The boards of the first British edition, as noted above, are 22.5cm in height. There is a variant issue, however, the boards of which are only 21.5cm in height, with the text block trimmed one centimeter at the bottom, and the topedge dyed blue. Except for these differences and the printer's marks noted below on page (1), the two versions are otherwise identical in all respects. This variant appears to be the first issue for the American market, with a different dust jacket, as noted below in the description of the first American edition.)

Front board: (blank)
Spine: (gilt lettering) (single rule)/ENGLISH/LITERATURE/IN THE/SIXTEENTH/CENTURY/EXCLUDING/DRAMA/C. S. LEWIS/(seal of the university)/OXFORD/single rule
Rear board: (blank)
Endpapers: (off-white)

Page (i): OXFORD HISTORY OF/ENGLISH LITERATURE /*Edited by*/F. P. WILSON *and* BONAMY DOBRÉE
Page (ii): THE OXFORD HISTORY OF/ENGLISH LITERATURE/*Edited by*/F. P.WILSON AND BONAMY DOBRÉE/(list of titles I through XII in the series)/(*The titles of some volumes are provisional*)
Page (iii): ENGLISH LITERATURE/IN THE/SIXTEENTH CENTURY/EXCLUDING DRAMA/BY/C. S. LEWIS/FELLOW OF MAGDALEN COLLEGE, OXFORD/*The Completion of*/THE CLARK LECTURES/*Trinity College, Cambridge*/1944/OXFORD /AT THE CLARENDON PRESS/1954
Page (iv): *Oxford University Press, Amen House, London E.C. 4* /GLASGOW NEW YORK TORONTO MELBOURNE WELLINGTON/BOMBAY CALCUTTA MADRAS KARACHI CAPE TOWN IBADAN/*Geoffrey Cumerlege, Publisher to the University*/(short rule)/PRINTED IN GREAT BRITAIN
Page (v): PREFACE/When I began this book ... for submitting to certain
Page (vi): vi PREFACE/... petty pilfrages ... and Miss Joy Davidman for help with the proofs./C. S. L.,/MAGDALEN COLLEGE /OXFORD/7 October 1953
Page (vii): CONTENTS/(Introduction, Books I through III, Epilogue, Chronological Table, Bibliography, and Index)
Page (viii): (blank)
Pages (1) through 696: (text and index)

Dust jacket: (light brownish yellow paper imprinted in blue and brown) Key to the true first edition, first printing jacket is a tiny (7/54) in blue at the bottom of the back panel. So many printings of this book have been made that later dust jackets are commonly found.
Front panel: (in 11.5cm x 20cm single rule border subdivided into three sections) (first section, in brown) *Oxford History of*/ENGLISH LITERATURE/ EDITED BY/F. P. WILSON AND BONAMY DOBREE (second section, in blue) English Literature/in the/ Sixteenth Century/excluding Drama/*The completion of*/THE CLARK LECTURES/*Trinity College, Cambridge, 1944*/C. S. LEWIS/(third section, in brown) Oxford: At the Clarendon Press

<u>Spine</u>: ENGLISH/LITERATURE/IN THE/SIXTEENTH /CENTURY/excluding Drama/C. S. LEWIS/(logo)/OXFORD
<u>Back panel</u>: (10 volumes listed, with tiny (7/54) in blue at the bottom)
<u>Front flap</u>: (publisher's blurb with two Lewis titles below: THE ALLEGORY OF LOVE @ 18s. net and A PREFACE TO PARADISE LOST @9s. 6d. net
<u>Back flap</u>: (12 country addresses for Oxford University Press, followed by the then name of the publisher, Geoffrey Cumerlege)

56. (First American edition)
ENGLISH LITERATURE IN THE SIXTEENTH CENTURY EXCLUDING DRAMA.
As noted in 55 above, the first edition sold in the United States was the trimmed-down edition printed in Britain but dyed blue on the top-edge, in a dust jacket on the back panel of which was the U.S. address: Oxford University Press, 114 Fifth Avenue, New York 11, New York. There were two versions of this jacket, the only difference being on the front flap. On one, a price of $7.00 is shown, with no price shown on the other.

KEY TO FIRST EDITION: The first American printing is identified by "First Published 1954/PRINTED IN THE UNITED STATES OF AMERICA" at the bottom of the verso of the title page, and the top edge is not dyed.

The same jacket, with the New York address on the back panel, was presumably used for this printing as well. Except for these two changes, the text block is identical to that printed in Britain.

This book was reprinted so often, both in the US and the UK, that one has to check book and jacket carefully to determine a true first printing.

57. THE MAGICIAN'S NEPHEW.
London: The Bodley Head, May 2, 1955.
183 pp   14cm x 20.3cm   Light green cloth

Although this was the sixth of the series to be published, by the time he had written it Lewis felt that *The Magician's Nephew* should be read first, to be followed by *The Lion, the Witch and the Wardrobe* in the same order in which the first five were published, then ending with *The Last Battle.*

The Bodley Head took over the publication of the hardcover editions of the last two books in the series, when Collins began publishing the paperbacks of the first five volumes.

The publisher William Collins & Sons bought Geoffrey Bles in 1953, and although Collins began publishing Lewis paperbacks in 1955, they retained the Bles imprint on hardcover books until Jocelyn Gibb, managing director of Bles, retired in 1974. Collins then published a new edition of the first five Narnia books in 1974.

KEY TO FIRST EDITION: (On back of title page)
First Published 1955
Front board: (blank)
Spine: (lettered in silver)
THE/MAGICIAN'S/NEPHEW/(filigree)/C. S. LEWIS
/THE/BODLEY/HEAD
Rear board: (blank)
Endpapers: (blank)
Page (1): THE MAGICIAN'S NEPHEW/logo of Bodley Head
Books
Page (2): (blank)
Page (3): THE/MAGICIAN'S NEPHEW/by/C. S. LEWIS/1955
/THE BODLEY HEAD/LONDON
Page (4): First Published 1955/*This book is copyright ...*
.*(etc)*/Printed in Great Britain by/THE PITMAN PRESS, BATH/for
JOHN LAND THE BODLEY HEAD LTD./28 Little Russell Street,
London, W.C.1
Page(5): CONTENTS/(Chapters I through XV)
Page (6): TO/THE KILMER FAMILY

(The Kilmers were a Washington, D.C. family whose eight children corresponded with Lewis in 1954, shortly before publication of *The Magician's Nephew*. Many of the letters from Lewis to the children may be found in *Letters to Children*, by Dorsett and Mead, Macmillan, 1985.)
Pages 7 through 183: (text)

Dust jacket:
Front panel: (white lettering on green background) THE MAGICIAN'S/NEPHEW/(picture in orange and black of two children holding candles, about to enter a doorway)/*A Story for Children by*/C. S. LEWIS
Spine: (white lettering on green background) THE/MAGICIAN'S/NEPHEW/C. S. LEWIS/(picture of flying horse in black on white background)/(logo of Bodley Head Books)
Back panel: (lettered in black on white background, in a double-ruled border in black within a green decorative border) (black-and-white montage)/*TALES OF NARNIA*/(single green rule)/(first five titles)/Published by GEOFFREY BLES LTD./(green decorative diamond, as in previous green rule)/Forthcoming/THE LAST BATTLE/to be published by/THE BODLEY HEAD
Front flap: (lettered in black) *THE MAGICIAN'S NEPHEW*/(single green rule)/(publisher's blurb)/(lettered in green) *Jacket by Pauline Baynes*/(lettered in black lower left corner) 3/3275 (on a slant in right corner) 8s 6d net
Back flap: (logo of Bodley Head Books)/If you would like ... /THE BODLEY HEAD/28, LITTLE RUSSELL STREET/LONDON, W.C.1/*Printed in Great Britain for*/*John Lane The Bodley Head*

58. (First American edition) **THE MAGICIAN'S NEPHEW**
New York: Macmillan, October 4, 1954
(Hooper gives this publication date, which would have been seven months prior to the British publication. However, the book shows the publication year as 1955.)
175 pp   14cm x 20cm   Light green cloth

KEY TO FIRST EDITION: On the back of the title page:
First Printing

Front board: (in black) (illustration of Digory opening a door)
Spine: (lettered horizontally in black) C. S. Lewis THE
MAGICIAN'S NEPHEW Macmillan
Rear board: (blank)
Endpapers: (blank)
Page (i): (half-title) THE MAGICIAN'S NEPHEW
Page (ii): (list of first six volumes of the Chronicles of Narnia)
Page (iii): THE/MAGICIAN'S/NEPHEW/*By C. S. Lewis*
/ILLUSTRATED BY PAULINE BAYNES/THE MACMILLAN
COMPANY/*New York*
Page (iv): (copyright information)/First Printing/PRINTED IN THE
UNITED STATES OF AMERICA
Page (v): TO/THE KILMER FAMILY
Page (vi)): (blank)
Page (vii): *Contents* (with chapters 1 through 15)
Page (viii): (blank)
Pages 1 through 167): (text)

Dust jacket: (All except flaps with dark green background)
Front panel: (lettered in black) THE MAGICIAN'S/NEPHEW
/(colored illustration in orange-brown and black of two children
entering a doorway)/*A Story for Children by*/C. S. LEWIS
Spine: (lettered in black horizontally) C. S. Lewis THE
MAGICIAN'S NEPHEW Macmillan
Back panel: (colored illustration of a guinea pig with a ring tied to it,
in black and orange-brown)
Front flap: (title, author and publisher's blurb)/Ages 10-
14/*Illustrated by Pauline Baynes*/(price of $2.75 parallel to right
edge of flap (The flap is clipped at the top corner, with a long,
shallow clipping of the bottom corner, just above which is the price.)
Back flap: (list of the first six volumes of the Chronicles of Narnia)

In the collection at Taylor University is another rare variant jacket in
which the front flap corners are not clipped and which has no price. It
also differs from the jacket as described above by being dark green
except for the flaps, with the front illustration colored in yellow, and
the illustration on the back in a clearly defined white oval, with
much darker black detail in the guinea pig figure.

59. SURPRISED BY JOY/*The Shape of My Early Life***.**
London: Geoffrey Bles, 1955.
224 pp   15cm x 22cm   Gray cloth

<u>**KEY TO FIRST EDITION:**</u> (on back of title page)
First published in 1955
<u>Front board</u>: (blank)
<u>Spine</u>: (lettered in silver) (on yellow background 2.5cm x 5.6cm)
(triple rule)/Surprised/by/Joy/(3 dots)/C.S./Lewis/(triple rule)/
Geoffrey/Bles
<u>Rear board</u>: (blank)
<u>Endpapers</u>: (blank)
<u>Page (1)</u>: (half-title) SURPRISED BY JOY/The shape of my early
life
<u>Page (2)</u>: *Also by C. S. Lewis*/(7 titles – The Screwtape Letters
through Christian Behaviour)/*For Children*/(four titles – The Lion,
the Witch and the Wardrobe through The Horse and His Boy)
<u>Page (3)</u>: SURPRISED BY JOY/The shape of my early life/by/C. S.
LEWIS/*Surprised by joy — impatient as the wind*/WORDSWORTH
/*LONDON*/GEOFFREY BLES/1955
<u>Page (4)</u>: *Printed in Great Britain … ./First published in 1955*
<u>Page (5)</u>: To/DOM BEDE GRIFFITHS, O.S.B.
<u>Page (6)</u>: (blank)
<u>Page 7-8</u>: Preface
<u>Page 9</u>: Contents (with chapters I through XV)
<u>Page (10)</u>: (blank)
<u>Pages 9 through 224</u>: (text)

Dust jacket: All gray background except for flaps
<u>Front panel</u>: (lettered in white) C. S./Lewis/(lettered in gray on
yellow ovaloid background) SURPRISED/BY JOY/The Shape of
My Early Life/(lettered in white) Recommended by the Book
Society
<u>Spine</u>: (lettered in gray on a yellow background) C. S./Lewis/(cross)
/Surprised/by/Joy/(lettered in white) Geoffrey/Bles
<u>Back panel</u>: *Also by C. S. Lewis* (followed by 12 titles, from The
Screwtape Letters 23rd impression @ 7s 6d to Transpositions @ 2s
6d)

<u>Front flap</u>: (publisher's blurb)/*Jacket design by John R. Biggs*/15s. net
<u>Back flap</u>: (blank)

60. (First American edition) **SURPRISED BY JOY.**
New York: Harcourt, Brace & World, February 1, 1956.
248 pp   15cm x 21cm   Bright green cloth

KEY TO FIRST EDITION: On back of title page:
first American edition **1956**

<u>Front board</u>: (blank)
<u>Spine</u>: (lettered in silver) C. S. LEWIS/(triple rule)/*Surprised*/*by Joy*/(triple rule)/HARCOURT,/BRACE AND/COMPANY
<u>Rear board</u>: (blank)
<u>Endpapers</u>: (blank) (followed by blank sheet)
<u>Page (i)</u>: (half-title) SURPRISED BY JOY
<u>Page (ii)</u>: (list of Lewis titles)
<u>Page (iii)</u>: C. S. LEWIS/(single rule)/SURPRISED BY JOY/*THE SHAPE OF MY EARLY LIFE*/(single rule)/*Surprised by joy – impatient as the wind*/–WORDSWORTH/HARCOURT, BRACE AND COMPANY/NEW YORK
<u>Page (iv)</u>: (copyright information)/*first American edition* 1956 /LIBRARY OF CONGRESS CATALOG CARD NUMBER: 56-5329/PRINTED IN THE UNITED STATES OF AMERICA
<u>Page (v)</u>: TO/DOM BEDE GRIFFITHS, O.S.B.
<u>Page (vi)</u>: (blank)
<u>Page (vii)-viii</u>: *Preface*
<u>Page ix</u>: *Contents* (with chapters I through XV)
<u>Page (x)</u>: (blank)
<u>Page (1)</u>: (a second half-title)
<u>Page 2</u>: (blank)
<u>Pages 3 through 238</u>: (text, followed by 3 blank sheets before the endpapers)

Dust jacket:

Front panel: (green background) (lettered in yellow) Surprised/By Joy/(in a black box) (lettered in yellow) The Shape of My Early Life/C. S. LEWIS/In this book C. S. Lewis tells of his search for joy, a spiritual journey which led him from the Christianity of his early years into atheism, and then, back to Christianity.

Spine: (lettered in white) *C. S. LEWIS*/(lettered in white in a black box) *Sur-/prised/By/Joy/Harcourt,/Brace and/Company*

Back panel: (a very formal full-page photograph of Lewis by Walter Stoneman) The second and subsequent printings of the book had a much more interesting full-page photograph by John S. Murray of Lewis lighting a pipe, with a wreath of smoke curling up toward his face.

Front flap: (author, title, and publisher's blurb, with price of $3.50)

Back flap: (biographical sketch)/*Jacket design by Philip Grushkin*/HARCOURT, BRACE & COMPANY/383 Madison Avenue, New York 17, N.Y.

61. THE LAST BATTLE.
London: The Bodley Head, March 19, 1956
184 pp   14cm x 20.3cm   Medium blue cloth

KEY TO FIRST EDITION: (on back of title page)
First Published 1956

Front board: (blank)
Spine: (lettered in silver) THE/LAST/BATTLE/(filigree)/
C. S. LEWIS/THE/BODLEY/HEAD
Rear board: (blank)
Endpapers: (blank)
Page (1): THE LAST BATTLE/(logo of Bodley Head Books)
Page (2): Other books by C. S. Lewis/(Chronicles of Narnia and the
Space Trilogy)
Page (3): THE LAST BATTLE/A STORY FOR CHILDREN/*by*/
C. S. LEWIS/*Illustrated by*/Pauline Baynes/1956/THE BODLEY
HEAD/LONDON
Page (4): First Published 1956/(copyright and printing statements as
shown for The Magician's Nephew)
Page (5): CONTENTS
Page (6): (blank)
Pages 7 through 194: (text)

Dust jacket:
Front panel: (on gray-blue background which extends into spine)
(lettered in black) THE/LAST BATTLE/(illustration of Lucy and
Mr. Tumnus in front of a wall under two trees, in gray blue and
brown on a round white background about 9cm in diameter)
/(lettered in white) *A Story for Children by*/C. S. LEWIS
Spine: (lettered in black on gray blue background)
THE/LAST/BATTLE/(lettered in white) C. S. LEWIS/(picture of a
unicorn in gray-blue and black on a white background/((in black)
(logo of Bodley Head Books)
Back panel: (lettered in black on white background, in a double-
ruled border in black within a green decorative border) (black-and-
white montage)/*TALES OF NARNIA*/(single green rule)/(first five
titles)/Published by GEOFFREY BLES LTD./(green decorative

diamond)/THE MAGICIAN'S NEPHEW/ published by/THE BODLEY HEAD
Front flap: (title and publisher's blurb lettered in black)/ (lettered in green) *Jacket by Pauline Baynes*/(lettered in black lower left corner) 3/3301 (on a slant in right corner) 9s 6d net
Back flap: (logo of Bodley Head Books)/If you would like ... /THE BODLEY HEAD/28, LITTLE RUSSELL STREET/LONDON, W.C.1/*Printed in Great Britain for/John Lane The Bodley Head*

62. (First American edition) **THE LAST BATTLE**
New York: Macmillan, September 4, 1956
175 pp   14cm x 20cm   Light blue-green cloth

KEY TO FIRST EDITION: (on back of title page)
First Printing

Front board: (6cm x 3.5cm figure of two men and a unicorn 3.5 cm above the bottom edge)
Spine: (lettered in black horizontally)
C. S. Lewis   THE LAST BATTLE   Macmillan
Rear board: (blank)
Endpapers: (blank)
Page (i): THE LAST BATTLE
Page (ii): *The Chronicles of Narnia*/(seven titles)
Page (iii): *The*/*LAST BATTLE*/BY C. S. LEWIS/*With illustrations* /*BY PAULINE BAYNES*/*New York*/
THE MACMILLAN COMPANY
Page (iv): (copyright information)/*First Printing*/PRINTED IN THE UNITED STATES OF AMERICA
Page (v): CONTENTS
Page (vi): (blank)
Pages 7 through 174: (text followed by two blank sheets before the free endpaper)

Dust jacket:

Front panel: (dark gray-blue background extending through spine and rear panel) (IDENTICAL TO FRONT PANEL ON THE BRITISH EDITION)

Spine: (horizontally) (lettered in white) C. S. Lewis (lettered in black) THE LAST BATTLE   Macmillan

Back panel: (unicorn in gray-blue and black, in 4.5cm x 7.5cm white oval)

Front flap: (price in upper right corner) $2.75/(title and publisher's blurb)/*Illustrated by Pauline Baynes*/*Ages 10-14*

(lower right corner clipped by publisher)

Back flap: (publisher's blurb with brief description of the story in the previous six titles)

63. TILL WE HAVE FACES.
London: Geoffrey Bles, September 10, 1956
320 pp   5.25cm x 7.5cm   Dark blue cloth

KEY TO FIRST EDITION: On the back of the title page:
First published 1956
Front board: (blank)
Spine: (lettered in gold) C. S. LEWIS/(filigree)/*TILL WE
/HAVE/FACES/A Myth/Retold/*GEOFFREY BLES
Rear board: (blank)
Endpapers: (blank)
Page (1): TILL WE HAVE FACES/(brief commentary by Lewis)
Page (2): (blank)
Page (3): (quotation from Shakespeare) *Love is too young to know
what conscience is*
Page (4): (list of Lewis books)
Page 5: (title page) C. S. LEWIS/Till We Have Faces/*A Myth
Retold/LONDON/*GEOFFREY BLES/1956
Page (6): (printing information)/*First published 1956*
Page 7: TO/JOY DAVIDMAN
Page (8): (blank)
Page (9): PART ONE
Page (10): (blank)
Pages 11 through 320: (text)

Dust jacket:
Front panel: (Pictorial dust jacket by Biggs extending over the spine,
lettered in yellow and white on a black background, with a female
statue and flowing blood) *Till We/Have Faces/*C. S./Lewis/(in lower
right corner) BIGGS '56
Spine: (lettered in yellow) *Till We/Have/Faces/A/Myth/Retold
/by/C. S. Lewis/Bles*
Back panel: (on white background) (printed in red) *About this
book/*(printed in black) C. S. Lewis has based his novel '*Till We
Have Faces/*on the classical myth of Psyche and Cupid ...
Dr. Lewis writes: 'The central alteration in my own version consists
in making Psyche's palace invisible to normal, mortal eyes .../

(lettered in red) GEOFFREY BLES LTD/52 DOUGHTY STREET, LONDON, W.C.1

Front flap: (lettered in red) C. S. LEWIS *writes*:/(lettered in black) "This reinterpretation of an old story has live in the author's mind ... ever since he was an undergraduate ... "/The author takes his title from the book itself. "How can the gods meet us face to face till we have faces?" ... /(in red) 15s. *net*

Back flap: (reviews of *Surprised by Joy*)/(lower left corner) APT/h50

64. (First American edition) **TILL WE HAVE FACES**
New York: Harcourt, Brace and Company, September 10, 1956
319 pp   14.5cm x 21cm   Red cloth

KEY TO FIRST EDITION: On back of title page:
First American edition 1957

Front board: (blank)
Spine: (lettered in silver) C. S. LEWIS/TILL/WE/HAVE/FACES/ HARCOURT, BRACE/AND COMPANY/(in black) statue of Psyche
Top-edge: (dark purple)
Rear board: (blank)
Endpapers: (blank)
Page (i): TILL WE HAVE FACES/(two sword-fighting figures)
Page (ii): (list of 20 Lewis books)
Page (iii): TILL WE HAVE/FACES A MYTH RETOLD/C. S. LEWIS/*Love is too young to know what conscience is*/HARCOURT, BRACE AND COMPANY – NEW YORK
Page (iv): (copyright information) *first American edition 1957* /Drawings by Fritz Eichenberg/LIBRARY OF CONGRESS CATALOG CARD NUMBER: 56-11300/PRINTED IN THE UNITED STATES OF AMERICA
Page (v): TO JOY DAVIDMAN
Page (vi): (blank)
Page (1): (full-page illustration of two figures facing each other)
Page (2): (blank)
Pages 3 through 313: (text)

Dust jacket:
Front panel: (pictorial dust jacket by Fritz Eichenberg in red, blue, green, brown, and black, with left half filled with picture of Psyche) (lettered in white) TILL/WE/HAVE/FACES/A NOVEL BY /C. S./LEWIS
Spine: (on pictorial red background, lettered in white) C. S./LEWIS /(single black rule)/TLL/WE/HAVE/FACES/(in white on blue background) HARCOURT,/BRACE AND/COMPANY
Back panel: Wonderful full-page informal photo by John S. Murray of Lewis lighting up a pipe, with a large wreath of rising smoke
Front flap: (top right corner) $4.50/TILL WE HAVE FACES/ (publisher's blurb)
Back flap: (publisher's blurb)

65. REFLECTIONS ON THE PSALMS.
London: Geoffrey Bles, September 8, 1958
160 pp.   13.5cm x 20.5cm   Maroon cloth

KEY TO FIRST EDITION: There is no notation as such, but I have never seen a second printing.

Front board: (blank)
Spine: (lettered in yellow) *Reflections/on the/Psalms/*(dot)/
C.S./LEWIS/BLES
Top-edge: Dark green-blue
Rear board: (blank)
Endpapers: Gray
Page (i): REFLECTIONS ON THE PSALMS
Page (ii): (list of 19 books by Lewis)
Page (iii): *Reflections on the Psalms/by/C. S. LEWIS/Geoffrey
Bles/*LONDON
Page (iv): (printing information)/(copyright symbol)/
C. S. LEWIS, 1958
Page (v): TO/AUSTIN AND KATHERINE/FARRER
Page (vi): (blank)
Page vii: *Contents*
Page (viii): (blank)
Pages 1 through 151: (text)
Page (152): (blank)

Dust jacket:
Front panel: (gray-green, as on spine and back as well, with a dark green harp in the background) (lettered in white) C. S. LEWIS/ (lettered in orange)*Reflections/*(lettered in white) *on the/*(lettered in orange) *Psalms/*(lettered in white)
Spine: (in dark green box) (lettered in orange) *Reflections/on the/ Psalms/*(lettered in white)/C. S. LEWIS/(lettered in dark green) BLES
Back panel: (in an orange box) (list of 13 titles of Lewis religious books)
Front flap: (publisher's blurb)/*Jacket designed by Elizabeth Andrewes/*12s. 6d. net
Back flap: (brief note on C. S. Lewis)

66. (First American edition) **REFLECTIONS ON THE PSALMS**
New York: Harcourt, Brace & World, November 5, 1958
159 pp   14.5cm x 21cm   Red cloth

KEY TO FIRST EDITION: On the back of the title page:
first American edition

Front board: (gold design upper right)
Spine: (in black) *C. S. Lewis*/(horizontally in gold) REFLECTIONS
ON THE PSALMS/(in black) *Harcourt/Brace/and/Company*/(gold
design)
Rear board: (blank)
Endpapers: (green-blue) (blank)
Page (i): (half-title) REFLECTIONS ON THE PSALMS
(The copy at Taylor University is inscribed: *W. H. Lewis 1959.*
Although C. S. Lewis never visited the United States, his brother
Warnie, and author in his own right, made several trips to New York
to his American publisher. This copy was very likely signed at such
a time.)
Page (ii): (list of Lewis books)
Page (iii): C. S. LEWIS/*Reflections on the Psalms*/(decorative
figure)
Page (iv): (copyright information)/*first American edition/Library of
Congress Catalog Card Number: 58-10910*
Page (v): TO/AUSTIN AND KATHERINE/FARRER
Page (vi): (blank)
Page (vii): CONTENTS (with chapters I through XII)/*The Book of
Common Prayer is Crown Copyright. The extracts are reproduced
by permission.*
Page (viii): (blank)
Pages 1 through 151: (text)

Dust jacket: (pictorial dust jacket by Jennyee Wong, all on maroon
background except for flaps)
Front panel: (in white) *Reflections/on the/Psalms*/(design with
three crosses)/C. S. LEWIS/*Author of "The Screwtape Letters"/and
"Surprised by Joy"*
Spine: (lettered in gold) C. S./(horizontally) *Reflections on the
Psalms*/ (Harcourt, Brace logo)/*Harcourt,/Brace/and/Company*

Back panel: (six excerpts from the book)
Front flap: (upper right corner) $3.50/C. S. LEWIS/(in maroon)
Reflections/on the/Psalms/(publisher's blurb)
Back flap: (John S. Murray photograph of Lewis lighting his pipe, with a wreath of smoke rising toward his face)/(publisher's blurb)

67. THE WORLD'S LAST NIGHT.
New York: Harcourt, Brace & World, February 10, 1960
123 pp   14.5cm x 21.3cm   Medium blue cloth

KEY TO FIRST EDITION: On back of title page: **first edition**

Front board: (decorative piece in upper right corner, in gold)
Spine: (in black) *C. S. Lewis*/(horizontally in gold) THE WORLD'S
LAST NIGHT/(in black) *Harcourt/Brace/and/Company/*(gold
decorative piece
Rear board: (blank)
Endpapers: (blank, yellow, followed by one blank white sheet)
Page (i): THE WORLD'S LAST NIGHT/AND OTHER ESSAYS
Page (ii): (blank)
Page (iii): (list of Lewis books)
Page (iv): (blank)
Page (v): (title page) The World's Last Night/AND OTHER
ESSAYS BY/C. S. Lewis
Page (vi): (copyright information)/first edition/(identification of
source of each essay)
Page (vii): CONTENTS
Page (viii): (blank)
Page (1): (another half-title) THE WORLD'S LAST NIGHT AND
OTHER ESSAYS
Page (2): (blank)
Pages 3 through 113: (text) (followed by one blank sheet – i.e., two
blank pages)

Dust jacket: (decorative jacket by Jennyee Wong, all in dark
turquoise except flaps)
Front panel: (in red) THE/*World's/Last Night/*INCLUDING A NEW
"SCREWTAPE" DIALOGUE/C. S. LEWIS/AUTHOR OF "THE
SCREWTAPE LETTERS" AND/ "REFLECTIONS ON THE
PSALMS"/(black, red, and white design with cross in center)
Spine: (in black) C.S./LEWIS/(horizontally in red) *The World's Last
Night* AND OTHER ESSAYS/(H-B logo)/(in black) *Harcourt,
Brace and/Company*

Back panel: (descriptions of three Lewis books: SURPRISED BY JOY, TILL WE HAVE FACES, and REFLECTIONS ON THE PSALMS
Front flap: $3.00 (in upper right corner)/(publisher's blurb)/*Jacket design by Jennyee Wong*/(publisher's address)
Back flap: (John S. Murray photograph of Lewis lighting his pipe, with a wreath of smoke rising toward his face)/(publisher's blurb)

There was no British first edition.

68. THE FOUR LOVES.
London: Geoffrey Bles, March 28, 1960
160 pp.   14cm x 20.5cm   Gray cloth

KEY TO FIRST EDITION: (on back of title page)
First Published in 1960

Front board: (blank)
Spine: (lettered in red) THE/FOUR/LOVES/(filigree)/C.
S./LEWIS/BLES
Rear board: (blank)
Endpapers: (orange)
Page (1): THE FOUR LOVES
Page (2): (list of 20 books by Lewis)
Page (3): *The Four Loves/by/C. S. LEWIS/That our affection kill us not/nor dye.*   DONNE/*Geoffrey Bles*/LONDON
Page (4): (publishing information and copyright) *First Published in 1960*
Page (5): TO/*Chad Walsh*
Page (6): (blank)
Page 7: *Contents*
Page (8): (blank)
Pages 9 through (160): (text)
Dust jacket:
Front panel: Decorative jacket by Harvey, divided into four rectangles of four different colors – yellow, red, maroon, and white – overlaid with silver swirls, each with a word: Affection, Friendship, Eros, Charity, and, in a large silver circle on a white background: THE/FOUR/LOVES/(single rule)/C.S. LEWIS
Spine: (all lettering in black) (on yellow) C. S./Lewis/(single wide silver rule)/(on white) THE/FOUR/LOVES/(single wide silver rule)/ (on maroon) BLES
Back panel: (same overall design as on front, but lettered only in the central circle in black with 10 Lewis titles)
Front flap: (publisher's blurb)/ *Jacket design by Michael Harvey 12s 6d net*
Back flap: (blank except for publisher's note at bottom)

69. (First American edition) **THE FOUR LOVES.**
New York: Harcourt, Brace & World, July 27, 1960
192 pp   14.5cm x 21cm
(Two binding variations have been noted: (1) all black cloth and
maroon endpapers;(2) black cloth on the spine, extending one inch
front and back, with maroon paper covering the rest of the boards.)

KEY TO FIRST EDITION: On the back of the title page, buried in
copyright information at the bottom: *First American edition*

Front board: (blank on all-black-cloth copy; blind-embossed design
across cloth and paper one-third down from the top)
Spine: (lettered in gold) (horizontally) C. S. LEWIS/(at right angle)
Harcourt,/Brace and/Company/(horizontally) THE FOUR LOVES
Rear board: (small blind-embossed H-B logo near spine)
Endpapers: (as noted above)
Page (1): THE FOUR LOVES
Page (2): (list of Lewis books at bottom of page)
Page (3): C. S. LEWIS (vertical design of four decorative circles)
THE FOUR LOVES/*That our affections kill us not, nor dye/* –
DONNE/*Harcourt, Brace and Company/*(H-B logo)/*New York*
Page (4): (copyright information at bottom, with *First American
edition* imbedded)
Page (5): TO CHAD WALSH
Page (6): (blank)
Page 7: CONTENTS (with six chapters)
Page (8): (blank)
Page (9): (horizontal design as on p. (3))/CHAPTER I
Page (10): (blank)
Pages 11 through 192: (text)

Dust jacket: (pictorial jacket by Betty Anderson)
Front panel: (on white background) (in black) C. S. LEWIS (in red)
THE FOUR LOVES/*Author of "The Screwtape Letters"/*(vertical
design of four multi-colored circles)
Spine: (on black background) (horizontally) (design with crosses in
four circles/(in white) C. S. LEWIS/ (in red) THE FOUR LOVES
Back panel: (excerpts from the book on red background)

Front flap: (on white background) (in upper right corner) $3.75/(publisher's blurb)
Back flap: (WASHINGTON STAR review and publisher's blurb)

70. STUDIES IN WORDS.
Cambridge: Cambridge University Press, September 9, 1960
249 pp.   13.5cm x 20.5cm   Dark blue cloth

KEY TO FIRST EDITION: (at bottom of title page) **1961**

Front board: (blank)
Spine: (lettered in gold) (in 2.5cm x 3cm black box at top of spine) (single rule) C. S. LEWIS/(star)/STUDIES/IN/WORDS/ (single rule)/(university seal)/CAMBRIDGE
Rear board: (blank)
Endpapers: (blank)
Page (i): STUDIES IN WORDS
Page (ii): TO/STANLEY AND/JOAN BENNETT
Page (iii): (title page) STUDIES IN/WORDS/BY/C. S. LEWIS /*Professor of Medieval and Renaissance English*/in the *University of Cambridge and*/*Fellow of Magdalene College*/(university seal) /CAMBRIDGE/AT THE/UNIVERSITY PRESS/1960
Page (iv): (publishing information and copyright) 1960
Page v: CONTENTS
Page (vi): (blank)
Page vi: PREFACE
Page (ix): (blank)
Pages 1 through (240): (text)

Dust jacket:
Front panel: (bright red, as on spine and back as well) (lettered in black) C. S. LEWIS/(lettered in yellow) *Studies/in/Words*/(lettered in black) CAMBRIDGE UNIVERSITY PRESS (along the right edge, from top to bottom, lettered in black) NATURE/ SAD/WIT/FREE/SENSE/ SIMPLE/CONSCIOUS /CONSCIENCE
Spine: (lettered in black) C. S. LEWIS/(star)/(lettered horizontally in yellow)/*Studies in Words*/(star)/CAMBRIDGE

Back panel: (lettered in black) (description of ENGISH EXAMINED by Susie L. Tucker)

Front flap: (yellow background) (lettered in black) (publisher's blurb)/(lower right corner) 21s net

Back flap: (yellow) (blank)

There was no American first edition, the one sold in the U. S. having been the British edition. The dust jacket had the U.K. price, *21s. net*, in the lower right corner of the front flap, and the U.S. price, $3.95, in the upper right corner. Many copies will therefore have one or the other price clipped, depending upon where the book was sold.

71. THE SCREWTAPE LETTERS AND SCREWTAPE PROPOSES A TOAST.

London: Geoffrey Bles, February 27, 1961.
158 pp.   14 cm x 20.5 cm   Gray cloth

KEY TO FIRST EDITION: On back of title page:
THIS NEW EDITION 1961

Although the writing of *The Screwtape Letters* had come easily to Lewis, he found the experience unpleasant. "Though it was easy to twist one's mind into the diabolical attitude, it was not fun, nor not or long. The strain produced a sort of spiritual cramp." He therefore resisted requests to write more Screwtape letters – until 1959, when the American magazine, the *Saturday Evening Post*, invited him to write a Screwtape lecture or "address." The idea appealed to him, and *Screwtape Proposes a Toast* appeared in the issue of December 19, 1959, as a toast by Screwtape at the "annual dinner of the Tempter's Training College for Young Devils." Bles reprinted the letters with the addition of this one, and with a new and additional Preface by Lewis.

Front board: (blank)
Spine: (red lettering) C. S. LEWIS /THE/SCREWTAPE/LETTERS /AND/ SCREWTAPE/PROPOSES/A TOAST/BLES
Rear board: (blank)
Top edge of pages: (maroon)
Endpapers: (blank)

Page (1): (half-title)
Page (2): *Also by C. S. Lewis*/(15 titles: THE FOUR LOVES ...
TILL WE HAVE FACES
Page (3): (title page) The Screwtape Letters/and/Screwtape Proposes
a Toast/by/ C. S. LEWIS/*Fellow of Magdalene College, Cambridge*/
with a new Preface/London/GEOFFREY BLES/1961
Page (4): *The Screwtape Letters* are reprinted by kind permission of
The/ Guardian, and *Screwtape Proposes a Toast* by that of *The/
Saturday Evening Post*, with some changes/ALL RIGHTS
RESERVED/THE SCREWTAPE LETTERS: FIRST PUBLISHED
1942/23RD EDITION 1954/THIS NEW EDITION 1961/© THE
SCREWTAPE LETTERS, C. S. LEWIS, 1942/©SCREWTAPE
PROPOSES A TOAST, HELEN JOY LEWIS, 1960
Page 5 through (157): (PREFACE and text)
Page (158): PRINTED IN GREAT BRITAIN BY THE
WHITEFRIARS PRESS LTD./LONDON AND TONBRIDGE

Dust jacket:
Front panel: (red lettering on gray background) C. S. LEWIS/(within
a rounded border on black background) (white lettering)
THE/SCREWTAPE/LETTERS/&/(red lettering) SCREWTAPE/
PROPOSES A/TOAST (end of border)/(black lettering) *With a
New Preface*
Spine: (black lettering) C.S./LEWIS/(within a rounded border)
(white lettering on black background) THE /SCREWTAPE
/LETTERS /&/SCREW-/TAPE/PROPOSES/A/TOAST
(end of border)/BLES
Back panel: (black figure of Screwtape with a spider over its head,
on gray background)/(red lettering) *His Abysmal Sublimity Under-
Secretary /Screwtape, as imagined by the author,/C. S. Lewis*
Front flap: On its first appearance THE SCREWTAPE LETTERS
... "Screwtape Proposes a Toast'. / 12s. 6d. *net*
Back flap: (Publisher's blurb about the author, followed by a list of
16 books and their prices) THE FOUR LOVES 12s 6d ... TILL WE
HAVE FACES *a novel* 15s / *All prices are net*
(APT/X327 appears on a line by itself at the bottom.)

72. THE SCREWTAPE LETTERS AND SCREWTAPE PROPOSES A TOAST. (First American edition)
New York: Macmillan, 1961.
158 pp.   14 cm x 20.5 cm   Red cloth

KEY TO FIRST EDITION: (none – reprints are noted as such)

Front board: (blank)
Spine: (lettered in gold) LEWIS / (horizontally) THE SCREWTAPE LETTERS & SCREWTAPE PROPOSES A TOAST/MACMILLAN
Rear board: (blank)
Endpapers: (blank)
Page (i): The/Screwtape Letters/ (single rule)/ Screwtape/ Proposes a Toast/by/C. S. LEWIS/The Macmillan Company, New York
Page (ii): Reprinted with some alterations by kind permission of/ "The Guardian"/Copyright ▣ C. S. LEWIS 1961 / Screwtape Proposes a Toast/Copyright ▣ Helen Joy Lewis 1959/From The World's Last Night by C. S. Lewis./Reprinted by permission of Harcourt, Brace & World, Inc./All rights reserved ... from the Publisher./Printed in the United States of America/ Library of Congress catalog card number: 62-16314
Page (iii): PREFACE
Page (xi): (half-title) I. The Screwtape Letters/(quotes from Luther and Thomas More)
Page (xii): TO/J. R. R. TOLKIEN
Pages (xiii – xiv): PREFACE
Pages 11 through 160: Text

(Note: I have supplied page numbers i through xiv for identification purposes only. These pages are not actually numbered – note the very peculiar and illogical page sequence!)

Dust jacket:
Front panel: (on red background) (black lettering) C. S. LEWIS /(on black spider-like background) (white lettering) THE/SCREWTAPE /LETTERS/(red lettering) and/SCREWTAPE/PROPOSES/A TOAST /with a new/preface/by the author

<u>Spine</u>: (on red background) (black lettering) C. S. LEWIS / (yellow lettering) THE SCREWTAPE LETTERS/AND SCREWTAPE PROPOSES A TOAST Macmillan

<u>Back panel</u>: (floral design) Other titles for your C. S. Lewis shelf (floral design) / (16 Lewis titles)

<u>Front flap</u>: (price at top) $4.95/(in red on white background) *"A witty Baedeker of modern sin ... an immediate bestseller ... a minor masterpiece of modern religious prose."* Time/(publisher's blurb, continued on back flap)

<u>Back flap</u>: (continued from front flap)/ *is as old ... an unfashionable orthodoxy against the heresies of his time."*/Jacket design by Ellen Raskin/MACMILLAN PUBLISHING Co., INC./866 Third Avenue, New York, N.Y. 10022

The "Revised Macmillan Paperback Edition" of 1982 contains "a hitherto unpublished piece by C. S. Lewis that serves as a Preface to 'Screwtape Proposes a Toast.'" This Preface was originally planned for the 1961 edition, but eventually omitted.

This American edition presents an additional puzzle. Although the volume was published in 1961, every dust jacket I have seen for it contains the note on the back flap that Lewis "died while the new edition of this book was on the press" and reprints an obituary comment from *Time*. Perhaps further research will bring more light to bear on this curious discrepancy.

73. A GRIEF OBSERVED.

London: Faber and Faber, September 29, 1961
62 pp   13.5cm x 20.5cm   Gray with a weave pattern

KEY TO FIRST EDITION: On back of title page:
First published in mcmlxi

Front board: (blank)
Spine: (horizontally in gold) A GRIEF OBSERVED – N. W.
CLERK   FABER
Rear board: (blank)
Endpapers: (blank)
Page (1): (blank)
Page (2): (blank)
Page (3): A Grief Observed
Page (4): (blank)
Page (5): (title page) A Grief Observed/by/N. W. Clerk/FABER &
FABER/24 Russell Square/London
Page (6): *First published in mcmlxi*/(publisher and printer
information) /copyright 1961 by N. W. Clerk
Pages 7 through 60: (text, followed by one blank sheet – two blank
pages)

Dust jacket: (Light blue background throughout
Front panel: (in light blue on gray background) *A Grief/Observed/*(in
black) N. W. Clerk
Spine: (in black on gray background) *A Grief Observed N. W. Clerk*
(in black) *Faber*
Back panel: (advertisements for THOUGHTS FOR MEDITATION
and THE SWORD OF THE SPIRIT)
Front flap: (title, author and publisher's blurb)/8*s* 6*d*/*net*
Back flap: (advertisement for THE TESTAMENT OF
IMMORTALITY)

74. (First American edition) A GRIEF OBSERVED.

Greenwich, Connecticut: The Seabury Press, 1963
60 pp   14cm x 21cm   Quarter gray cloth around spine, with green-
gray vertical wavy stripes on off-white paper

KEY TO FIRST EDITION: Other than the copyright date of **1961**, there is no indication of reprinting.

Front board: (blank)
Spine: (horizontally in silver) CLERK (dot) A GRIEF OBSERVED (dot) SEABURY
Rear board: (blank)
Endpapers: (blank)
The pagination is identical to that of the British first edition, with the text having been printed exactly as it appears in the British edition. Only the title page and its verso has been changed.
Title page: N. W. Clerk/A Grief Observed/(logo of The Seabury Press)/GREENWICH – CONNECTICUT/1963

Dust jacket: (dark gray throughout, except for flaps, which are light gray)
Front panel: (in white) A GRIEF/OBSERVED/N. W. CLERK /(curly-cue design)
Spine: (horizontally in white) CLERK (dot) A GRIEF OBSERVED (dot) SEABURY
Back panel: (exactly the same as the front panel)
Front flap: $2.00 (in upper right corner/(publisher's blurb)
Back flap: (blank)

With the true identity of the author concealed, the book sold poorly, and the publisher apparently had many copies still on hand by the time Lewis died. When permission was granted by the Lewis estate to reissue the book identifying Lewis as author, the publisher put the new jackets on the surplus copies, so the book itself still showed N. W. Clerk as author. The new jacket is almost identical to the original jacket, except that C. S. LEWIS appears above the curly-cue, with the title beneath. The front and back flaps are filled with the publisher's blurb, with the $2.00 price still on the front flap.

When the stock of the original first edition books was exhausted, the publisher reissued the book, stating it to be the first American printing – which it certainly was not.

75. AN EXPERIMENT IN CRITICISM.

Cambridge: Cambridge University Press, October 13, 1961
152 pp.   12.cm x 20cm   Blue cloth

KEY TO FIRST EDITION: (bottom of title page) **1961**

Front board: (blank)
Spine: (lettered in gold on 1.5cm x 4 cm black background near top
of spine) (single rule)/C. S. LEWIS/(double rule) AN
/EXPERIMENT/IN/ CRITICISM/(double rule)CAMBRIDGE/
(single rule)
Rear board: (blank)
Endpapers: (blank)
Page (i): (blank)
Page (ii): (blank)
Page (iii): AN EXPERIMENT IN /CRITICISM
Page (iv): (blank)
Page (v): (title page) AN/EXPERIMENT IN/CRITICISM/BY/C.S.
LEWIS/
(seal of the university)/CAMBRIDGE/AT THE UNIVERSITY
PRESS/1961
Page (vi): (publication and copyright information) 1961
Page (vii): CONTENTS
Page (viii): (blank)
Pages 1 through (144): (text)

Dust jacket:
Front panel: (lettered in white on alternating orange and black
rectangles) (from top to bottom) *C. S. LEWIS/An/Experiment/
in Criticism/Cambridge*
Spine: (lettered horizontally in white) (on black background) *C. S.
LEWIS* (on orange background) *An Experiment in Criticism*
Back panel: (description and reviews of *Studies in Words*)
Front flap: (publisher's blurb) (U.K. price in lower right corner) *15s.
net* (U.S. price of $2.95 in the upper right corner, which may have
been clipped by a British bookseller)
Back flap: (blank)

76. (First American edition) **AN EXPERIMENT IN CRITICISM**

The American edition is identical to the British edition, with two notable exceptions – it is bound in orange cloth, and the lettering on the spine is horizontal in black: C. S. LEWIS An Experiment in Criticism

The same dust jacket was used on both editions, with the U.K. price, *15s. net*, in the lower right corner of the front flap, and the U.S. price, $2.95, in the upper right corner. The U.K. price may have been clipped by the American bookseller.

77. THEY ASKED FOR A PAPER.
London: Geoffrey Bles, February 26, 1962
219 pp   14.5cm x 22cm
Two binding variations have been noted: (1) tan cloth with black lettering on the spine, and salmon-colored top-edge; (2) shiny black weave-design cloth with silver lettering on the spine, and undyed top-edge. Priority is unknown, but my guess favors (1) as having precedence.

KEY TO FIRST EDITION: 1962 on bottom of title page and copyright date on back of title page

Front board: (blank)
Spine: (except for black on tan cloth and silver on black cloth, both are lettered identically) *C. S. LEWIS/* (short single rule)/THEY /ASKED/FOR A/PAPER/*BLES*
Rear board: (blank)
Endpapers: (light blue) (blank)
Page (i): THEY ASKED FOR A PAPER
Page (ii): (list of Lewis books)
Page (iii): (title page) C. S. LEWIS/(single rule)/They Asked for a Paper/PAPERS AND ADDRESSES/1962/GEOFFREY BLES, LONDON
Page (iv): (copyright date 1962) (publisher's addresses in Australia, New Zealand, Canada, and South Africa)
Pages v and vi: Acknowledgments

Dust jacket: (decorative jacket by Michael Harvey) (all except flaps on brown background with vertical strip of white between spine and front and back panels)
Front panel: (in white) THEY/ASKED/FOR A/PAPER/(design in red) /(in green) C. S. Lewis/ (in red) *Harvey*
Spine: (in green) C. S./Lewis/(design)/(in white) THEY/ASKED /FOR A/PAPER/BLES
Back panel: (blank)
Front flap: (publisher's blurb in brown)/*Jacket designed by Michael Harvey* (price of 16s net in lower right corner)
Back flap: (list of 16 Lewis books, from THE SCREWTAPE LETTERS AND SCREWTAPE PROPOSES A TOAST @ 12s 6d to THE PILGRIM'S REGRESS @9s 6d)

There was no American first edition.

78. BEYOND THE BRIGHT BLUR.
New York: Harcourt, Brace & World, December 25, 1963
32 pp   12.5cm x 19.5cm   Gray cloth with purple around spine

KEY TO FIRST EDITION: (on back of title page)
FIRST EDITION

This was a limited edition sent as a New Year's greeting by the publisher to "friends of the author and the publisher." It contained excerpts from Lewis's last book, *Letters to Malcolm*, to be published early in 1964, and was issued in a plain translucent glassine dust jacket with a wrinkled surface, which tended to yellow with age. Laid in was a plain white card, imprinted in red: *With the Season's Greetings from Harcourt, Brace & World, Inc.*

It is alleged to have been limited to 350 copies, of which I have purchased many over the years – so many of which have appeared on the market in recent years that I wonder if some I've purchased recently were those I had sold earlier!

Front board: (gray cloth blind-stamped with a 4cm decorative wreath near the top center, with 1.5cm of the purple cloth wrapped around the spine)
Spine: (lettered in gold) C. S. LEWIS   (publisher's logo) BEYOND THE BRIGHT BLUR
Rear board: (blank)
Endpapers: (blue) (blank)
Page (1): ANNO MCMLXIII/BEYOND THE BRIGHT BLUR/*is taken from*/LETTERS TO MALCOLM: CHIEFLY ON PRAYER /*by C. S. Lewis*/*which will be published*/*in the year 1964*/*This limited edition*/*is published*/*as a New Year's greeting*/*to friends*/*of the author*/*and his publisher.*
Page (2): (blank)
Page (3): C. S. LEWIS/BEYOND/THE BRIGHT/BLUR/(purple wreath)/*Harcourt, Brace & World, Inc. New York*
Page (4): (copyright information)/FIRST EDITION
Page (5): BEYOND THE BRIGHT BLUR
Page (6): (blank)
Pages 7 through 30: (text)
Pages (31, 32): (blank)

79. LETTERS TO MALCOLM: CHIEFLY ON PRAYER.

London: Geoffrey Bles, January 27, 1964

160 pp   14cm x 20cm   Dark olive-green cloth

KEY TO FIRST EDITION: On back of title page:
First Published in 1964
Front board: (blank)
Spine: (lettered in gold) (on 2cm x 5cm black background)
C. S./LEWIS/(single rule) LETTERS/TO/MALCOLM
/CHIEFLY/ON/ PRAYER/BLES
Top-edge: Dark blue
Rear board: (blank)
Endpapers: (light olive green) (blank)
Page (1): (blank)
Page (2): (blank)
Page (3): LETTERS TO MALCOLM: CHIEFLY ON PRAYER
Page (4): (list of 21 Lewis books)
Page (5): (title page) LETTERS TO MALCOLM:/CHIEFLY ON
PRAYER/by/C. S. LEWIS/GEOFFREY BLES (dot) LONDON
Page (6): (copyright and printing information) First Published in
1964
Page (7): (warning)
Page (8): (blank)
Pages (9): (another half-title) LETTERS TO MALCOLM:
CHIEFLY ON PRAYER
Page (10): (blank)
Pages 11 through (160): (text)

Dust jacket:
Front panel: (lettered in gray) *C. S. LEWIS*/(single red rule)/(lettered
in black) *LETTERS/TO/*MALCOLM (with large M in red)/(lettered
in gray) *CHIEFLY/ON/PRAYER*
Spine: (lettered in black) *C.S./LEWIS*/(single red rule)
/LETTERS/TO/MALCOLM/(lettered in red) *CHIEFLY/ON
/PRAYER/*(lettered in black) *BLES*
Back panel: (red) (blank)
Front flap: (publisher's blurb) *Jacket design by Michael Harvey/*
(price in lower right corner) 12s. 6d. net
Back flap: (blank)

80. (First American edition)
LETTERS TO MALCOLM: CHIEFLY ON PRAYER.
New York: Harcourt, Brace & World, February 12, 1964
128 pp   14cm x 21cm   Bright blue cloth

KEY TO FIRST EDITION: (on back of title page)
First American Edition
Front board: (blind-embossed figure in 6cm circle – probably representing a stained glass church window)
Spine: (lettered horizontally in gold) *C. S. Lewis* LETTERS TO MALCOLM: CHIEFLY ON PRAYER (publisher's logo) (under the above line of type: *Harcourt, Brace & World)*
Rear board: (blank)
Endpapers: (light gray) (blank)
Page (1): LETTERS/TO MALCOLM/CHIEFLY/ON/PRAYER
Page (2): (list of 24 Lewis books)
Page (3): (title page) LETTERS/TO/MALCOLM:/CHIEFLY/ON PRAYER/(same circular figure as on front cover)/C. S. LEWIS /HARCOURT, BRACE & WORLD, INC., NEW YORK
Page (4): (copyright and printing information) *First American Edition*
Page 5: (another half-title) LETTERS/TO MALCOLM/CHIEFLY/ON/PRAYER
Page (6): (blank)
The text begins with page 3, not page 7, for some odd reason and ends with page 124

Dust jacket:
Front panel: (on background of white six-petal design over four 7cm circles, two of which are blue and two tan) (lettered in blue) C. S. LEWIS/(lettered in black) Letters to Malcolm:/Chiefly on Prayer /Reflections on the relationship between man/and God by the author of *The Screwtape Letters*
Spine: (horizontally) (in black) C. S. LEWIS ((in tan) Letters to Malcolm: Chiefly on Prayer (logo in blue) (in black) Harcourt, /Brace & World
Back panel: (full-page photo by John S. Murray of Lewis lighting his pipe)
Front flap: (publisher's blurb) (price in upper right corner) $3.50

<u>Back flap</u>:(biographical sketch of Lewis)/*Jacket design by Ellen Raskin*

Letters to Malcolm was Lewis's last book, written while terminally ill, only six months before his death on November 22, 1963. On July 18, 1963, he wrote to a lady in New York who had requested an appointment with him in late August:
I can give you no assurance as to what I will be doing by the end of August. After a long illness I am now suffering a relapse and at present waiting to be admitted to hospital as soon as there is a vacancy. One of my complaints is anaemia. This, tho painless, has a most debilitating effect on the mind; so that even if I were technically "well" again, you would find yourself confronted with , almost, an imbecile. Thanks for the kind things you say, but look for no help from me. I am but a <u>fossil</u> dinosaur now. Yours sincerely, C. S. Lewis

The first copy of *Letters of Malcolm* acquired for my collection had belonged to Dr. Donald Coggan, Archbishop of Canterbury and Head of the Church of England – an advance copy sent to him by Jocelyn Gibb, Lewis's editor at Geoffrey Bles. Laid in was the printed publisher's slip, "With the compliments of Mr. Jocelyn Gibb." Gibb had crossed out the printed "Mr." and written this poignant note, *"Publication of both these will be on 27 Jan 64. I hope you will like them. Sad, oh sad, that it is CSL's last. Jock Gibb 9 Jan 64"*

81. THE DISCARDED IMAGE: An Introduction to Medieval and Renaissance Literature.
Cambridge: Cambridge University Press, May 7, 1964
242 pp   13cm x 21cm   Black cloth

KEY TO FIRST EDITION: At the bottom of the title page: **1964**

Front board: (blank)
Spine: (in gold) *The/Discarded/Image*/C. S. LEWIS/*Cambridge*
Top-edge: Light blue-gray
Rear board: (blank)
Endpapers: (blank)
Page (i): (half-title) THE DISCARDED IMAGE
Page (ii): (blank)
Page (iii): THE/DISCARDED/IMAGE/ AN INTRODUCTION TO/MEDIEVAL AND RENAISSANCE/LITERATURE/BY/C. S. LEWIS/(logo)/CAMBRIDGE/AT THE UNIVERSITY PRESS/1964
Page (iv): (publishing and copyright information)
Page (v): *To*/ROGER LANCELYN GREEN
Page (vi): (blank)
Pages vii and viii: CONTENTS
Pages ix and (x): PREFACE
Pages 1 through (232): (text)

Dust jacket: (orange background throughout)
Front panel: (colorful jacket by Will Carter) (in three boxes with black background) (first box in orange) C. S. LEWIS/(second box in red) *The Dis-/carded/Image*/(in orange) AN INTRODUCTION TO MEDIEVAL/AND RENAISSANCE LITERATURE
Spine: (horizontally in black box) (orange) *The Discarded Image* (red) *C. S. Lewis* (orange) *Cambridge*
Back panel: (description of AN EXPERIMENT IN CRITICISM)
Front flap: (title, author, and publisher's blurb, continued on back flap)/ (lower right corner) 22s 6d
Back flap: (blurb cont'd)/*Jacket design by Will Carter*

There was no American first edition, the one sold in the U. S. having been the British edition. The dust jacket had the U.K. price, 22s 6d, in the lower right corner of the front flap, and the U.S. price, $3.95, in the upper right corner. Many copies will therefore have one or the other price clipped, depending upon where the book was sold.

Although *The Discarded Image* was not published until after Lewis's death, it was a compilation of lectures given over a period of many years before his eventual resignation of his professorship at Cambridge.

The remaining books in this bibliography were published under the direction of the Lewis estate, most of them edited by Walter Hooper. Although most of them contain poems, essays, or lectures that were previously unpublished, in the interest of conserving space I have not given them the exhaustive descriptive coverage of the books published or in the process of being published in his lifetime. I have also not included paperback editions for which there were no preceding hardcover editions.

Books published by Cambridge University Press were only in one edition, with both British and American prices on the dust jacket, to be clipped as appropriate if the seller so desired.

When publishers use a string of letters or numbers to designate the printing, the first printing will have "1" or "A", which will be dropped with the next printing.

82. POEMS.
(Edited by Walter Hooper)
London: Geoffrey Bles, October 26, 1964
Blue cloth with gold type on spine; title and author on burgundy background
First edition: 1964 at bottom of title page
Price on front flap of dust jacket, lower right corner: 16s. net

83. POEMS. (First American edition)
New York: Harcourt, Brace & World, March 24, 1965
Orange-red and off-white cloth with bronze type on spine
First edition: First American edition 1965, on back of title page
Price on front flap of dust jacket, upper right corner: $4.50

84. STUDIES IN MEDIEVAL AND RENAISSANCE LITERATURE.
(Edited by Walter Hooper)
Cambridge: Cambridge University Press, June 9, 1966

Orange-red cloth with gold type on spine
First edition: 1966 at bottom of title page
Prices on front flap of dust jacket: *$5.95 in U.S.A.*, upper right
corner – *30s. net in U.K.,* lower right corner

85. LETTERS OF C. S. LEWIS.

(Edited, with a Memoir, by W. H. Lewis)
London: Geoffrey Bles, April 18, 1966
Maroon cloth with gold type on spine; title on blue background
No indication of first edition
Price on front flap of dust jacket, lower right corner: 30s. net

86. LETTERS OF C. S. LEWIS. (First American edition)

New York: Harcourt, Brace & World, November 16, 1966
Black cloth with silver type on spine
First edition: First American edition, on back of title page
Price on front flap of dust jacket, upper right corner: $5.95

87. OF OTHER WORLDS *Essays and Stories.*

(Edited by Walter Hooper)
London: Geoffrey Bles, September 5, 1966
Orange red cloth with gold type on spine
No indication of first edition
Price on front dust jacket flap, lower right corner: 16s net

88. OF OTHER WORLDS *Essays and Stories* (First American edition)

New York: Harcourt, Brace & World, February 22, 1967
Olive cloth with dark green-blue and gold lettering on spine
First edition: First American edition 1967, on back of title page
Price on front dust jacket flap, upper right corner: $3.95

89. CHRISTIAN REFLECTIONS.
(Edited by Walter Hooper)
London: Geoffrey Bles, January 23, 1967
Dark orange cloth with gold type on spine
First edition: 1967 at bottom of title page
Price on front flap of dust jacket, lower right corner: 18*s net*

90. CHRISTIAN REFLECTIONS. (First American edition)
Grand Rapids, Michigan: Eerdmans, 1967
Dark blue cloth with white type on spine
No indication of first edition
Price on front flap of dust jacket, upper right corner: $3.95

91. SPENSER'S IMAGES OF LIFE.
(Edited by Alistair Fowler)
Cambridge: Cambridge University Press, November 2, 1967
Burgundy cloth with gold type on spine; title and author on maroon
background
First edition: 1967 on title page
Price on front flap of dust jacket: $3.95 in upper right corner,
                                        21s. net in lower right corner

92. LETTERS TO AN AMERICAN LADY.
(Edited by Clyde S. Kilby)
Grand Rapids, Michigan: Eerdmans, 1967
Red cloth with black type on spine
The first edition has no specific indication, but in the absence of a
dust jacket, its height of 22cm and woven cloth distinguishes it from
the shorter Book Club edition with smooth cloth.
Price on front dust jacket flap: $3.95

93. LETTERS TO AN AMERICAN LADY. (First British edition)
London: Hodder and Stoughton, June 1969
Dark red cloth with gold type on spine
First edition: First printed in Great Britain 1969, on back of title
    page
Price on front flap of dust jacket, upper right corner: 25s. (£1.25)
(Britain was switching to decimalized currency at this time – see
#98)

94. A MIND AWAKE *An Anthology of C. S. Lewis.*
(Edited by Clyde S. Kilby)
London: Geoffrey Bles, March 4, 1968
Olive green cloth with gold type on spine
First edition: First Published 1968, on back of title page
Price on front flap of dust jacket, lower right corner: 25s. net

95. A MIND AWAKE *An Anthology* ... (First American edition)
New York: Harcourt, Brace & World, December 3, 1969
Gray cloth with white type on spine
First edition: FIRST AMERICAN EDITION 1969, on back of title
    page
Price on front of dust jacket: $5.75 in upper right corner

96. NARRATIVE POEMS.
(Edited by Walter Hooper)
London: Geoffrey Bles, October 27, 1969
Black cloth with gold type on spine, with title and author on light
blue background
First edition: First Published in 1969, on back of title page
Price on front flap of dust jacket, lower right corner: 25s. net

97. NARRATIVE POEMS. (First American edition)
New York: Harcourt, Brace, Jovanovich, February 23, 1972
Blue cloth with silver type on spine
First edition: First American edition 1972, on back of title page, with string of letters ABCDE below
Price on front flap of dust jacket, upper right corner: $5.95

98. SELECTED LITERARY ESSAYS.
(Edited by Walter Hooper)
Cambridge: Cambridge University Press, December 4, 1969
Bright blue cloth with gold type on spine; title and author in gold rectangle
First edition: 1969 on title page
Price on front flap of dust jacket: $7.95 in USA, upper right corner,
                  50s. (£2.50) net in U.K., lower right corner

99. GOD IN THE DOCK.
(Edited by Walter Hooper)
Grand Rapids, Michigan: Eeerdmans, November 30, 1970
Black cloth with white type on spine
No indication of first edition
Price on front flap of dust jacket, lower right corner: $6.95

100. UNDECEPTIONS. (First British edition of *God in the Dock*)
London: Geoffrey Bles, 1971
Gray cloth with gold & red type on spine; title on red background
First edition: First Published in 1971, on back of title page
Price on front flap of dust jacket, lower right corner: £2.25 net
                             (45/--)

101. THE DARK TOWER *And Other Stories.*
(Edited by Walter Hooper)
London: Collins, February 28, 1977
Black cloth with silver type on spine
First edition: First published 1977 (on back of title page:
Price on front dust jacket flap: £3.95 net

102. THE DARK TOWER *And Other Stories.* (First American edition)
New York: Harcourt, Brace, Jovanovich, April 18, 1977
Gray cloth on spine with black type; aqua cloth on boards
First edition: First American edition 1977, with string of letters
        ABCDEFGHIJ below
Price on front flap of jacket, upper right corner: $6.95

103. THE JOYFUL CHRISTIAN: *127 Readings from C. S. Lewis.*
(Edited with a Foreword by Henry William Griffin)
New York: Macmillan, 1977
Black cloth with red-gold type on spine
First edition: First printing 1977, on back of title page
Price on front flap of dust jacket: $7.95

104. THEY STAND TOGETHER.
(Edited by Walter Hooper)
London: Collins, April 19, 1979
Ochre cloth with gold type on spine
First edition: First published 1979, on back of title page
Price on front flap of dust jacket, in lower right corner: £8.95

105. THEY STAND TOGETHER. (First American edition)
New York: Macmillan, 1979
Light blue cloth on spine with gold type; gray paper-covered boards,
First edition: First American Edition 1979, on back of title page
Price on front dust jacket flap, upper right corner: $13.95

106. C. S. LEWIS: THE VISIONARY CHRISTIAN: 131
Readings (Selected and Edited by Chad Walsh)
New York: Macmillan, 1981
Ivory cloth with blue type on spine
First edition: String of numbers 10 9 8 --- 3 2 1 on title page
Price on front flap of dust jacket: $10.95

107. OF THIS AND OTHER WORLDS.
(Edited by Walter Hooper)
London: Collins, September 6, 1982
Dark brown cloth with gold type on spine
First edition: First published 1982, on back of title page
Price on front flap of dust jacket, lower right corner: £7.95 net

108. ON STORIES: and Other Essays on Literature.
(First American edition of Of This and Other Worlds)
New York: Harcourt, Brace, Jovanovich, June 24, 1982
Maroon cloth on spine with gold type; red paper-covered boards
First edition: First edition, on back of title page, with string of letters
     ABCDE beneath
Price on front flap of dust jacket, upper right corner: $9.95

109. BOXEN: *The Imaginary World of the Young C. S. Lewis*
(Edited by Walter Hooper)
London: Collins, May 28, 1985
Olive cloth with gold type on spine
First edition: First published in Great Britain 1985, on back of title
     page
Price on front flap of dust jacket, right lower corner: £7.95

110. BOXEN: *The Imaginary World* ... (First American edition)
San Diego: Harcourt, Brace, Jovanovich, October 17, 1985
Brown cloth on spine with gold type; yellow paper-covered boards
First edition: First American edition, on back of title page, with
     string of letters ABCDE beneath
Price on front dust jacket flap, right upper corner: $13.95

111. LETTERS TO CHILDREN
(Edited by Lyle W. Dorsett and Marjorie Lamp Mead)
New York: Macmillan, April 11, 1985
Navy blue cloth on spine with silver type; blue paper-covered boards
First edition: String of numbers 10 9 8 --- 3 2 1 on back of title page
Price on front flap of dust jacket, upper right corner: $9.95

112. LETTERS TO CHILDREN (First British edition)
London: Collins, October 31, 1985
Dark red cloth with gold type on spine
First edition: First published 1985, on back of title page:
Price on front dust jacket flap: £6.95, on publisher's sticker at bottom, with corner clipped

113. LETTERS – C. S. LEWIS – DON GIOVANNI CALABRIA
(Translated and edited by Martin Moynihan)
London: Collins, January 1989
Marbled blue paper with title on front on white background
First edition: First published 1988, on back of title page
No dust jacket

114. ALL MY ROAD BEFORE ME: *The Diary of C. S. Lewis 1922-27.*
(Edited by Walter Hooper)
London: HarperCollins Publishers, April 18, 1991
Off-white cloth with gold type on spine
Back of title page: First published in Great Britain in 1991 by
        Collins Religious Group
Price on front dust jacket flap, lower right corner: £19.99

115. ALL MY ROAD BEFORE ME: *The Diary of C. S. Lewis 1922- 27.* (First American edition)
San Diego: Harcourt, Brace, Jovanovich
Yellow paper on boards; blue cloth with gold type on spine
First edition: First U.S. edition, on back of title page, with string of
        letters ABCDE below
Price on front flap of dust jacket, in upper right corner: $24.95
                                    (HIGHER IN CANADA)

116. C. S. LEWIS: ESSAY COLLECTION AND OTHER SHORT PIECES.
(Edited by Lesley Walmsley)
London: HarperCollins *Publishers*, 2000
Green cloth with gold type on spine
First edition: First published in Great Britain in 2000 by
HarperCollinsPublishers, plus string of numbers:
      1 3 5 7 9 10 8 6 4 2, on title page
Prices on front dust jacket flap: UK £25 CAN $54.95 at bottom

This book gathers in one volume 135 essays, letters, and short stories that were previously published between 1939 and 1996, but are no longer easily obtainable. There was apparently no American edition.

117. C. S. LEWIS: COLLECTED LETTERS, Vol. I – Family Letters 1905-1931.
(Edited by Walter Hooper)
London: HarperCollins *Publishers*, 2000
Black cloth with gold type on spine
First edition: First published in Great Britain in 2000 by
HarperCollinsPublishers, plus string of numbers:
      1 3 5 7 9 10 8 6 4 2, on back of title page
Prices on front dust jacket flap: UK £25 CAN $54.95 at bottom

118. C. S. LEWIS: COLLECTED LETTERS, Vol. I – Family Letters 1905-1931.
(First American edition, published in 2004 concurrently with the first British edition of Volume II)
San Francisco: HarperSanFrancisco, 2004
Cream-colored cloth with gold type on spine.
First edition: FIRST EDITION, plus string of numbers:
      10 9 8 7 6 5 4 3 2 1, on back of title page
Prices on front dust jacket flap: USA $34.95 CAN $53.95 in upper right corner

**119. THE COLLECTED LETTERS OF C. S. LEWIS, Vol. II –
Books, Broadcasts, and the War 1931-1949.**
London: HarperCollins *Publishers*, 2004
Black cloth with gold type on spine.
First edition: First published 2004, plus string of numbers:
    1 3 5 7 9 8 6 4 2, on back of title page
Price on front dust jacket flap: (electronically encoded)

120. (First American edition)
**THE COLLECTED LETTERS OF C. S. LEWIS, Vol. II –
Books, Broadcasts, and the War 1931-1949.**
San Francisco: HarperSanFrancisco, 2004
White cloth with silver type on spine
Back of title page: FIRST EDITION, plus string of years and
numbers:
    04 05 06 07 08 RRD(H) 10 9 8 7 6 5 4 3 2 1 at bottom
Prices on front dust jacket flap: USA $34.95 CAN $53.95 in upper
right corner

**121. C. S. LEWIS: COLLECTED LETTERS, Vol. III--
Narnia, Cambridge and Joy 1950-1963**
London:HarperCollins,2006

122. (First American edition)
**THE COLLECTED LETTERS OF C. S. LEWIS, Vol. III
Narnia, Cambridge and Joy 1950-1963**
San Francisco: HarperSanFrancisco, 2006

Volume III includes a Supplement containing letters
not included in Volumes I and II.

ALPHABETICAL INDEX OF FIRST EDITIONS

www.ingramcontent.com/pod-product-compliance
Lightning Source LLC
Chambersburg PA
CBHW021826090426
42811CB00032B/2043/J